SIGNATURE KILLERS

Robert D. Keppel is the Chief Criminal Investigator for the Washington State Attorney General's Office. He has a Ph.D in Criminal Justice from the University of Washington and has been an investigator or consultant to over 2,000 murder cases and over 50 serial murder investigations, including the Atlanta Child Murders and the Green River Murders.

William J. Birnes is the president of Shadow Lawn Press in Los Angeles, California

Also by Robert D. Keppel with William J. Birnes

The Riverman

SIGNATURE KILLERS

Robert D. Keppel with
William J. Birnes

arrow books

Published by Arrow Books in 1998

7 9 10 8 6

First published in the United Kingdom in 1998 by Arrow Books

Arrow Books
The Random House Group Limited
20 Vauxhall Bridge Road, London SW1V 2SA

Random House Australia (Pty) Limited
20 Alfred Street, Milsons Point, Sydney,
New South Wales 2061, Australia

Random House New Zealand Limited
18 Poland Road, Glenfield
Auckland 10, New Zealand

Random House (Pty) Limited
Endulini, 5a Jubilee Road, Parktown 2193, South Africa

The Random House Group Limited Reg. No. 954009

www.randomhouse.co.uk

A CIP catalogue record for this book
is available from the British Library

Papers used by Random House are natural, recyclable products made from wood grown in sustainable forests. The manufacturing processes conform to the environmental regulations of the country of origin

ISBN 0 09 927772 7

Phototypeset by Intype, London Ltd
Printed and bound in Great Britain by
Cox & Wyman Ltd, Reading, Berkshire

Acknowledgments

It is something more than twenty-two years since I first started investigating and studying the crime-scene patterns of sexually oriented serial killers. In that time frame, changes of one kind or another have occurred, although not such as to alter the course of these predators.

Schools of thought concerning the etiology of the serial killer that were once considered to be firmly entrenched somewhere within biological, sociological, and psychological theories have now become tentative and provisional. It goes without saying that books and papers dealing with serial killers have grown to shape what is known about them. But those very references have at times been very shallow and devoid of information that would help us really understand the behavior of the serial killer. I can say with impunity that I have met highly dedicated people who have been contributing in their own way to a greater understanding of these predators.

Many of the contributors are law-enforcement officers, prosecutors, criminologists, psychiatrists, psychologists, and authors. I mentioned some of them in *The Riverman*, but a handful are worthy of further recognition here because of their thankless work in the area of signature killers.

First of all, fortuitous circumstances intervened when I met Richard Walter, of Lansing, Michigan. Richard and I took separate paths, he as a prison counselor interviewing many sex murderers, and myself as a homicide detective investigating many sexual-related murders. We ended up with very similar beliefs about signature killers. His expertise and thoughtful editing of this book were vital to me in expressing the characteristics of the signature killer in a clear and understandable way. For this, I am forever grateful.

The case materials for this book were provided by people who recognized the importance of relating the rare phenomenon of signature killers to others.

They were Deputy Chief Ed Denning, Bergen County Prosecutor's Office, Hackensack, New Jersey; and Vernon Geberth (retired NYPD), author of the book *Practical Homicide Investigation: Tactics, Procedures, and Forensic Evidence* in the murders of Richard Cottingham; Sgt. M. A. Rogers and Lt. C. R. Owens, Shreveport Police Department, and Rebecca Bush, Assistant District Attorney, Caddo Parrish, Louisiana, in the Nathaniel Code cases; Lt. Joe Swiski, Delaware State Police, for the Steven Pennell murders; Daniel Lamborn, Deputy District Attorney, San Diego County, California, for the Cleophus Prince murder cases; Donald R. Couury, Senior Assistant Attorney General, Commonwealth of Virginia, for the murders of Timothy Spencer; and Rebecca Roe and Jeff Baird, King County Prosecutor's Office, Dale Foote and Marv Skeen of the Bellevue Police Department, and Larry Peterson of the King County Police, Seattle, Washington, for the killings of George Russell.

Two individuals have paved the way for others by giving expert testimony about signature murder in the trials of convicted murderers. Former FBI agent and supervisor of the FBI's Behavioral Sciences Unit and author of the book *The Mindhunter*, John Douglas, was the first person to offer testimony in the Steven Pennell, Nathaniel Code, Cleophus Prince, and George Russell cases. Special agent Larry G. Ankrom gave testimony in the Cleophus Prince murder trial.

I especially thank Pierce Brooks, former LAPD homicide detective, for his encouraging words for me to write this book. Brooks was the first to recognize publicly through his work on the Harvey Glatman murders that killers have similarities from one murder to the next, and those similarities are reflected by the killer's own personal signature.

This book would be no book without the support and encouragement of true-crime writer extraordinaire, Ann Rule. She recognized that *Signature Killers* was 'something special.' Her writings are far too voluminous to mention here, but anyone who reads this book should know Ann well.

Ann's editor, former publisher at Pocket Books, Bill Grose, was instrumental to the entire process of our writing this book because he reviewed the material we'd submitted, rethought the book we wanted to do, and decided that it was something Pocket wanted to publish. We thank him for his insight.

I am grateful to Amelia Sheldon, my former editor at Pocket, because she so carefully edited this manuscript and was responsible for the book in its final form. Thanks also to my new editor, Tris Coburn, who stepped in at the end of last year to steer this manuscript through the shoals of the publication process.

Finally, my writings once again have been supplemented by one of the brightest literary agents around, Bill Birnes. He diligently pored over the manuscript, enhancing it and polishing my police-eze. For this, I am forever grateful.

ÐA COM OF MORE UNDER MISTLEOÞUM
GRENDEL GONGAN, GODES YRRE BÆRRE
– Beowulf

Alone, alone, all, all alone
Alone on a wide, wide sea!

– Samuel Taylor Coleridge,
The Rime of the Ancient Mariner

Foreword By Ann Rule

As recently as 1982, there was only one term used to describe murderers who killed many victims: 'mass murderers.' This phrase was correct for only *one* genre of multiple killers – the psychotic maniac who opens fire in a crowded fast-food restaurant, on a campus, or, yes, in a post office. The mass murderer is usually suicidal, a paranoid schizophrenic who dies in the midst of the terror he has created.

Then, in the early 1980s, we began to use the appellation 'serial killer,' which came from Pierce Brooks, whom author Bob Keppel calls his 'mentor.' Brooks saw that there were killers who were quite sane, medically and legally, who murdered again and again and again – until they were either captured or dead. He called them 'serial killers.'

Identifying and delineating multiple murderers into categories may seem a gruesome task without reward or purpose. It is not. Once the break between 'mass' and 'serial' murder took place, it became apparent to the most intelligent and innovative detectives and criminologists that there were subgroups within these two classifications of killers. For instance, a 'spree killer' might be considered a serial killer at warp speed; the spree killer often erupts and murders a victim a day for a week or two.

Bob Keppel, who is the antithesis of the 'television detective,' has spent more than two decades studying the motivations and methods of the multiple murderers among us. He is not a 'seat of the pants instinct' detective, and he is not a 'profiler' in the ordinary sense of the term, although he often works with other detectives, encouraging them to 'profile' their own cases. Having known and written about Bob Keppel since his very first homicide case, I would call him a scientist-criminologist-psychologist-computer genius-detective. It was Keppel who used an embryonic computer of the 1970s to winnow Ted Bundy's name out of 2,000 or more suspects in the Northwest's 'Ted Murders' of that era. Even then, he could see that computers were going to be a vital tool for the investigation of major crimes.

And it was also Bob Keppel who was smart enough to let Ted Bundy *think* he was outsmarting Keppel; who better to impart wisdom about serial killers than a serial killer himself? Keppel listened and nodded and remembered the words of Bundy, one of America's most infamous murderers, then about to face the electric chair. 'What I learned from Bundy and others like him is that the process of the murder for these guys goes on longer than our perception of it,' Keppel recalls. 'One of them told me, "the murder ain't over until *I* say it's over." '

Signature Killers, which Bob Keppel has written with Bill Birnes, is the result of massive research into the murky minds of sadistic killers. It is a tour de force. As you read, you will go along with Keppel and figuratively peer over his shoulder as he reads through the private files of the most shocking murders in criminal history. It is definitely not for the fainthearted or those with delicate stomachs. Even though I have been writing about murder for as long as Keppel has been solving homicide cases, I found that I often had to put this book down and go out and plant geraniums in the sunshine. Frankly, I could not read it at night.

Beyond its shocking presentation of sadism and the workings of aberrant minds, *Signature Killers* offers so much more. For anyone who ever wanted to sit down with a detective's detective and ask questions, this is a treasure trove. Bob Keppel has come up with theories of murder that no one else has yet discovered. He speaks of the 'psychological calling cards' that signature killers leave behind, often all unknowingly. It is these often subtle similarities that allow detectives and the profilers who work with them to use computers most efficiently.

Some of the signature killers Keppel discusses are familiar names – headline names – and some are known only to the police jurisdiction where their crimes occurred. I found that I learned something new about killers whom I thought I knew well.

Signature Killers is not a quick read. I would suggest that it is an important book written to be used as a textbook on multiple murder for serious students of the criminally aberrant personality. And yet it will also be of tremendous interest to professionals in the field and to readers who have pondered, as I have, the bizarre intricacies of the murderous mind. I would venture to say there is not another existing work on this level. It may ask more questions than it answers.

Saying that, I suspect Bob Keppel would agree with me. He has been asking questions about murder for a long time now. He asks for *more* study – more in-depth interviews with serial offenders. Computers are only as accurate as the information fed into them. Keppel feels that a serial personality can sometimes be detected early on – long before it evolves into the serial murder phase.

'We're only scratching the surface,' he comments. 'There is so much more we need to learn and understand. I mean – *What if we could somehow prevent this?*'

In *Signature Killers*, Bob Keppel has more than

'scratched the surface.' Keppel and Bill Birnes have taken us a long way toward understanding the phenomenon of signature murder – toward understanding *all* murder – and that knowledge will certainly protect the reader and those he or she cares for. This book will make you think – perhaps more than you wanted to. It will frighten you, and it will shock you. But, until we understand the mechanisms of multiple murder, we cannot begin to work our way backward to its roots and tear them out before they sprout.

Introduction

The tension in this part of the city made residents and visitors alike sick to their stomachs as they walked past the flapping yellow tape marked Crime Scene – Do Not Enter and saw the police units on every corner and the reflections of red and blue lights dancing across the rain-streaked building walls. It had almost become a ritual by now, the warnings on the eleven o'clock news, the ominous headlines on page one of the local papers: 'Madman Still at Loose.' And the warnings: everyone's at risk; women shouldn't go out alone; there's only safety in numbers. It doesn't matter what city this is. It can be anywhere from Seattle to Miami. It's all the same scene.

In the darkness, unnoticed, a man in a black turtle-neck, long-sleeved pullover shirt, and maybe even in navy blue woolen watch cap slipped sideways in one motion through a sliding glass door and was swallowed up by the silence of the night. The streets behind him were deserted. As the figure crossed just outside the circle of a halogen streetlamp, a flicker of his shadow etched itself across a concertina wire fence deep within an otherwise pitch black alley. Behind him, on the other side of the sliding glass door, he had left the bloody corpse of a still-lovely young woman, beautiful even dead.

A rope, carefully turned in dog collar fashion around her neck and knotted at the base of her throat, was evidence of the cruel and fatal control a demented killer had during the last moments of his helpless victim's life, just another in a series. With over fifty stab wounds bunched together in her left chest, her body was a road map of the killer's ritualistic and obsessive need for overkill. In a final fit of necropohilic fantasy, so as to acid-etch into his memory an image for his private moments, the killer placed a long-stemmed rose between her lips and carefully scalpeled out her right breast with a surgeon's skill, a totem to fuel his later fantasies. That night, behind the sliding glass door in that first-story apartment, a woman was terrorized, slaughtered, defiled, and then arranged in a pose more frightful than one ever conceived by those who created Hannibal Lecter or Freddie Kruger and it was real.

We have lost count of the number of times a terrorized public has suffered through the menacing presence of a crazed killer on the loose, grazing on a local population of victims until he is caught, dies, or simply moves on to his next feeding ground. The more bizarre the murders, steeped as they always are in grisly details, the deeper the threat to the community. And most people don't know this, but almost every citizen in what police cite as high-risk groups has, at one time or another, been placed in jeopardy by an invisible stalking killer: lone travelers, men or women, in a strange city at night; gay men simply minding their own business; children walking home from school or waiting at the bus stop; children, especially toddlers, who momentarily stray from their parents in shopping centers or even supermarkets; college coeds who believe too much in the security of their own campuses; or prostitutes cruising the streets in a red-light district. The cases in which these high-risk victims are killed become sensationalized. Newspaper editors slug in highly charged headlines such as 'Torso Killer,' 'Boston Strangler,' 'Nightstalker,' and 'Trash Bag Killer' in an effort to personalize or brand-name the elusive murderer for their lead stories until the identities of the killers become known. In naming a killer with phrases that include the words 'strangler,' 'ripper,' 'butcher,' 'slasher,' 'stalker,' or even 'trash bag' and 'torso,' the media types rarely understand that these very words pinpoint the actual pathological symbols each killer sees as his true nature, his psychological driver, the engine that gives the feeling of control over others and his environment that he obsessively seeks.

Of course, the thought of mutilating a beautiful woman repulses most of us. Any normal person would shrink from the mere thought of the violence itself. Many of us who actually reach the throes of a fury-driven passion on occasion will still recoil before committing an act of serious violence, because we have been socialized against it. We fear what we might do – the beast within – even more than we fear the legal consequences of our violent passions. But to a compulsive killer, the acts of mutilation and overkill give him a sense of control and domination over his sexually degraded victim. They are the framework of his psychopathological imprint – something he must act out, something that drives him to kill time and time again.

Killers like that strike as though they are invisible, nameless phantoms who just pop out of nowhere and disappear without leaving a trail. Only the most experienced homicide investigators can recognize the common denominators and predictable changes from one crime scene to the next in a series of murders, even before the victims' acquaintances and relatives are traced. They can find the one central thread, the 'calling card' of the multiple killer that is present in all of the homicides. This is what homicide detectives call 'the signature' of the killer. It lies within the very nature of the killer that his signature will be recreated in each and every murder he commits. Homicide detectives who know how to find a killer's signature and understand what that signature means are usually more successful in solving serial crimes than their counterparts who proceed, sometimes unthinkingly, along traditional paths.

When what are apparently signature murder cases in the state of Washington cross county lines or overwhelm a local police force; when serial murder cases in another state require an outside pair of eyes to bring them into focus; when the brutality of a homicide makes even the most veteran detectives shudder – that's when the phone rings on my desk. It's my job to pull together the different threads in a signature murder case, especially if the killer's a serial, and help set up the task force to bring these monsters in. I try not to rely on prepackaged psychological profiles, courtesy of amateur behavioral scientists. I look, instead, for what I call the components of a signature murder, the pieces of crime-scene evidence and victim profile that tell me what this guy is after and where he's going to strike again. I want the task force to be there to catch him.

As a specialist in signature murder, I see the most grisly and horrifying aspects of the homicide and daily face the devastating and demoralizing truth about what one human being can do to another. I see the frailty not only of the victim but of the killer, his weakness and hopelessness etched in dried blood with every knife stroke and each bruise on the victim. Like Joseph Conrad's Kurtz, I travel up a river of blood into the very heart of darkness, the deep-frozen center of a signature killer's soul. I must go there to recreate the working record of the last hours of the victim's life after she had the extreme misfortune of crossing the path of a signature serial killer trolling for his next target.

Signature Killers

CHAPTER I

The Calling Card of a Signature Killer

What are the trademark traces of a signature killer and how do we know when one has struck? Not surprisingly the elements that comprise a signature murderer personality are elements that we find in many unhappy and disturbed people. In the case of a serial signature killer, these elements are distorted to the extreme. In 1975 when I was the lead investigator in the 'Ted' murders in King County, Washington, I didn't really know what would lead us to the killer. I realized we had victims who were so similar to each other in looks, they could have been sisters. I also soon discovered that we had an assailant capable of taking his victims off so surreptitiously, he could do it in the midst of a crowded beach or on a busy barroom dance floor. It was only when we revisited the cases months later that we understood the common threads that ran in patterns through his murders. In retrospect we saw that they were there even when he consciously and deliberately changed his methods of operation to throw us off or to experiment with new ways of getting sexual thrills. These common threads that extend from crime to crime have come to be known as the signature.

WHAT IS A SIGNATURE KILLER?

The killer's signature is his psychological 'calling card' that he leaves at each crime scene across a spectrum of several murders. I have come to recognize individual calling cards from the thousands of crime scenes I've investigated of the hundreds of serial killers whose paths I've crossed. So my life and work as a homicide detective have taught me to look for the unusual – what is rare – that makes one murder so very different from another. By that method, when one sees something rare in one murder and recognizes the same thing a week later, those unusual acts in two murders are often the signature of a lone killer. For example, when the killer in one murder intentionally leaves the victim in a position so the victim will be found open and displayed, posed physically spread-eagled and vulnerable; when he savagely beats that victim to a point of overkill and violently rapes her with an iron rod, you have to consider that fundamentally unusual. After a second murder in which the killer does the same things, even though he may slightly modify one or two of the features, there is little doubt in my mind that the two murders are related. The killer has left his signature.

Most people confuse MO, or modus operandi, with signature, as if the two were the same thing. They're not. An MO, the definitions for which go back to the seventeenth century, is simply the way in which a particular criminal operates. If he commits breaking and entry burglaries by using a glass cutter to get through a door and suctions the glass away so it doesn't fall to the ground and make noise, that's his MO. If he uses flypaper instead of a suction cup to hold the glass fragments together so they don't make noise, that's a different MO. When police find flypaper traces at a crime scene, they go back to their files and look for breaking-and-entry burglars who've used flypaper, and from there they form a list of suspects.

Certain criminals operate only at night; others like to watch particular ATM machines in isolated locations where they wait for a specific victim type, such as a lone woman or an elderly person. Still others like to frequent crowded events where they pick pockets and steal pocketbooks, then fade away into the mob of people. Basically, an MO accounts for the type of crime and property involved. It includes the victim type, the time and place the crime was committed, the tools or implements used; the way the criminal gained entry or how he approached or subdued his victim (this includes disguises or uniforms, ways he represented himself to a victim, or if he used props such as a bike or pair of crutches), whether he used associates, and any distinguishing trademarks he might have left (such as poisoning a guard dog or using a special pick to break a lock, or even engaging in conversation with the victims). Sounds pretty straightforward, doesn't it? It is, for most crimes.

However, the MO is not the only evidence to go by, although many police investigators act as though it is. I've found in a lot of the cases I've worked that police detectives rely so much on MO that if the MO changes even slightly from one crime to the next, they go off looking for a different criminal even when there are other striking similarities linking the crimes. For example, let's say that we find a series of killings in which there are three white women who are victims and one black woman. Even though the crimes may be similar – all on or near university campuses, all committed in isolated areas within ten to fifteen miles of one another, all cases of rape murder – the fact that one young victim was black while the others were white usually causes police to hunt for two suspects. That's what happened in Rochester, New York, in 1989 during the Arthur Shawcross case. The killer attacked both black and white prostitutes as well as other women who crossed his path who weren't prostitutes. The different victim types sent the police in different directions, at times looking for at least three separate killers. But it was a lone killer, ex-convict and parolee Arthur Shawcross, who confessed to all the murders.

Also, criminals aren't always as stupid as people make them out to be. I've interviewed career criminals who spend long stretches of their lives in prison where they frequent the prison libraries to read the very same law enforcement textbooks police read in their academy courses. Crooks, rapists, and killers all read about 'techniques of investigation,' 'crime-scene management,' 'interviewing the suspect,' 'identification of stolen property,' and 'the fundamentals of criminal MO.' The bad guys will readily admit to me that after they read a book on MO, they deliberately change their MO from crime to crime when they are on the street again. Sounds simple, but it throws police, trained rigidly in MO investigation, right off the track. And the bad guys are rightfully proud of this because, like George C. Scott's famous line from *Patton*, they proclaim to anyone who will listen, 'I read your book.'

SIGNATURE VERSUS MO.

Because it can change, it is foolish simply to say that because there are different MOs in a number of cases otherwise related by time, place, or area, homicides can't be related. That's what kept the police in the Atlanta child murders, and the Arthur Shawcross murders in Rochester, New York, running around chasing phantoms for so long. However, there are other crime-scene indicators that relate murders even when the MO changes. Many sexually sadistic repetitive killers, for example, go beyond the actions necessary to commit a murder. The

MO of the killer can and does change over time as the killer discovers that some things he does are more effective. The FBI's John Douglas of the Behavioral Sciences Unit in Quantico has said that the modus operandi of a killer is only those actions which are necessary to commit the murder.

Beyond the MO, there are many, many killers not just satisfied with committing the murder and going on their way. They have a compulsion to leave their own personal stamp. The killer's personal expression takes the form of his unique signature, an imprint left by him at the scene, an imprint the killer is psychologically compelled to leave to satisfy himself sexually. In Ted Bundy's lingo, it's whatever the killer 'gets his rocks off on.' The core of a killer's imprint will never change. Unlike the characteristics of an offender's MO, the core remains constant. However, a signature may evolve over time, such as in cases where a necrophilic killer performs more and more post-mortem mutilation from one murder to the next. The FBI's behavioral scientists say that the signature elements of the original personal expression don't change, they just become more fully developed.

John Douglas once described the nature of the signature as the person's violent fantasies which are progressive in nature and contribute to thoughts of exhibiting extremely violent behavior. As a person dreams and thinks of his fantasies over time, he develops a need to express those violent fantasies. Most serial killers have been living with their fantasies for years before they finally bubble to the surface and are translated into deeds. When the killer finally acts out, some aspect of the murder will demonstrate his unique personal expression that has been replayed in his fantasies over and over again. On the same subject, retired NYPD homicide detective Vernon Geberth wrote that it's not enough for these types of murderers just to kill, the murderer must act out his fantasies in some manner over and beyond inflicting death-producing injuries. From my experience, I've seen lust killers who have a need to bludgeon to the point of overkill, others who carve on the body, or signature killers who leave messages written in blood. Some rearrange the position of the victim, performing postmortem activities which suit their own personal desires. In each of these ways, they leave their psychopathological calling card at the crime scene.

I begin to look at murder scenes as a series when I see the same type of extraordinary violence similarities. This physical evidence is usually accompanied by my gut instinct which tells me there's more that's alike than different. But another homicide investigator might look at the evidence and say the killer used a pipe wrench as a blunt instrument here, a ballpeen hammer there, and in this third crime we can't even figure out what weapon he used. Maybe the killer draped a pair of underpants on the victim's left leg. In the next crime scene, the underpants were on her right leg or maybe still on the bed. These are differences, I'll agree. Yet, in each case, I will argue that the victim was obviously beaten well beyond the point of death by an assailant whose violence seemed to increase in frenzy while he was attacking her. Also, the killer seemed preoccupied with the victim's clothing and took some time to arrange the crime scene, even though there might have been people living just upstairs. When I compare evidence like this, I see overwhelming similarities. These are the psychological calling cards the killer actually *needs* to leave at each scene. These constitute his signature and remain relatively constant from crime to crime, even when the killer deliberately changes his MO because of situational circumstances or as an attempt to throw us off his trail.

Through the years since Bundy, I became increasingly aware of the nature of serial murder cases in which the killer seemed to be acting in an unconscious pattern when it came to victim profile, exercising control over the victim, inflicting wounds of specific types, postmortem activity with the victim's body, and disposing the body. Even though the killer varied his MO, things about the crimes were eerily the same. What was this pattern? The more serial cases I examined or consulted on, the more aware I became of the pattern. I was intrigued as well as disturbed. Instinctive homicide investigators were able to home in on the patterns also, but didn't take conscious notice of it. I knew there had to be something there beyond the MO of the serial killer, something that told us more about the murderer than he wanted us to know, something that would allow us to make predictions not only about where the killer had come from and where he had been, but where he would go and what he might do next. The more research I did, the more it became clear that the killer was not just committing one crime in a series, but that each crime was a different act in a drama that had been going on throughout his entire life. The individual act contained the same plot, same characters, and same dialogue, and came to the same conclusion. But the psychodrama itself was an evolving story. If you knew the story, you might know how to stop the killer.

But first you had to know what to look for. For me, that object lesson in reading beyond the obvious elements of the crime scene took place in 1977 at my very first signature murder case. There I learned that to find the core of a killer's signature, I had to be educated and alert to the changes in a killer's modus operandi and ever cognizant of those features of a killer's calling card that never change. I had to train myself to look for the similarities that relate the core identities of the crime, and not get hung up on the differences that the killer was leaving behind to throw me off his trail. My instructor was a sadistic serial killer named Morris Frampton.

THE MURDER AT THE SOUTH PARK MARINA

The morning of August 9, 1977, started out at sixty-one degrees on the way to such a bright, sunny day in Seattle that all personnel on duty in the Major Crimes Unit of the King County Police were wishing they were any place but inside the Courthouse. Sgt. Bob Schmitz, on call-out duty, received a call from the Communications Center at about 7:45 A.M. that someone had discovered the body of a woman who'd been killed at the South Park Marina. He immediately cleared all available teams out the detective's bull pen and sent us to the crime scene.

When the news of the marina murder hit, I had already been locked in the 'Bundy Room' for the better part of three years. I spent the majority of my time investigating cases in which the psychological characteristics of Ted Bundy had long since been hidden by decomposing bones found at two separate crime scenes and monitoring the Ted Bundy cases in Utah and Colorado. With the discovery at the South Park Marina, I would investigate the fresh corpse of a homicide victim bearing the telltale psychopathological marks of a vicious killer. It would be my first signature case, the importance of which could not be underrated because it was my introductory lesson to the paradigm of the signature killer, a phenomenon relatively unknown at that time. But, partly because I was working on the Ted Bundy case and partly because I had been reading the works some criminologists had been writing about the signature of murder, I had prepared myself for these types of cases by consulting with clinical psychologists and forensic psychiatrists about the subject.

Within one quarter of an hour after we were dispatched from the bull pen, we arrived at the front gate to the marina. The marina was located at Sixteenth Avenue South and South Dallas Street, just one block outside the city limits of Seattle. Nestled among industrial buildings, the marina serves boat owners who moor their small craft on the Duwamish River. I peeked through an eight-foot-high chain-link fence and got my first glimpse at the bloody remains of what once looked to have been a beautiful woman. Her face was still etched with the pain and injuries from what was surely an horrendous beating, a reality later attested to by an autopsy report that methodically listed her eighty-one injuries.

Maybe the killer thought that he had gotten away clean with the murder, but the police had a witness. Within fifty feet of the entrance, and inside the gate of the South Park Marina, Sharon Adams was asleep, all alone in her trailer which she shared with her husband who worked the late shift out at Boeing. At 3:05 A.M., she was startled out of sleep by the throbbing of an idling engine and grabbed her electric clock off the nightstand to read the time. The engine idled for about another minute, then it was shut off. Sharon heard crashing noises and the sound of metal being kicked. At first she thought she heard a child, but then decided it was the voice of a woman moaning and whimpering. She heard the sound of skin on skin, which she described as the slapping sound of sexual intercourse, rhythmic, repetitive. Frightened, she dressed just in case she needed to get away from whoever it was. Then she heard the woman's voice again, this time pleading, 'Don't, I'm already dead.' Things outside were quiet for a minute, then she heard the sound of two doors slamming and an engine turning over. With the noise of tires spinning out in gravel, the killer's car left the scene. Adams stayed put, locked inside the trailer with no telephone. Only when officers arrived, after the manager had called them upon seeing a dead body, did she come out to tell her story.

The unidentified dead woman was laid out in a supine position and was located about thirty feet southeast of the gate on top of a small sandpile. She was nude, strangled with a black piece of elastic that was tightly wound around her neck. In the rising morning sun, her body didn't glisten because of all the injuries that broke the smooth surface of her skin. I did notice that most of her injuries had been inflicted before death. You could tell this because predeath wounds bleed out very profusely and the bruises around the breaks in the skin are often a bright raspberry color or bluish red. Postmortem wounds rarely bleed out, and the bruises around them are a yellowish brown or deep brown. The victim we found at the marina had been tortured by the constant beating of a sadistic maniac. She was left with her legs spread, as though the killer wanted her to be found that way, fully exposed in a humiliating pose. Was there some message in the positioning of her body in plain view? I would soon discover that there was. The inner portions of her thighs were bruised by the blunt instrument used to rape her. Her left arm was obviously broken since it bent into the shape of an *S*. The back of her head was savagely beaten in, and the weapon's mark was indelibly etched across her back. You could clearly see the marks on the back of her body in a linear fashion which corresponded exactly to the corrugations in a piece of rebar found within fifteen feet of the body. In the frenzy of the attack, the killer had forgotten to take it with him.

Physical evidence was abundant at the crime scene. According to Locard's principle of transference, the killer would have taken blood and hair from the victim and sand from the pile with him or on him. He left his murder and rape weapon, a five-eighths-inch-wide piece of pipe about two feet long with a piece of rebar bent so it was wedged or stuck inside the pipe. The entire weapon was about four feet long. The killer's vehicle left tire impressions. A yellow spongy material was strewn all over the scene and was spread to a location in line with the suspect vehicle's trunk. The killer's car struck the gatepost upon entering the South Park Marina. Therefore, in accordance with Locard, there were two types of paint transfer, green paint transferred *to* the post *from* the suspect's vehicle and gray and blue transferred *from* the post *back onto* the killer's car. Surely with all that evidence we could identify the killer, but we had to find him quickly before he cleaned up his vehicle.

Neither I nor the other detectives at the scene had ever seen such a brutal murder. This type of sexually related killing was extremely rare. In the history of murder in Seattle, there was only one other, committed by the same killer two weeks before the discovery at the South Park Marina.

The murder case at the South Park Marina was not only a whodunit but also a who-is-it, the worst of all possible combinations for homicide investigators, because in this instance you're really searching for two identities instead of one. Before you can identify the killer, you usually have to identify the unknown victim, and that can take weeks or even months. But this time we caught a break. Within hours of clearing the scene, I received crucial information which led to the identity of our victim. News of the murder had spread quickly to Seattle detectives who, in checking police reports from the previous shift, came up with a 'found property' report which detailed the discovery of a purse in the International District where prostitutes were known to hook. At 1 A.M. that same day, an anonymous caller frantically reported that he just saw a female beaten by a large man with bushy hair and glasses. The assailant also tore off her clothes and stuffed her into the trunk of a dark-colored car. By the time police arrived – just before three in the morning – the car was gone. All police found was a purse belonging to a Rosemary Stuart, also known as Rosemary Park. She was a slender white woman, five feet four inches and 104 pounds, who used two dates of birth – December 17, 1950 or 1951 – and had a rap sheet listing multiple arrests for prostitution. Her fingerprints, taken when she was booked, matched those taken at the autopsy from the body at the South Park Marina. We had our victim.

THE MURDER OF IANTHA BUCHANAN

When I called to thank the Seattle detectives for the information, they told me they had recorded another fatal attack on a prostitute recently. This time, they said, they were investigating the murder of Iantha Buchanan, a black female prostitute.

King County Medical Examiner Dr. Donald Reay estimated that Buchanan's murder took place July 30, 1977, sometime between 2:00 and 4:00 A.M., exactly nine days prior to the murder of Rosemary Stuart. Her body was discovered lying on top of the cement foundation of a building construction site about five miles from the South Park Marina. From my review of the case and the crime-scene photographs Seattle detectives gave me, I could see that with the exception of the location and the victim's race, the same psychopathological aspects in the killer's character were present here as in Rosemary Stuart's murder.

This happened to be my first serial murder investigation where the killer was racially indiscriminate in his choice of victims. This is becoming increasingly common in prostitute murder cases – especially serial murders – where the issue is not the race of the victim or the race of the killer, but the vulnerability of prostitutes who are already working outside the law, seeking to attract potential customers, and placing themselves under the predator's control as an unwitting process of their business.

Like Stuart, Buchanan had suffered a terrible beating with multiple blows so devastating it was clear that the killer was out not only to kill her, but to destroy her. She died from multiple blunt impact injuries to the head.

She had fractures of the vault and base of the skull, extensive cerebral cortical contusions, and extensive fractures of the facial bones. She also received blunt impact injuries to the neck and trunk and suffered from a broken right clavicle. Drag marks in blood on the newly dried concrete surface showed that the killer dragged her from the front of the building to the back. Like Stuart had been, Buchanan's body was graphically posed in the corner of the building. She was lying on her back with her pubic region fully and deliberately exposed. One leg was propped up against the rear wall and the other propped up against the side or intersecting wall. Her feet were twenty-three inches from the floor. She was partially nude with her panty hose on her left leg but removed from the right leg. Intertwined in the nylons was her underwear. Her red skirt was pulled up and covered her face. She was wearing a black blouse, but it had been ripped open, exposing her chest. At the scene but several feet away from the body, detectives found the victim's bra. This was one of the most physically degrading displays of a victim I had ever witnessed.

This sight of a bludgeoned victim lying fully exposed at the crime scene was also extremely disturbing even to the most seasoned Seattle homicide detectives, because it was obvious to all that the killer was performing a ritual act of violent retribution on women to the point where the identity of the victim seemed far less important than the fact that she was female. The Buchanan and Stuart murders went far beyond pure and simple homicide into a realm investigators call 'overkill.' The repeated infliction of injuries was so intense that murder was incidental to the actual wounds. The infliction of injuries was itself the purpose of the crime. Cops have seen overkill before, but this was different. The level and sheer intensity of violence the murderer inflicted upon Buchanan's and Stuart's bodies was beyond anything detectives had ever seen.

Seattle police quickly identified Buchanan from the ID cards in her black purse they found at the scene. She was twenty-seven years old, five feet seven inches tall, and a slight 127 pounds. She would have been physically very easy to control for a large man the size of Stuart's killer. Detectives quickly determined that alleged local pimp Marcus Jackson, her live-in boyfriend, was the last person to have seen her alive at about 9:45 P.M. They had left their apartment together on July 29 to work the streets in downtown Seattle, and Jackson lost sight of her as she walked away. Typically, she would make contact with a trick, agree on a price, and then direct the trick to the Moore Hotel, where the couple maintained two 'trick' rooms. She would walk ahead of the trick, meet him by the elevator, and then take him to one of the rooms. Jackson claimed that Buchanan would not turn tricks inside a vehicle. But something happened that night to change her usual methods. Whatever it was had proved fatal.

THE SIGNATURE ANALYSIS IN THE BUCHANAN AND STUART CASES

There was no official signature analysis completed on these two cases in 1977 because we didn't know anything about signature analysis back then. Now, as I look back on these two murders after having investigated and consulted in thousands of homicides since then, signature analysis seems clear to me. Therefore, the analysis presented here reflects that experience. It allows me to examine the Buchanan and Stuart murders and render an informed opinion about their killer and his signature.

To my mind, both the Stuart and Buchanan cases display the classical signature of the sexually sadistic serial killer. Homicide cops in these cases knew what they were looking at even if they didn't know what to call it.

That's why initially, the detectives had linked the two murders only by their gut instincts based on what they observed, not on any observable combination of events that directly related the two cases. Without calling it a signature case, the obviousness of the overkill in both murders led detectives to suspect that the killer was the same, even though for the purposes of signature analysis, one must examine the Buchanan case first and discover the subtle changes in MO from that case to the Stuart case.

If you took the individual MO factors in both cases separately, no matter which case occurred first, and totally neglected the evolving signature of the killer, you would develop the false theory that they were killed by different people because, according to traditional homicide theory at that time, prostitute killers did not routinely cross racial boundaries: white prostitute killers killed only white prostitutes and black prostitute killers killed only black prostitutes. Therefore, police would assume that they were looking for two different killers, one white and the other black.

However, to understand those two murders in their true context, you would first have to examine the characteristics of murders throughout the last ten years in the Pacific Northwest. This is what police routinely do when they investigate bizarre sex crimes such as the South Park Marina murder, because they need to establish a pattern background for what types of murders occurred within a particular area. In this case, the analysis showed that no other homicides resembled the unique characteristics of Stuart and Buchanan. Those two murders, committed within nine days and five miles of each other, within the same jurisdiction, and exhibiting the same degree of violence inflicted upon the body, were truly rare in occurrence. In fact, they were unique. But we could learn this only after we had conducted an examination of the frequency of similar cases throughout history for our particular region. This is what the signature analyses of homicide cases sometimes requires.

Stepping away physically from the multitude of details at each scene by examining two-dimensional photographs and the three-dimensional descriptions of external evidence of injuries from the autopsy reports, you get more than a glimpse of the core of the killer's signature. The overpowering sight of bodies lying in positions reflecting the killer's fantasy of a degraded victim – legs splayed grotesquely exposing the pubic area of each woman as if mocking their sexuality, the massively fractured skulls which suffered multiple fatal trauma wounds, and the fact that the victims' bodies were intentionally, almost ritualistically, displayed in areas where the killer knew each victim would obviously be found – represents the repetitive core of this killer's signature. In the average person's mind, the killer didn't have to perform all those things just to commit murder. There was something more going on in the killer's mind than simple homicide. As the noted California psychiatrist, Dr. Park E. Dietz, once said about sexually related murder at a homicide seminar I attended, sexual sadists who commit these crimes do so to 'fulfill their sexual desires.' Even if the killer commits other crimes such as robbery, felony-murder, or drug trafficking, it is only the sexual murder that 'objectifies his basic sadistic pathology.' I would add that you can see the difference in the intent of the crimes from the nature of the killer's signature. He always displays his psychological stamp at the crime scenes even though aspects of the crime he commits or the method he uses may change from crime scene to crime scene.

In the Frampton case, the abduction of a black woman, Iantha Buchanan, and then a white woman, Rosemary Stuart, shows a change in the killer's modus operandi. Police usually link victims of the same race to the same killer because traditional sexual violence theories teach that statistically, blacks kill blacks and whites kill whites.

But we now know that when it comes to a serial prostitute killer, streetwalkers and those whom he perceives as prostitute types are his victims and fair game no matter what their race. The serial attacks upon prostitutes actively hooking on street corners is the basic calling-card signature of a killer who knows exactly how such women can be picked up and ultimately controlled. Prostitutes' vulnerability and willingness to get picked up is the profile that attracts the killer and drives him into a sexual frenzy.

The killer in the Buchanan and Stuart cases used the very intimate method of choice for many sexually sadistic killers: a frantic, hands-on, extreme bludgeoning. In this signature trait, the hammering away at the victim strike after strike actually increases his sexual fury throughout the crime. The killer becomes more intense and whips himself deeper into a violent, trancelike state with each blow until his fury is expended. The blows themselves and the stripping away of the victim's humanity with each massive bone-smashing wound only incite the killer to greater violence. What's even more telling is that the killer escalates the overkill from victim to victim. He's on a continuum of violence throughout his criminal career, which will result in a greater number of fatal injuries to his victims as the killer extends his series. For example, the number of intimate injuries – actual blows administered by the killer's hand to the victim – increased from the Buchanan murder to the Stuart murder, indicating to me that the escalation itself of overkill injuries – wounds inflicted beyond those necessary to cause death – was the killer's true gratification, not the inflicting of injuries upon any specific victim. The feeling of additional thumping of fatal injuries in which the killer felt the resistance and texture of the victim's body and his administering of torture to terrify his victim satisfied his lust for the crescendo of violence, total mastery over the victim, and his sexual satisfaction aroused by intense fury. As we will see with other signature killers presented and following here, the acts of stabbing, beating, and thumping on victims reduces the victim herself to an almost meaningless thing in the killer's mind. She becomes only an asset of opportunity.

The overkill sexual murderer is usually incapable of sexual orgasm without performing violent acts. He probably only reaches a climax, if he ever reaches climax at all, when the victim is dead and displayed. It is just as likely that the overkill signature killer is hardwired so perversely in the neural circuitry of his primal brain that sex becomes violence and violence becomes sex, in such a way that the killer never reaches climax at all, or if he does it's much later and in private. Many times in cases like these, the fury expanded in carrying out violence is the only physical or psychological release the killer experiences.

The last trait of the Buchanan/Stuart killer's signature was the way he inserted foreign objects into the victim's sexual orifice. He experimented with this and it looked as though he was evolving a methodology of how he would defile his victims. Step one in the Buchanan case was to pose her in plain view. This was a core element of his signature that he repeated in the Stuart murder and would have repeated with subsequent victims. The next stage in this evolution, once the victim has been posed with her legs spread, is to insert a foreign object into the victim's vagina. This stage is considered a sexual perversion that evolves over time from one murder to the next in cases where the killer is posing his victims. There was no evidence of sexual insertion of a foreign object in the Buchanan case, but there was such evidence in the Stuart case. The killer's sexual experimentation in the Buchanan case was to pose her in a bizarre state of undress after ripping her clothing off. The killer ripped the clothes off Stuart, too, but had evolved his method into a more violent act of defilement by inserting the rebar into her vagina.

These sexual acts of violent disrobing, ripping of clothing, and foreign object insertion were derived from the killer's need to cause pain and terror and to humiliate each victim by leaving them in a state of utter defilement. This is how I knew the same killer had committed both crimes even though Stuart's murder was more violent than Buchanan's. The killer was simply getting more frantic and was experimenting with his own bizarre sexual fantasies. You could actually see these fantasies evolving from one crime to the next. I knew from the escalation of violence in the Buchanan and Stuart murders that he would kill again very soon.

CATCHING THE KILLER

By now, leads in the Buchanan-Stuart murders were coming into the investigation fast and furious. A service station attendant reported seeing a white male with blood all over him, but with no visible signs of injuries, drive his green 1969 Dodge Charger into a service station. The man was six feet three inches tall and dripping blood from his face, hands, and clothing. The service station attendant fixed the man's taillights while the man washed up in the restroom. The attendant discovered that three taillight bulbs were broken out from the inside of the trunk. Had Rosemary Stuart tried in vain to attract police attention to the car by breaking out the lights as she was being transported in the trunk of the car? The attendant described the car in detail: a two-door with a bench front seat instead of bucket seats, automatic transmission, black upholstery, two small yellow tires that were hooked together hanging from under the dash on the passenger side. There were beer bottles on the back floorboards and two beer bottles on the front passenger side. The car was really dirty with a throaty, labored idle as if it were in need of a tune-up.

In the trunk, the man noticed a pillow containing yellow foam stuffing. The witness said the driver of the car claimed to have been worked over and rolled for his money. This had to be our guy: tall, bushy hair, glasses, and driving a green car. Officers searched the restroom and recovered bloodstains, foam rubber, and hair samples. This evidence would eventually be compared to evidence found at the scene. Samples taken at the gas station matched the victim's hair and blood and the foam-rubber particles located at the scene.

We next searched Stuart's house in north Seattle where we discovered from her car registration that she probably drove a white Chevrolet. We confirmed this fact with her landlord, who also said she had a small child. But where were the car and child? We found out that Rosemary Stuart's child had been turned into child protective services because she never returned to pick her up from the babysitter. Next, knowing that Stuart liked to hang out in the International District, we searched those areas up the hill from the district that had free parking for Stuart's car. I drove up to the Yesler Terrace Apartments and found the white Chevrolet. Inside the car, I found the first few pages from the classified ads section of the *Seattle Times* newspaper. We would find the remaining pages of that same exact section to that newspaper several days later in a green Dodge Charger belonging to the killer. We would discover that the pages in the killer's car came from the remaining pages of the classifieds section left in Stuart's car.

For the next several days, in response to our all-points bulletin, police officers throughout King County and Seattle stopped vehicles and identified the drivers of 1969 green Dodge Chargers and beat-up reddish colored pickup trucks. At about 3:50 in the afternoon on August 14, 1977, Seattle police plainclothes officers Robert Avery and Jules Werner, working 2 William 96 in west Seattle, observed a 1969 black-over-green Dodge Charger heading westbound on Admiral Way. They followed the vehicle for about two blocks when the driver made a left-hand turn without signaling and failed to yield the right of way to an oncoming vehicle that had to brake and swerve wide to avoid an accident. Now, having a traffic violation they could use to pull the suspect vehicle over and identify the driver from what they knew from the homicide bulletins, the officers stopped the car in the 3200 block of Fifty-ninth Avenue Southwest just as the driver pulled in behind a rust-colored pickup truck. Driver Morris Frampton explained to the officers that the truck had a flat tire, and they were going to fix it and tow the truck home. Both Avery and Werner knew that a beat-up reddish colored pickup truck was a suspect vehicle in the Buchanan homicide and an assault on another prostitute. What a coincidence! The car they were looking for just happened to pull in behind another homicide suspect vehicle they were also looking for.

Werner checked the bulletins and recognized that the driver, Morris Frampton, fit the composite drawing. The officers had learned from my alert that the suspect Charger had a yellow wire dangling down under the dashboard on the passenger side. It was in plain view on the car they had just stopped. They were also looking for fresh damage on the car that the Charger would have received from striking the gatepost at the South Park Marina. It was there on the right front fender, and Officer Werner saw what appeared to be dried blood on the car's passenger seat. As he passed by the pickup, Werner noticed several pieces of rebar in plain view in the bed of the truck and knew from the APB that rebar was listed as a weapon in the county homicide case. With all this information, the officers placed Morris Frampton under arrest and turned him over to homicide detectives.

Ultimately, this arrest would end the search for the man who committed two murders and three vicious assaults.

At the Seattle Police impound building, Frampton's vehicles sat in picturesque display, teeming with the physical evidence of his murders. The Washington State Patrol Crime Laboratory tested both vehicles for trace evidence. They meticulously retrieved one piece of physical evidence after another that placed Rosemary Stuart in the Charger's trunk and also showed that car had been at the South Park Marina.

The most telling evidence discovered on the outside of the car was the paint transfers on the left front fender. Vertically, the scratches on that fender were exactly the same height as the scratches on the South Park Marina gatepost. The contact with the post caused dark green paint from highest portion of the damage to be transferred from the car. A lower scratch on the fender received the gray and blue paint from the gatepost. The mathematical possibilities of the transfer of paint coming from any place other than the South Park Marina were so far reaching that they elevated this evidence almost to the significance of a fingerprint.

A curious combination of evidence was also found on the top and near the headlight of the right front fender. Wedged in previous damage were small pieces of sand, traced back to the sandpile, caked with the victim's hair and blood. Crime-scene specialists guessed that when Frampton ran back to his car in a hurry to escape, he braced his hand on the fender as he ran around the front end of the car. That effort to support his weight transferred to the fender multiple traces of evidence which had accumulated on his left hand. Locard's theory of transference – the perpetrator leaves physical evidence of himself at the crime scene and takes physical evidence from the crime scene with him – was working overtime.

Upon reaching the undercarriage of the car, evidence

technicians found bloodstains that were eventually compared to and matched Stuart's blood type. On the lowest chrome sideguard on the car, a large swipe-type stain was found. It was clear, as we reconstructed the sequence of events leading to her murder, that at some point during the assault, Stuart tried to crawl under the man's car in a futile attempt to protect herself from his homicidal rage.

Lying on the rear seat of Frampton's Charger for all to see were pages from the classified ads section in the *Seattle Times* newspaper of August 9, 1977, the missing pages from the same section of the newspaper found in Stuart's Chevy. We surmised that Stuart had kept the classified section with her because an ad in it listed the telephone number of the babysitter she had left her child with that night.

The dankness of the impound garage usually depresses the spirits of anyone who enters. But this day was different. The Dodge Charger was perched on the lift in all its splendor with the white-coated laboratory personnel surrounding it as if they were ministers at an altar waiting for the oracle to give up its secrets. Their greatest discoveries would come from the Charger's trunk. There they found a cornucopia of incriminating evidence against Frampton. At first glance, tiny particles of yellowish foam rubber littered the inside. One would have thought that Frampton would have cleaned it out by then in case he were caught. But such wasn't the case. Each of those pieces matched in type, color, and consistency with the same particles I retrieved at Stuart's death scene. Mixed in with the spongy material was hair that was eventually found to be microscopically indistinguishable from the head hair of Rosemary Stuart. Bloodstains left by swiping motions covered the inner surface of the trunk lid. And then, incredibly, the victim's fingerprint was found etched in one of the bloodstains. It was like Christmas in August for members of the crime laboratory.

They had found enough physical evidence to put this guy away forever.

After pursuing for so long the evidence in the Ted Bundy cases and never finding anything that could link him to crime scenes in Washington State, the Stuart murder was astonishingly different. Frampton was considered a serial killer, and it had been common knowledge that such killers leave very little in the way of trace evidence that could link them to any one victim. But this was not the case with Frampton, because he was caught before he could clean evidence out of his car and his truck. Also, Frampton was an overkill signature killer, unlike Bundy who was a control-freak necrophile. Bundy didn't leave his victims out in the open where they could be found, until he got to Florida. In Washington, Colorado, and Utah, far from leaving his victims exposed the way Frampton did, Bundy took such pains to hide them that all we had were missing-person reports, not homicides.

I would learn from the Frampton case that when a signature killer is subsumed by his signature, he gives up control and the evidence will be there to catch him. Signature overkillers, in the act of smashing and splattering their victims, can be so taken over by the act of violence that they sometimes give up control and can never retrieve the evidence they leave. This is the aspect of overkill that is so important – in the act of violence, these killers surrender control. In surrendering control, they give up the aspect of invisibility that usually makes serial killers so difficult to catch.

Frampton was a classic example of a signature killer who was a sexual sadist. He didn't just kill his victims, he 'overkilled' them. And in these particular murders he first tortured his living victims to experience their terror and dread, and then enjoyed such postmortem activities as posing his victims' dead bodies and humiliating them by exposing them in plain view. The Morris Frampton case was the first in what would eventually become my specialty – the psychologically bizarre world of signature murder, its types, and its components.

HOW RAMPANT IS SIGNATURE MURDER?

Signature killers, the single largest subcategory of serial killers, are driven by such a primal psychological motivation to act out the same crime over and over again that their patterns become obsessive. All signature murderers seek some form of sexual gratification, and their crimes are expressions of the ways they satisfy that need. For example, inasmuch as most of the killers exert little or no control over their own existences or perceive themselves deep down inside as being life's losers and the victims of society, they gratify their sexual urges by demonstrating control over their murder victims. Whether that control manifests itself as necrophilia, bondage, humiliation, the torture of living victims, or the posing of dead victims, it is the control itself that supplies the killer with his gratification. The events leading up to the ultimate moment of control supply him with the excitement of anticipation.

In many ways, the behavior of signature killers so mirrors the behaviors of other types of addicts that it is important to see how the crime plays itself out as a progression of escalating, but linked, violent events. Like all addicts, signature killers work from a script, engaging in repetitive behavior to the point of obsessiveness. Their calling cards at the crime scenes – how they choose their victims, control their victims, mutilate or manipulate the bodies, and dispose of bodies – all display similar types of pathological deviance and repeat themselves no matter how their method of operation changes. Signature killers change their MOs, often experimenting with different ways of dealing with their victims and satisfying their sexual cravings. They often take mementos or souvenirs with them from their victims. The killers impart to these items a special kind of power to reinvigorate their excitement over taking the victim. When the excitement subsides over time, the killers go out hunting again, taking new mementos to sustain their fantasy life after the murder by reenergizing their sexual thrill so as to allow them to continue to experience the excitement of the crime they committed.

You can very often determine what type of psychological signature the killer has left by examining the crime scene, understanding the profile of the victims, and recreating the process of the crime. For example, prostitute killers fall into specific categories, child predators fall into another, and so do killers of gay young adults such as John Gacy and Jeffrey Dahmer.

Gacy picked up adolescent boys and young men at bus stations in Des Plaines, Illinois, with the offer of jobs at his construction firm. He was married and hated his compulsion for young boys, especially boys on the run or in trouble. Thus, he cruised for runaways, duped them into believing he was providing money and work, brought them back to his house, and killed them when they were under his control. He buried their bodies in his basement to hide their corpses. Gacy was convicted and executed for his crimes.

Jeffrey Dahmer, saying that he was a photographer looking for models, picked up young gay men in downtown Milwaukee with offers of money for a quick photo shoot. He brought his victims back to his apartment where he drugged them, killed them, and then dissected and cannibalized them. Jeffrey Dahmer *controlled* rather than killed, posing his victims for photos while they were unconscious before he killed them and cut up their bodies. He stored their body parts throughout his apartment and even painted the bare skulls of his victims for use as ritualistic decorations. Dahmer was murdered while serving a life sentence for multiple murder in a Wisconsin penitentiary.

Both Gacy and Dahmer, although they both killed young men, had different signatures. Gacy romanced and then murdered his victims, whom he buried beneath his house to dispose of them. Dahmer enjoyed cutting up his dead victims, devouring their flesh, and creating pieces of art from their skulls. He enjoyed living with his victims' remains.

The infamous Seattle serial killer Ted Bundy could not be intimate with his victims until after they were dead. If he had established a relationship with a woman, he did not kill her. It was only the women he observed from afar, or who happened to cross his path when he was cruising for victims, whom he murdered. And even then, Bundy's murders were a quick dispatch. It was the bodies he wanted to control, not the living victims.

New York's Arthur Shawcross was a ladies' man who hated women in the last phase of his career in Rochester. He threw police off his trail because instead of killing only prostitutes in the Lake Avenue district near the Genesee River, he killed any woman who put herself into his power and then threatened him afterward. Shawcross was the subject of an intense search in the Rochester area from 1989 through 1990, and was caught only after a police helicopter spotted him eating his lunch on a bridge over the Genesee River directly above the frozen corpse of his most recent victim.

Similarly, Seattle's Green River killer from the 1980s, and my personal nemesis, is a prostitute murderer who wants to be the last person to subdue the hooker he picks up off the Sea-Tac strip. Whether he or one of his copycats poses as a cop, a friendly caretaker in a familiar-looking cab, or even a medical doctor or social worker, it's the ruse he uses to trick an otherwise alert victim that turns him on. The Green River murders, the subject of a number of books and reality television shows, is one of the longest ongoing homicide investigations in the United States.

Different killers have different signatures. Killers who pulverize their victims leave one type of calling card, while killers who torture living victims or who play with corpses leave another. Some killers go through different signature phases during the same crime, smashing or crushing the life out of their victims with many fatal wounds and then posing their bodies as if to play with them after the violence of overkill has been expended. Some killers are less intimate with their victims than others, or display their hatred of an aspect of themselves in their victims instead of their need to be sexually satisfied.

Whatever the specific signature or signatures we determine from the crime scene, they all fall into one or more of the basic traits of sexual sadism – control, humiliation, progression, posing, torture, overkill, necrophilia, and cannibalism – that we see in the succeeding chapters. It is the combination of these that often gives us enough of a handle on whom we're looking for that we know where he might strike next, or when, like the Green River killer, he's probably passed us by. Each of these types of signatures is a clue not only to what the murderer does, but what he wants, what he seeks, and what drives him from victim to victim. Hidden among the evidence, often gleaned from the marks and wounds on the victim's body, or clues left at a body dumpsite, these signatures are the only ways the killer truly expresses himself. But if you're smart, you can figure out what the killer is really after.

During the course of my career, I've become so concerned over the dramatic rise in what I see as signature crimes, including murders, that I've made it my business to research this area extensively. From my first encounter with Morris Frampton to cases I'm working on to this very day, I've seen a pattern of growing violence so extraordinary and so dangerous that I realized we had to look over the horizon to see where this continuum of violence was taking us. There are ominous warning signs about the future confronting us. Though certain murders may be on the decrease, as the FBI statistics tell us, I believe signature crimes are rising quietly but dramatically. Where are these signature criminals coming from? Why are they literally pouring onto the streets in greater numbers than ever before? Can we ever figure out what makes a signature killer and can we prevent that series of events? For my answers I began at the very, very beginning of signature murder investigation in America, long before anyone called it signature crime. I began in Los Angeles at a time of coonskin caps, flintlock cap guns, the Mouseketeers, and the opening of Disneyland. I began right in the middle of the 1950s with celebrated LAPD homicide detective Pierce Brooks and the sad victims who fell prey to the 'Lonely Hearts Club killer.'

CHAPTER 2

The Discovery of Signature

Harvey Glatman, The Lonely Hearts Killer, and William Heirens, 'Stop me Before I Kill Again!'

There is a mystery surrounding the nature of signature murder. It perplexed investigators long before I began my career and well before there was the behavioral science unit of the FBI and the profilers who work up cases of serial killers for local police. The patterns of a signature murder crime scene are so bizarre they send shivers down your back, even if you've seen hundreds of crime scenes. What is obvious at these sites is the meticulous care the killer took in posing or positioning the body, the precise way a bondage killer tied his victim, the animalistic frenzy with which a killer delivered blunt trauma wounds to a corpse, or the murderer's precise placement of pricking wounds. You can sense the time and the care each killer took, and that is what makes you feel the most nauseated. Many police agencies want to turn away from such scenes and hope that a crime like this is a one-time-only occurrence. But the more experienced among us realize that the type of guy who leaves this kind of scene kills again and again.

My mentor, celebrated LAPD homicide detective Pierce Brooks, a pioneer investigator in the field of signature murder and one of the first people to talk about catching repetitive killers by examining their behavior at crime scenes, once said that serial signature killers can't be rehabilitated and really can't be cured in the way most people understand the word. They're habitual killers, Brooks said, who turn their murders into rituals during which they gain extreme sexual pleasure by humiliating, defiling, and ultimately destroying their victims. These people are different from the rest of us. Pierce Brooks led me into the labyrinth of serial signature murder through his analyses of cases and his presentations of crimes which forced one to look beyond the rational into the bizarre and surreal. His work and his cases are where any investigation into the nature of signature murder must begin. Brooks, a veteran of the infamous 'Onion Field' murder, trailblazed research into the infant science of criminology in America, developing the techniques that would lead to today's methods of investigating signature murders. In an era when most police didn't even know what a serial killer was, and if they did, they wouldn't have necessarily known what to do about it, Brooks was applying his skills to gruesome signature homicide cases. One of the most famous he worked on was 'the lonely hearts murders,' the signature crimes of Harvey Glatman, which challenged the investigative skills of police in southern California.

The name Harvey Glatman sounds more like that of an accountant or a lawyer, maybe someone who sat next to you in eighth-grade biology, than the cunning predator who rampaged through southern California in the late 1950s looking for lonely women. And indeed, Glatman did look just like television's beloved Mr. Peepers. He was slight, studious, and intense behind his large, round glasses – not the least bit menacing. In fact, maybe because of his large coyote ears, he looked harmless and funny. At least that's how he appeared to his victims, especially Shirley Bridgeford.

THE 'LONELY HEARTS KILLER' AND THE MURDER OF SHIRLEY BRIDGEFORD

Shirley Bridgeford had joined a 'lonely hearts club' in Hollywood because she was looking for companionship. Many unattached women did the same thing during the fifties in southern California. What she didn't know was that the intelligent Glatman, representing himself as a photographer for a lonely hearts magazine, enticing good-looking women to pose for him, was really a bondage-crazed sadist setting clever traps for his intended victims. With offers of money – what amounted to a modeling fee – to women flattered by the attention from a professional photographer, Glatman established both his ruse and method of operation. He lured unwitting victims into allowing themselves to be handcuffed or bound. At that point, they were helpless and Glatman was free to translate his sexually sadistic fantasies into homicides.

Glatman got Shirley Bridgeford's name in March 1958, when he contacted the lonely hearts club she had joined. Because that was the purpose of the club, a kind of a members-only singles bar, it was easy for Glatman to get anything he wanted. He didn't even have to show his driver's license to the young woman at the desk, and used the alias George Williams of Pasadena. That became his new identity. Then, posing as a photographer and giving the false name – his modus operandi – he phoned Bridgeford and made an appointment to meet her on the following Saturday night at her home in the San Fernando Valley. When Shirley Bridgeford came to the door, she saw a harmless-looking photographer who offered to take her for a drive in his car so they could get to know each other. Who had ever heard of a serial killer at a lonely hearts club? What had she to fear?

Glatman acted comfortably within his ruse, asking her

what she wanted to do, and then suggested that they just drive.

'Well, where do you want to go, just ride around?' he asked her. 'Drive for a while, is that right?'

And the couple drove for a couple of hours on the warm March night toward Oceanside until they parked off the highway in a secluded area. The conversation was innocuous at first, and then, in Glatman's words, 'We did some necking.' Glatman tried as hard as he could to push Shirley Bridgeford into having sex with him, but she began to push him away. So he took her for a bite to eat at a roadside restaurant when she said, 'It's getting pretty late. We should be starting back.'

But they didn't start back. Instead of driving back to Los Angeles up the coast highway, Glatman drove her east into the chaparral where he again pulled off the road.

'I wanted to see how far I could go with her and so we started necking again,' he told police. 'But I couldn't go as far as I wanted.'

He tried to push by tentatively raising the subject of sex and then trying to persuade her to have intercourse. When Shirley refused and then pulled away from his advances, Glatman pulled a gun from his glove compartment and told her to shut up. As she sat there looking at the gun and wondering what was going to happen next, Glatman promised her he wouldn't hurt her if she did what he said. They were miles from anywhere and any screams would have died in her throat beneath the sound of a gunshot. Bridgeford agreed to do whatever Glatman wanted. So he took her in the back seat and they had sex.

Now, with Shirley Bridgeford his silent victim and with the cover of darkness as his friend, Glatman drove southeast to a desert area in San Diego County where he stopped and waited until the sun came up. Glatman had already decided to kill Shirley in the same way he had killed a previous victim, Judy Dull. By telling Judy that he wanted to shoot some pictures as illustrations for mystery stories in a magazine he was working for, he persuaded her to pose as a victim with bound hands and feet. When he had securely tied her up with his favorite ropes, and she was completely defenseless, he killed her.

As in the Judy Dull murder, Glatman used the pretext of wanting to take bondage photos to tie up Shirley's hands and feet. He still had the gun, but he'd convinced her that if she only did what he told her, she wouldn't get hurt. So she acquiesced to his every demand. Once tied, Glatman posed his victim in the sand and then, after taking several pictures, he fastened a rope to the cord around Shirley's ankles, and pulled it tight so as to bend her knees up to her chin. He placed his knee into the small of her back, looped the rope twice around her neck, and pulled as hard as he could for five to ten minutes until, struggling as hard as she could, she went into convulsions and then stopped breathing. Glatman took his rope, left his dead victim in the isolation of the desert, and drove back to Los Angeles as quickly as he could, stopping along the way at various places only to throw away Shirley's purse and its contents. This would become a common modus operandi among repetitive killers like Ted Bundy, who fifteen years later would discard the belongings of his victims in similar fashion alongside roadways. Glatman kept about thirty cents in coins from Shirley's purse.

Glatman said later that his only purpose in calling Shirley Bridgeford up for a date was to have sexual intercourse with her either with her consent or by force. Murder wasn't on his mind at first, he said, until he pulled out his gun and knew he had committed a felony. But that was a lie, and the consent he said he sought was only self-serving rubbish. If he had to use force, he also admitted, he was prepared to kill her to avoid arrest. But judging from his sexually deviant behavior in photographing women in undergarments while bound and gagged in various degrading and humiliating positions, his plan had to have been to kill them in the first place. It was clear from what he did to women before he actually killed them that in Glatman's mind his victims were already dead from the moment he picked them up. Glatman was almost completely impulsive and repeated a pattern of behavior as if it were a matter of habitual need. He even told homicide investigators that when he and Shirley first parked before he tried to seduce her, he had reached the conclusion that he would have to kill her for his own safety. Murder was on his mind from the very first moments.

In July 1958, Glatman changed his MO significantly in response to a changing situation when it seemed as though fate had simply thrown another victim his way. Glatman's approach to women, like that of the most cunning of long-term serial killers, had always been dynamic and completely flexible depending on his access to and the susceptibility of unwitting victims. He played to his victims' needs and fantasies to lure them into a trap. Until he met victim number three, Ruth Mercado, most of the women he spoke to were looking only for companionship. But Mercado was different: she was looking for employment in the very career Glatman was offering. Glatman came across her name in a classified ad Ruth Mercado had placed in a local paper seeking work as a model. When Glatman read it, he immediately modified his MO and contacted her directly through the number in the ad. This time, instead of using the lonely hearts club as a cover, he had an even better cover to preserve his anonymity. Serial killers are opportunists, and Glatman seized upon the chance to contact a potential victim who was already looking for a photographer. Her defenses would be completely down.

Glatman called the number in the ad and made a date with Ruth to visit her at her apartment in the evening and interview her for the assignment. To Ruth, nothing seemed out of the ordinary. When he showed up at her door looking not the least bit threatening, the unsuspecting Mercado invited him right in. But just as soon as the door closed behind him, Glatman pulled a gun from his pocket and told her to keep quiet and do exactly as he said. He then ordered her to go to the master bedroom. He had gained control over her just like he had with Bridgeford and Dull, using a cover story to get them alone where he could spring his trap. Now he took even greater control, control that aroused him sexually. He bound her hand and foot and gagged her to keep her silent. Then he warned her, gesturing with his gun, that if she struggled or made any noise, it would be the end of her. She got the message and stayed put while Glatman checked out the apartment like a nervous cat burglar. Since Glatman had never taken anyone from a building before, he had to plan as he went along, changing his MO in each and every minute detail from the script he used with Dull and Bridgeford. This was all new to him, and he made sure his victim's apartment had a back door just in case he had to get out of there fast.

He came back to the bedroom where Mercado was just waiting, tied up and shaking in terror.

'Don't do anything foolish,' he ordered. 'I'm going to untie you.' Then he told her they were going to have sex right then and there, but she'd be all right if she didn't give him any trouble.

'Now, where's your money?' he demanded.

She pointed him to a stack of twenty or twenty-five dollars in bills on the dresser, which he stuffed into his pocket. Then he untied her and forced her to have sex with him again and again until she fell asleep. He waited in the darkness, listening to her heavy breathing, until just after midnight when he tied her hands behind her back, put a coat over her shoulders to hide her hands and arms, guided her to his car where he pushed her down into the seat, and drove her southeast from Los Angeles toward the desert in San Diego County.

When they arrived at the isolated location he had chosen, he pulled her out of the car and arranged her, just as he did with Shirley Bridgeford. Acting out his sexual compulsion to memorialize the control he exercised over his victims, Glatman took five or six pictures of Mercado with her hands and feet tied and in poses similar to those in the Shirley Bridgeford pictures. Not only was he satisfying himself sexually through the photography, he was creating a totem that would help him relive the excitement when he wasn't killing. At the same time, he was documenting his own signature for investigators, much like Jeffrey Dahmer in Wisconsin and Wesley Alan Dodd in Washington State would do over thirty years later.

After spending most of the day in the desert with Mercado, he told her it was too risky to take her back to Los Angeles. He was going to have to kill her, he said, but first he wanted to take more pictures. He told her he was going to take some 'flashlight pictures,' but it was only a ruse. He forced her to pose again with her hands and feet tied, but he quickly looped a piece of rope from her ankles to bend her legs back, put his knee in the small of her back, and wound the rope twice around her neck. Like a cowboy securing his calf at a rodeo, he pulled it as tight as he could for about five minutes while she twitched and gasped for air. He waited until her heaves subsided and her breathing stopped. Then he left her in the desert where her body would eventually decompose to a stage of skeletal remains. As he drove back to Los Angeles after the murder, he tossed most of Ruth's belongings out of the car along the highway. He kept about ten dollars that was in her purse, a wristwatch, and a few personal items such as a wallet with identification papers and some articles of clothing.

The beginning of the end for Harvey Glatman's career

took place on the evening of October 27, 1958, when a motorcycle cop discovered Glatman struggling with a frightened Lorraine Vigil as he attempted to keep a gun on her and tie her up while they were parked on a side road in Orange County. The officer quickly intervened and realized that Glatman had used the gun in an unsuccessful rape attempt. He arrested the sullen Glatman, who was stopped at the high point of gaining control over another victim, and who made no statements to the police. It would be up to interrogators from three law enforcement agencies to wheedle a confession out of this strange, bookwormish, bespectacled character.

Initially Glatman agreed to take a lie detector test, during which he denied any involvement in the murders of Dull, Bridgeford, and Mercado. But the polygraph readings indicated he was being untrue, so it was up to the detectives to find a way to get him to confess. In the cat-and-mouse interrogation that followed, Glatman said about the polygraph test, 'I just wanted to see how it worked. I know you found those pictures in my apartment.' With that statement, Glatman revealed to Pierce Brooks and the two other detectives that there was incriminating evidence – the photographs he took of his victims – in a locked toolbox in his apartment, because he believed the police had already found them. Actually, the police were unable to open the toolbox without a search warrant, but they had to fake their knowledge of these photos to get Glatman to talk about them so they could use his response as the probable cause to get a search warrant to get them into the toolbox.

Pierce Brooks said that he and the other two police officers had to fake knowing about the photographs during the hours of interrogation as Glatman lapsed into his confession, because they needed him to talk about the crimes. He had already admitted to the murders. Now it was a matter of getting the physical evidence against him – they needed the bodies of the three victims.

Glatman became convinced that because the police already had the incriminating photos of the murders of his victims in their possession, things would go harder for him if he didn't tell them all they wanted to know. Accordingly, he confessed to everything.

Glatman directed Detective Pierce Brooks and the other homicide investigators to where in San Diego County he had killed Bridgeford and Mercado. The officers found the remains of the two victims where he said they were, but because the piercing hot desert sun had completely dried their bones and obliterated Glatman's signature of bondage, the prosecution never raised the accusation of signature murder against him at trial even though the descriptions of his murders were examples of a true signature. In their search of Glatman's apartment, police found a metal toolbox that contained Ruth Mercado's billfold, some of her clothing, and the chilling photographs he took of Bridgeford and Mercado when he posed them in the desert. In true signature killer fashion, these items had reignited Glatman's sexual thrills in between each episode of murder.

The photographs were an essential part of Glatman's personal signature of murder, and that was why their existence had taken on a life of its own during the interrogation and had actually forced Glatman into a confession. They were even more than souvenirs because, in Glatman's mind, they actually carried the power of his need for bondage and control. They showed the women in various poses: sitting up or lying down, hands always bound behind their backs, innocent looks on their faces, but with eyes wide with terror because they had guessed what was to come. Their after-death photos were even more horrifying to police because they revealed Glatman's true nature. They showed the ways the killer had positioned his victims, and the psychological depravity they evidenced was deeply revolting. That a human being could so reveal the depths of his own weakness and feelings of insignificance through photographs was something investigators had not seen before. What were they dealing with here? Was Glatman something less than human? LAPD homicide detective Pierce Brooks had to find the answer.

First of all, Brooks believed that Glatman's confession that he decided at certain points to strangle each girl for fear of being caught was nothing more than an attempt to conceal his real psychological need for killing. His signature photos depicted a far different story. They were images of Glatman's detailed methodology of murder which showed a sequence of terror by re-creating the entire psychological arc of the crime. He first photographed each victim with a look of innocence on her face as if she were truly enjoying a modeling session. The next series represented a sadist's view of a sexually terrorized victim with the impending horror of a slow and painful death etched across her face. The final frame depicted the victim's position that Glatman himself had arranged after he strangled her. Innocence, the horror at her realization of being trapped, and her complete acquiescence in death: these are the central phases of Glatman's signature of serial murder. The photos showed that Glatman did not kill the three women to cover up the abductions and rape, but was driven by the essential part of his underlying behavior. Glatman had to experience his euphoria of violence with all three poses for each victim. His story that he just picked each victim up with the idea to engage in consensual intercourse was a complete lie. His only motive from the outset was to torture and murder, to bring each woman to a secluded place where he could exercise total and absolute control, to engage in sexually sadistic ridicule and to punish them before and after death.

The nature of Glatman's signature crimes was uncovered by Pierce Brooks, who in so doing became the first law enforcement officer to recognize the importance of determining the killer's calling card to link similar murders. His early investigation of Glatman was the forerunner of VICAP, the FBI's serial murder tracking program which Pierce first conceived of as a way to organize the vast amount of disparate evidence in signature murder cases that often confounded the police.

The Glatman murders were similar in their psychological elements to murders that took place in Chicago six years earlier. Those were the infamous crimes of another reputed genius, triple-murderer William Heirens.

THE LIPSTICK MURDERER

'For heaven's sake, catch me before I kill more; I cannot control myself,' was scrawled in bright lipstick on a mirror by William Heirens at the bizarre scene of a killing in 1945. What sort of message was that? investigators wondered. Was the unknown killer on a mission of self-preservation, wanting someone to catch him? Did some playful news reporter pen the words, as some had believed? Was the killer exhibiting some perverted, personal expression of control over his helpless victim and the police? Perhaps the writing was the power of a hysterical fantasy, something he just had to do no matter what. Or was it a Sherlock Holmes clue leading directly to the identity of a demented killer?

Heirens, a seventeen-year-old university student with an IQ of 129, terrorized Chicago for two years. He viciously murdered two adult women and a six-year-old girl and committed twenty-six additional crimes that included burglaries, robberies, and assaults. His career began with simple break-ins, but he gave off indicators of his pathology when he stole women's undergarments and urinated and defecated in the homes he'd entered. Eventually, his fantasies of violent sexual crime escalated to murder. He killed two women who, he falsely confessed to police, had interrupted his masturbation.

On January 7, 1946, Heirens's MO changed dramatically when he moved from murdering adult females to kidnapping a six-year-old child, Suzanne Degnan, from her home on the south side of Chicago. He broke into the child's room and subdued Suzanne in her bed. But he wasn't quiet about it. After hearing strange noises, the child's mother called out to see if she was all right, almost discovering the crime in progress. But Heirens forced the frightened Suzanne to say that she was okay, and then waited in the darkness until he heard the mother walk away, probably believing her daughter had gone back to sleep. Heirens immediately killed the little girl in her own bed, rolled her up in a blanket, and carried her to another basement where he had sex with her and mutilated her. Suzanne's dismembered body was later discovered in a sewer catch basin. A ransom note which was found by the child's father was the only trace left by her abductor. It was a further sign of control over the circumstances that the killer felt he needed to exert. Afterward, Heirens nonchalantly returned to his dormitory room.

Understandably, it would have been very difficult for traditional homicide investigators, even in big-city departments, to connect the murder of Suzanne Degnan to the murders of the two women, because it is unusual for predators of children to attack adults. It is so unusual, in fact, that in the standard classifications of homicide types, child murderers are categorized separately from all other murders. When killers cross the boundary and extend their reach from adults to children or the other way around, it is considered an anomaly to be looked at very carefully.

In my own files, the anomaly was Ted Bundy's final murder of twelve-year-old Kimberly Leach, which was a deviation from his pattern of attacking only coed-aged victims. I surmised that Ted was so desperate when he was down and out in Florida, driving a stolen vehicle, and on the run from the Chi Omega sorority house murders that he selected the first victim of opportunity just to satisfy his overwhelming sexual frenzy. Had he been less desperate and more in control, he most likely would have stayed within his preferred victim profile.

Similarly, Richard Allen Davis, convicted and sentenced to the gas chamber for the nationally publicized murder of twelve-year-old Polly Klaas in Petaluma, California, was not known as a child molester, nor was the infamous Milwaukee serial killer Jeffrey Dahmer, even though he was still on probation for child molestation when his murder spree began. New York State's Arthur Shawcross was originally convicted and sent to prison for the murder of two children, but upon his parole twenty-five years later he began killing prostitutes in the city of Rochester. New York State troopers and local police were dumbfounded because the Shawcross pattern technically was not a part of the killer profile, because the FBI believed the Rochester killer to be between twenty-five and thirty. Shawcross was forty-five. Police also dismissed Shawcross as a suspect early on because, they said, he had no driver's license. We now know that there are no hard and fast rules when it comes to selecting among victim types, because a sexual serial killer goes for whatever's easiest. However, when the rules work, his signature will usually remain the same even though he moves into a new victim population. And that's where an analytical homicide detective will find the solution to the mystery of the murder.

Therefore, although the elements of Heirens's signature murders were obvious, you can't blame the police for not recognizing them, because the knowledge of signature killing wasn't even the language of law enforcement in the 1940s, especially in Chicago. First, for Chicago cops in a city with a history of traditional gangland hits or murder-for-hire contracts, Heirens's three murders were atypical. The characteristics of those cases did not match any others during that era. Second, despite Heirens's changing method of operation from attacking adult females to attacking a young child, his signature remained constant. At the core of Heirens's signature was his obsession with defecation and urination, which were the vivid illustrations of his overwhelming compulsion to demonstrate the helplessness of his victims and control over police officers pursuing him. In other words, his domination reflected an attitude of 'I shit on everybody.' And last, the messages he scrawled were the visual representations of his attempt to manipulate others even though the wording was different in each note. It's not the actual wording of the notes or the writing medium, but his compulsion to leave notes that was the signature.

Like many other serial killers, Heirens's crime spree was brought up short when he was accidentally apprehended for a crime not directly connected to murder. On June 26, 1946, Heirens was stopped in the act of burglarizing a building, by an off-duty police officer. Heirens tried to shoot his way out, but his pistol jammed and he was bludgeoned into submission with three flowerpots by a rookie police officer returning from a nearby beach. After he was in custody, another policeman alertly noticed that Heirens signed his name with a conspicuous curve flourish which was the same handwriting on the ransom note and message written in lipstick. According to latent fingerprint experts, his fingerprints matched latent prints found on the Suzanne Degnan ransom note. Also, his prints matched a bloody latent print found on the doorjamb where his previous victim Frances Brown was killed.

With a thorough and detailed analysis of each scene, the individual characteristics of Heirens's and Glatman's signatures could have been useful in connecting each of their murders more easily given what we know today. The examination of each crime scene must exhibit the cautious and meticulous search for physical evidence and psychological clues left by the killer that Sherlock Holmes so diligently searched for at the fictional crime scenes reported in the writings of Sir Arthur Conan Doyle.

The search for signature evidence reflects the words of Sherlock Holmes. A favorite literary piece of his was *The Book of Life*, a magazine which attempted to show how much an observant man might learn by an accurate and systematic examination of all that came his way. It struck Holmes's partner Watson as a remarkable mixture of shrewdness and absurdity. Its reasoning was close and intense, but the deductions appeared to be far-fetched and exaggerated, much like those of some detectives of modern times who are at first skeptical of linking cases that differ in modus operandi until they become experienced at recognizing the sometimes subtle differences a killer portrays from one murder to the next. As with Sherlock Holmes, so it is with the results of signature analyses of today. The results of both are so startling they mystify the uninitiated, until the processes by which they were arrived at are understood.

In *A Study in Scarlet*, Sherlock Holmes said, '. . . a logician could infer the possibility of an Atlantic or a Niagara without having seen or heard of one or the other. So all life is a great chain, the nature of which is known whenever we are shown a single link of it. Like all other arts, the Science of Deduction and Analysis is one which can only be acquired by long and patient study, nor is life long enough to allow any mortal to attain the highest possible perfection in it. Before turning to these moral and mental aspects of the matter which present the greatest difficulties, let the inquirer begin by mastering more elementary problems. Let him, on meeting a fellow-mortal, learn at a glance to distinguish the history of the man, and the trade or profession to which he belongs. Puerile as such an exercise may seem, it sharpens the faculties of observation, and teaches one where to look and what to look for. By a man's finger-nails, by his coat-sleeve, by his boot, by his trouser-knees, by the callosities of his forefinger and thumb, by his expression, by his shirt-cuffs – by each of these things a man's calling is plainly revealed. That all united should fail to enlighten the competent inquirer in any is almost inconceivable.' With that statement, Doyle had captured the essence of signature analysis at homicide scenes.

It was detective literature such as this and real-life cases such as Ted Bundy, Wayne Williams, Morris Frampton, Harvey Glatman, and William Heirens that kept nagging at me to find a common denominator that linked these types of killers. It wasn't just they were all serial killers or even that they were necessarily sexual predators. It was something else, something that Pierce Brooks had said about the way each serial killer's ritualistic symbolism changed very little from crime to crime that intrigued me. Pierce also called it the murderer's 'intrinsic personal touch' that remained constant even when such major components of method of approach and even body disposal changed. What motivated each killer emotionally? I kept asking. What was the drive that forced the killer to reveal something about his own individual character weakness in each and every crime? The more crimes I evaluated, the more the signatures stuck out at me like flashing beacons. But some of them repeated themselves and could almost be construed as related to one another even though the killers might be separated by thousands of miles and half a century. Could there be general patterns that encompassed all signature killers? I began to organize and categorize, looking for the broad strokes that related different killers. And I found myself poring over some of the most brutal cases from around the country in a siegelike search for answers, answers to a type of crime I saw as growing and threatening to overwhelm the same institutions I was sworn to protect.

CHAPTER 3

The Essence of Torture

Richard Cottingham, 'The Midtown Torso Killer'

At about the same time I was introduced to the world of the signature killer in the Morris Frampton case, another series of murders began in the New York metropolitan area that would put into sharp relief just what a signature killer does and how he behaves. Many people heard about this case through the newspapers because it was a lurid, bloody series of crimes so violent that it initially left NYPD and local New Jersey detectives dazed. What could the killer be after? What thrills was he seeking?

Killer Richard Cottingham belonged to a subgroup of sexually sadistic serial killers who try to quench their self-consuming need for sexual arousal by torturing their victims. In cases such as these, the victim's pain and terror stimulate the killer. The victim's reactions drive the killer into a frenzy, which in turn leads him to intensify the level of the victim's torture, and so the cycle continues until the killer's lust is momentarily satisfied. To reach this level of sexual gratification, most torture-killers must ratchet their excitement up to a peak by luring in victims, successfully capturing them, and then springing their traps. Most killers in this category are smooth talkers, beguilingly charming but deceitful and ultimately lethal. Torture-killers use all sorts of conventional and innovative approaches to con their victims into a false sense of security. They flatter and flirt, offer rewards, especially money, hold out the promise of satisfying exactly what they perceive the victim wants, and speak directly to the victim's needs. Killers like this are observant predators.

The killer's setup for the trap can take anywhere from a few minutes of casual conversation to a plan that takes weeks to unfold and includes elaborate ritual. But whatever the case, it's all a ruse made to look innocent and result in a victim who steps into the killer's world. Once the victim is isolated and completely under his control, often with the help of drugs, the killer begins the process of orchestrating 'the three *D*'s' that gratify him: dependency – the victim is forced to rely upon the killer for each moment of life while in captivity; dread – the victim is terrified at the pain and torture being inflicted; and degradation – the humiliated and defeated victim is reduced to begging for life or for the lives of other victims, usually children, and acknowledging by word and deed that he or she lives only to serve the killer's pleasure. Harvey Glatman's signature in which he forced his living victims to pose while painfully bound at the hands and feet is an example of this form of degradation. To facilitate this perversion of complete control, the killer will often use various props such as leather slave collars, handcuffs, cigarette lighters, whips, and adhesive or duct tape.

My good friend, NYPD homicide detective Vern Geberth, first alerted me to the fact that all of these core components were present in a bloodbath of an investigation dubbed the Midtown Torso Case by New York tabloids. After Geberth mentioned this to me, I could see that indeed, control freak Richard Cottingham was a classic example of this type of killer and the study of his crimes illuminated the motives and methods of a serial killer subtype. The more involved I became with the Cottingham case, the more I believed that it would lead me and other homicide investigators to some startling conclusions about the nature of similar crimes.

THE RICHARD COTTINGHAM MURDERS

From 1977 through 1980, a frightful series of crimes against women occurred in New York City and the northern New Jersey river towns. Several of the victims were found alive, having suffered vicious sexual assaults. Other were found dead, their corpses bearing signs of having been strangled, mutilated, and bitten, discovered in ragged hotels along West Forty-second Street in New York City and in similar no-frills motels near the Hudson River in northern New Jersey. All eight of the victims were white females in their twenties. NYPD detectives and local New Jersey police did not immediately determine one killer was responsible for the deaths, although the New York cops suspected three of the deaths in their jurisdiction could be related.

The murders were similar in their savageness and the fact that the victims all were prostitutes or prostitute look-alikes and act-alikes. The police soon determined the murders were the result of a perverted man's vivid fantasy life. The first known case in the series started with the brutal sex slaying of Mary Ann Carr.

Mary Ann Carr

At approximately 7:00 A.M. on December 16, 1977, the body of Mary Ann Carr was discovered by a hotel employee, left out in the open between a parked van and a chain-link fence sixty feet from the southwest entrance of the Quality Inn parking lot in Ledgewood Terrace, New Jersey. She was wearing a white nurse's uniform the left pant leg of which had a cut by a sharp instrument. On her right thigh was a clump of her hair that had been similarly cut. Her white nurse's shoes were missing, as were her coat and handbag. At the time of her death, Mary Ann Carr was only twenty-six years old, five feet five inches tall, 115 pounds, with artificially treated blond hair. She lived at the nearby Ledgewood Terrace Apartments.

The police discovered that Mary Carr suffered lacerations from a sharp instrument on her chest and feet. Marks on her wrists and ankles showed she had been handcuffed. A careful examination of her body revealed residue of white adhesive tape which had been stretched across her mouth. Further marks led detectives to believe she had been ligature strangled with a thin rope or cord which left a mark on the right side of her neck. There were recent bruises on her shoulders, arms, thighs, and right breast. The left cheekbone had a hemorrhage consistent with a blow from a blunt instrument, and there was a vicious human bite mark on her left breast. The official cause of death was mechanical asphyxia, a combination of suffocation by the adhesive tape and strangulation.

Mary Ann Carr was one of two Cottingham victims murdered in New Jersey. Reportedly, based on results of all the autopsies done in Bergen County over the last several years, only Mary Carr and Valerie Street, Cottingham's second New Jersey victim who would be found similarly murdered later, had the residue of adhesive tape around their mouths and marks from handcuffing on their wrists. Mary Ann Carr was last seen in the parking lot of her apartment, speaking to a man who looked like her husband, a white male thirty-two years old with light brown hair.

Karen Schilt

At seven in the morning of March 23, 1978, Patrolman Raymond Auger discovered the almost lifeless form of Karen Schilt, one of Cottingham's victims who survived the attack. Her account of what happened on the night of March 22, 1978, was absent of the most lurid details, but was the best she could recall after the trauma of her abduction and assault. All day up until six o'clock, she worked at Tuesday's, a restaurant-tavern located on Third Avenue near East Seventeenth Street just off Union Square in New York City. From there, the pregnant young woman briefly visited her boyfriend in a nearby hospital and returned to Tuesday's to work until eight o'clock. She had two drinks at the bar and left for another Third Avenue bar where she had two more drinks. It was there that she met a man who called himself John Schaefer. During the conversation, Schaefer was curious about his companion and asked Schilt if she was a 'working girl,' slang for a prostitute. She said no, but it didn't alter Schaefer's interest in her. Karen's description of Schaefer offered no unique features that would set him apart from most white males in the area: clean shaven, about thirty years old, five feet eight inches to five feet ten inches tall, medium to heavy build, with straight hair parted on the left side. She realized that sometime in her conversation with him, he claimed to live in New Jersey, near Hackensack, but he frequented bars on Third Avenue in the city, a thoroughfare which below Thirty-fourth Street was known as a hangout for streetwalkers.

At about nine o'clock and very soon into her conversation with Schaefer, Karen felt sick. Her stomach became queasy, she got weak in the knees, and the room started to spin as if she were going to faint. She put down the drink she'd been sipping, left Schaefer at the bar, and walked toward her apartment at 94 Third Avenue just off the corner of East Fifteenth Street. Schaefer followed her outside, and feigning a gentlemanly concern, tagged along behind her in his car until he saw her weaving. He stopped, opened the door, and asked her if she 'wished a ride home.' She said yes, stumbled inside the car, and almost immediately lost consciousness as she sank into the softness of the passenger seat.

Karen didn't know how long they'd been driving, but when she awoke and gained enough presence of mind to look around, she knew that they were nowhere near her apartment. In fact, when she looked out the window, she found they were driving along Route 80 in New Jersey. Schaefer then asked her if she had taken Tuinal. When she said no, he forced her to swallow three bluish and red Tuinal capsules. Very quickly, she passed out once again.

According to the *Physicians' Desk Reference*, Tuinal is a combination of equal parts of Seconal sodium and Amytal sodium, barbituric acid derivatives that occur as white, odorless, bitter powders. They are very soluble in water and alcohol. Tuinal is a central nervous system depressant, and in ordinary doses, the drug acts as a hypnotic. Tuinal takes effect in fifteen to thirty minutes after it has been taken and its effects can last from three to eleven hours. Prolonged, uninterrupted use of Tuinal may result in psychic and physical dependence. Back in the late seventies, before Rohypnol became easily available in Mexico, Tuinal was the drug most sexual assailants used if they could get it on the street. Tuinal was the date rape drug of choice because it dissolved quickly in any drink and was undetectable until the victim passed out. This is what happened to Karen Schilt.

Karen Schilt slept throughout the car ride. The next thing she recalled was awakening in the dark and feeling a burning sensation to her breast caused by Schaefer. In the midst of her turmoil, she heard Schaefer tell her that he currently lived, or had once lived, at the place where they were. Then Karen passed out again and only recalled awakening in Hackensack Hospital. She felt as if she were in a physical and mental cocoon and had no idea what had happened to her the night before or how close she had come to death.

Karen had been discovered earlier that morning by the Little Ferry police officer lying in the open, unconscious, and reduced to a state of near death. Raymond Auger had received a radio message directing him to the Ledgewood

Terrace Apartment complex on Liberty Street, which runs north-south off Route 46, a mile away from the intersection with Route 80. As the patrolman entered the eastern parking lot area, he saw a car parked facing a stockade fence. Partially hidden underneath that parked car was Karen Schilt. She was unconscious with her blouse pulled above her breasts and her slacks undone and pulled down to her knees. Karen resembled all other women attacked or murdered in this series: twenty-two years of age, five feet five inches tall, about 140 pounds, blue eyes, and artificially colored blond hair. She was missing her coat, purse, scarf, and a large silver ring.

Patrolman Auger checked the condition of the woman, noted her especially weak pulse and shallow breathing, and radioed for an ambulance. When it arrived, he helped local EMTs deliver oxygen and CPR to Karen in an attempt to revive her. After several moments, they established a steady but weak heartbeat and sped to Hackensack Hospital where the admitting emergency room physician documented her extensive injuries. What monster could have done something like this? The still unidentified woman had bruises on her legs and trauma to her elbow, her breasts had been severely scratched, and her left breast had been burned by a cigarette and savagely bitten, exactly like Mary Ann Carr. The hospital lab immediately did a blood workup and ran a toxicology screen to check for the presence of poisons or drugs, tests which revealed the presence of ethyl alcohol and the drugs amobarbital and secobarbital, the two constituents of the capsules commonly known as Tuinal. Now the doctors knew the cause of her stuporous condition, but they also knew she would survive the ordeal once the effects of the drugs wore off. When Karen awoke, she had only vague images in her mind of the night before and could only clearly remember feeling sick and weak and then riding in a car. The police investigation of the Karen Schilt case did not develop any viable leads and would remain inactive until Richard Cottingham's arrest in 1980.

Susan Geiger

On October 10, 1978, blond, five-foot-tall Susan Geiger was hooking along Eighth Avenue near the Alpine Hotel in New York City. She was ninety-six pounds, cute, and petite. This area, right around the theater district, was notorious for its high rate of prostitution, sex shops, and X-rated porn movie theaters. If you were a hooker you didn't have to wait long for a trick, and Susan was soon approached by a white male she described as about five feet ten inches tall, 170 pounds, with blue eyes, dirty blond hair, and no facial hair. The anxious john offered Geiger a flat two hundred dollars for sex that night, but she told him it was a no go. She was all booked that evening. So she gave him her telephone number and told him to call the next day if he wanted her. He called on October 11 and made a date.

Unknowingly, Susan Geiger had become a pawn in a very common ruse used by serial killers who target prostitutes. Richard Hansen from Alaska, the killer of eleven prostitutes, obtained telephone numbers of potential victims and called each of them later for a date. Then he would stake out the area where he was to meet them in advance of their appointment to assure himself that no one followed these women to the meeting site. Once convinced that he had successfully isolated the woman, he picked her up and made her his next victim.

At midnight, Susan Geiger met her trick right in front of the Alpine Hotel. They drove across town through still-heavy theater district traffic to Flanagan's Tavern on First Avenue between East Sixty-fifth and Sixty-sixth, just north of the Queensboro Bridge and the Roosevelt Island tram. It was in Flanagan's that the man finally introduced himself as Jim and told her he was married with young children and living over in New Jersey. He claimed that he worked with computers at an office somewhere nearby 'in the forties' and that he'd just gotten off work. He bragged to her that he just won a bundle from gambling, and to prove this, flashed a large wad of bills allegedly amounting to a few thousand dollars. For just a moment Geiger left the bar area, and when she returned, Jim handed her a screwdriver he'd just ordered and told her to keep stirring it with her straw. She recalled sipping at her drink, but then things got very hazy. In fact, she had just been drugged and she quickly fell into a drug-induced stupor, leaning heavily on Jim to keep from dropping to the floor. She didn't remember much after drinking the screwdriver, but did recall getting into Jim's car, a light-colored, older Thunderbird with a soiled interior. She remembered spelling out the letters of the word *Thunderbird* written into the dashboard in front of her, then she passed out. For brief periods throughout the morning, she regained consciousness and recalled being in a room with Jim sexually molesting her, and being physically unable to fight him off. She thought that Jim used a piece of green garden hose to beat her.

It was not until early afternoon on October 12, 1979, that Susan Geiger regained full consciousness. She found herself on the floor of room 28 of the Airport Motel in South Hackensack, New Jersey. She had experienced a brutal sexual attack with bleeding lacerations and bruises on her face, mouth, breasts, vagina, and rectum. She located her clothes and managed to dress. Still in shock and some denial about what happened to her, she realized that her gold earrings were missing because they had been ripped from her ears. She was also missing her handbag and its contents. Susan gathered what she could of herself and staggered out of the room and into the autumn afternoon daylight spilling across the motel parking lot.

Captain John Agar of the South Hackensack Police

Department was surprised, as he pulled into the Airport Motel parking lot, at the sight of a young white female in an obvious state of panic and confusion staggering around the motel court. He pulled up and asked her to identify herself. Even though she was intermittently confused and in obvious pain, she said her name was Susan Geiger and began her story about being beaten and raped. Agar noticed that her clothing was disheveled and her blouse was torn. He tried to follow what she was saying as she interrupted her story by periods of incoherence. Her bruised and swollen face was also severely scratched and her puffy lips were bleeding profusely. After examining her hands, Captain Agar observed that some of her artificial fingernails were missing. The experienced police officer concluded that Geiger was also still under the lingering influence of some kind of drug.

Agar opened up room 28 and immediately found an unmade bed and several broken artificial fingernails that matched Geiger's. There were also pieces of Geiger's clothing on the bed as well as two motel towels. He submitted these things for examination to the New Jersey State Police Laboratory in Little Falls where forensic chemists discovered seminal stains on the towels which had come from a male secretor who had type O blood.

Agar drove Susan Geiger over to Hackensack Hospital where an analysis of her blood confirmed the police captain's suspicions that the young woman had been drugged, specifically by amobarbital and secobarbital, the same drugs found in the blood of Karen Schilt. Like Schilt, Geiger was also pregnant. Emergency-room personnel concluded that a severe beating caused the general swelling of her face, bruises on her forehead, lacerations over her right eye, excessive spittle running over her mouth and lips, and a mucous buildup in her chest and stomach. She also had bruises on her left thigh and buttocks and abrasions and ecchymoses – tiny hemorrhages in ruptured capillaries that result from an external beating – on her right thigh. On her breasts were multiple contusions and abrasions. Her right breast had been 'savagely' bitten. Like Karen Schilt's investigation, Geiger's follow-up would be inactivated until Richard Cottingham's arrest in 1980.

Deedah Godzari and Jane Doe: The Mystery of the Headless Torsos

Hotel employees at the Travel Lodge Motor Inn at 515 West Forty-second Street in New York remembered that the resident in room 417 was secretive. He registered under the name Carl Wilson of Anderson Place in Merlin, New Jersey; detectives would later discover that both the name and location were bogus. The man checked in on November 29, hung his Do Not Disturb sign from the doorknob, and was rarely seen thereafter.

On Sunday, December 2, 1979, at about 9:00 A.M. hotel workers called the fire department because smoke was streaming out of room 417. Quickly, the New York firefighters from the local engine company extinguished the fire. In the smoky darkness of the room, they found a frightening discovery: the charred corpses of two women lying on separate beds, covered by bedsheets, who had been deliberately set on fire. Their bodies were nude and mutilated; their heads and hands, completely severed from their bodies, were not in the room. Worse yet, detectives felt the killer had gone to great lengths to remove evidence. Setting a fire as the last act in a murder was indicative that the killer did not want to leave any physical evidence that could be traced back to him. In processing the double-body recovery site, detectives realized that the killer left no fingerprints or any murder weapon. It made one detective comment to *New York Times* reporters that he had never seen a room cleaned out so thoroughly, considering the amount of mutilation that took place.

At the autopsy, it was revealed that each woman had been physically tortured and sexually abused while she was still alive. Later, the investigation would determine that both initially unidentified women had been abducted and killed at different times. Police later identified Deedah Godzari, a twenty-three-year-old prostitute, as one of the unlucky victims. The other young woman remains unidentified to this day, but authorities guessed that she was in her late teens. Initially police had so few leads to go on, they put this double murder down as just another unsolved prostitute homicide in Times Square.

Forty-second Street, stretching from the Chrysler and *Daily News* buildings in the east, under the Park Avenue overpass, straight across Bryant Park and Times Square, and past the Port Authority bus terminal on its way under the remains of the West Side Highway to the abandoned dockyards along the Hudson River, looked like a raw scar through Manhattan's midsection in the late 1970s. The days of Dick Powell and Ruby Keeler, Rogers and Hammerstein, and glittering Broadway opening nights were faded memories of twenty years ago in a city still barely crawling away from the edge of bankruptcy. From Sixth Avenue west you would have found microskirted hookers looking for tricks, crack dealers in doorways hawking nickel vials, strip joints, porn movie houses, massage parlors, seamy low-rent hotels, and some of the toughest bars on the East Coast. If it was for sale you could have found it here on West Forty-second Street. Citizen's committees in the Times Square area complained, a new reform candidate would announce for mayor, from time to time a congressional delegation swept through inspecting urban decay, or there'd be a brutal murder that shocked even the thickest-skinned New Yorker. These were some of the reasons the NYPD would periodically crack down on the illicit activities along Forty-second Street and flood the area with tactical street-crime combat units. But a couple of months would pass, a black-gray Northwest winter would come rolling up the coast and across the harbor, and the street would again turn into a virtual haven for the illicit. Areas such as this are perfect trolling grounds for the sexually sadistic serial killer because he blends in so well and remains virtually anonymous without any one of his potential victims suspecting imminent danger from the man whispering to them from the shadow of a doorway.

Beyond the terror of anyone who sees a headless, handless torso, the police have a tremendously difficult time pursuing leads related to the killer's identity. Based on the mutilated remains they discovered in the Forty-second Street Travel Lodge Motel, Manhattan South's elite homicide squad had two operating theories as reported in the *New York Times*. One was that the murderer was in a psychotic rage or that he feared the identification of the victims would incriminate him. And since there were two victims, police did not eliminate the possibility they were looking for more than one killer.

Investigators desperately approached the murder inquiry from two perspectives. First, detectives conducted a massive search of miles of abandoned piers and mounds of garbage piles for the heads and hands. They employed underwater divers and dredges out in the Hudson and along the river pilings near the hotel. Because police believed that the victims were prostitutes, they checked scores of streetwalkers and searched hundreds of missing-person reports for young women that matched the victims' descriptions.

Second, they had a description of the probable killer from hotel employees who said he was a white man with brown hair, thirty-five years old, five feet ten inches tall, and weighing 175 pounds. The detectives showed a composite sketch of the man to streetwalkers and interviewed any john matching the description. They also questioned prostitutes who had been approached by a customer who wanted an assignation at the Travel Lodge Motor Inn.

Common in cases where there was a physical description of the potential killer, detectives found many people who matched the composite and hung out on Forty-second Street. Police interviewed hundreds of potential suspects but would not find the right one for almost a year and a half. However, four months after the midtown torso cases, the nude body of a nineteen-year-old female was found in Bergen County, New Jersey. Police discovered she was a prostitute who had been sexually assaulted, mutilated and murdered, but her head and hands were not removed. Because of differences in MO with regard to geography and location, the cases were not immediately connected by police in New York and New Jersey. The identity of the killer in this case and the one responsible for the headless torso murders was still unknown.

Valerie Ann Street

The morning of May 5, 1980, began routinely for Mary Ann Sancanelli, a housekeeper at the Quality Inn in Hasbrouck Heights, New Jersey. She was in the midst of cleaning room 132 and noticed that the bed on the south side of the room had not been slept in, but its bedspread was pulled partially down as if to cover something at the foot of the bed. The other bed had been slept in. As she tried to vacuum underneath the made-up bed, her vacuum hit something underneath the mattress frame. When she picked up the cover, she gasped and her eyes widened in shock at the sight of the dead body of Valerie Ann Street. Mrs. Sancanelli phoned the police.

Valerie Street was pretty. She was nineteen years old, five feet four inches tall, weighed 135 pounds, and had blue eyes and shoulder-length, artificially colored, strawberry blond hair. Investigators observed that she must have died an excruciatingly painful death. Her hands were handcuffed tightly behind her back, as evidenced by the deep indentations from the cuffs left on her wrists.

Right away, detectives noticed that across her neck were two deep ligature marks. At the scene, investigators concluded that she had been gagged, because there was residue from pieces of white adhesive tape across her mouth. The examination at the scene revealed that her breasts had markings similar to other victims in the previous series of unsolved rapes; they were contused with her nipples severely scratched and bitten. She had also suffered blows to the shinbone areas of both legs. When she was discovered in the Quality Inn, all her clothing and all forms of identification were missing. Investigation revealed that Street had entered through the rear southwest entrance. One bit of promising evidence discovered was a latent print found on the ratchet side of the handcuffs. Police hoped it belonged to the killer.

On May 6, 1980, Dr. Louis V. Napolitano of the Bergen County Medical Examiner's Office performed the autopsy on Valerie Street in which he described her injuries as bizarre and startling. Initially, he found that she had sustained a blunt impact blow or blows which resulted in injuries to the back of her head and in contusions to her brain. The medical examiner could determine the telltale external signs of a beating by the large bruises she'd sustained from her right temple down to her right cheek. Within twenty-four hours of her death, Street received multiple bruises on her arms and shoulders. The most apparent wounds to Street's body, however, were the abrasions and lacerations to her breasts and nipples. Dr. Napolitano concluded she had been savagely bitten on her breasts. Valerie Street had been strangled with a thin strap or cord which had been pulled upward and from the right side of her neck. Street's cause of death was listed as mechanical asphyxia due to strangulation.

For over a month, Valerie Street's body lay unidentified in the county morgue because the killer had removed all her clothing and any identification she would have been carrying. The only objects foreign to the room where the housekeeper had found her were the handcuffs and a broken piece of an earring later identified as a pair the victim was known to wear. The killer had picked the room clean of evidence. Neither the other half of the broken-off piece of the earring nor its mate could be found. So, absent clues to the killer's identity, the police investigators quickly turned to establishing the young woman's identity.

The victim had registered at the motel as Shelley Dudley from Florida. She entered the lobby without baggage and requested a room some time between four and four-thirty on the afternoon of May fourth. While waiting for the desk clerk, who was occupied with his guest register, Shelley walked to her right in the general direction of the southwest entrance and came right back from that same direction to register at the desk. The clerk did not hear from her again until she called at about ten o'clock in the morning to keep the room for one more day. She never checked out.

Shelley Dudley was officially identified as Valerie Street through fingerprints on file with the state of Florida for an arrest and conviction for prostitution. Investigations further revealed that Street had left Florida on April 30, 1980. She arrived in New York and was seen by another prostitute named China on May third at 10 P.M. at the corner of East Thirty-second Street and Madison Avenue in New York City.

A fellow prostitute also saw Valerie three hours later, about one in the morning on May fourth, soliciting at that same corner at Thirty-second and Madison in New York only eight blocks from where Leslie O'Dell, Cottingham's final victim, would be picked up three weeks later on May 22. Cottingham's arrest and the solution to the Valerie Street murder would wait until then.

The Hotel Seville Case

It was a case of déjà vu for Manhattan South detectives on May 15, 1980, when they were again summoned by firefighters to a hotel room fire, this time in the Hotel Seville at 22 East Twenty-ninth Street just off Fifth Avenue. Inside the smoke-filled room, fire department personnel found the remains of Ann Reyner, nude, mutilated, and murdered. However, this time the killer did not remove the victim's head and hands, having instead incised and dissected out both of her breasts. And in open display, he neatly placed them side by side on the headboard of the bed. There was also evidence, again, of bondage and torture, and homicide detectives immediately linked this murder to the Midtown torso cases. This victim, like Deedah Godzari, was a high-class prostitute who ordinarily wouldn't have been operating out of this type of lower-class, seamy hotel. It was a mystery, just like the Godzari murder, but in only one week the case would be broken when detectives solved the case of Leslie O'Dell, who was brutally attacked and barely escaped death.

Leslie Ann O'Dell

On May 22, 1980, five-foot-four and blond Leslie Ann O'Dell, a prostitute working New York's east side, met a customer on East Twenty-fifth Street between Madison and Park avenues just north of Gramercy Park. The customer, who called himself Tommy, drove O'Dell to a bar where they spent a couple of hours drinking and talking before he told her that he was taking her over to Jersey, where they would spend the evening having sex. They stopped to eat at the New Star Diner in South Hackensack, New Jersey, only five-tenths of a mile from the Ledgewood Terrace Apartments and four-tenths of a mile from the Airport Motel. From there, the man drove

O'Dell to the Quality Inn Motel in Hasbrouck Heights, a mile down the road from the diner.

O'Dell's date parked the car in the rear of the motel and parked outside the southwest entrance. As though the chain of events were important to him, Tommy told O'Dell to wait there while he went back into the front entrance and until he came to the southwest entrance to get her. After a short time had expired, Tommy came out of the southwest entrance, opened his car trunk, and took out their things. As before, the man, with O'Dell at his side, entered the Quality Inn through the rear southwest entrance. He cautioned her not to be seen by anyone. After they got to room 117, Tommy left to move his car.

When Tommy returned to the room, Leslie O'Dell's torment began. First he ordered her to undress and get into bed facedown. At that point, Tommy lay on top of her and placed a knife at her throat, threatening to kill her if she uttered a sound. Without waiting for her to say anything, he handcuffed her wrists behind her back and then told her explicitly what he was going to do to her. He went on to say that he derived sexual satisfaction and enjoyment from torturing and beating women, and that he had done it many times before. She was a whore, he said; she had to pay for being a whore, and he was going to hurt her because she was a whore. As part of her torture, Tommy scraped the right side of her chest with his knife and threatened to burn her breasts as well as her pubic and anal areas and beat her with his belt. He then turned O'Dell over, raped her, bit her breasts like a savage, stabbed and scraped one breast with his knife, and lacerated her breastbone. He then forced her to perform fellatio upon him, all the time threatening her with further pain, humiliation, and more torture. It was clear that the verbal terrorizing of O'Dell was just as important to her assailant as was the physical torture. His sexual arousal relied on that. He repeatedly told her that he was going to hurt her if she refused any of his sexual commands or called out for any help or in pain.

Tommy then shackled O'Dell's ankles with another pair of handcuffs so she could not run away, and removed the first pair from her wrists. He ordered her to lick his entire body, which she did, and then he performed forcible anal sodomy upon her. Even more out of control now than he had been, and calling himself her 'master,' Tommy ordered her to kiss and lick his feet. Instinctively, O'Dell resisted. The man called Tommy grabbed her and she screamed in terror. In a fit of absolute rage, Tommy threw O'Dell on the bed and began strangling and suffocating her. She believed she was about to die. Then, as his hands grew tighter around her throat choking off her cries, he told her to shut up because if anyone came to the room, she was dead. But motel security officers heard O'Dell's screams and called police.

Motel personnel responding to O'Dell's screams burst into the room, interrupting Richard Cottingham's assault, and he fled the room to escape. However, the police had already responded, and before he could leave the motel he was caught and arrested by the Hasbrouck Heights police. During the initial search, police found in his possession an open roll of adhesive tape, handcuffs, leather slave collars, a leather mouth gag, a fake gun, a knife, liquor, and the Tuinal capsules which would eventually tie him to the unsolved cases in New York and New Jersey that police would soon identify as his previous rapes.

The Evidence Against Cottingham

The abduction and sexual assault of Leslie O'Dell was Richard Cottingham's undoing, and shortly after his arrest he sat across from Sgt. Bruce Werner and Investigator Edward Denning in an interview in the Hasbrouck Heights Police Department Detective Bureau. The two detectives found themselves facing a bespectacled and mustached man, five feet ten inches tall, 187 pounds, born November 25, 1946, the day after another infamous killer, Theodore Robert Bundy. They began by advising him of his constitutional rights, being careful to do this properly, because no one wanted a case of this level of brutality and magnitude to slip away on a successful arrest procedures appeal. In the cases of most serial killers, the rights admonishment is but a formality because they are quite familiar with all aspects of it. Cottingham was no exception.

Investigator Denning told Cottingham that he had the right to remain silent and asked if he understood that right. Cottingham acknowledged that he understood and was asked if he knew what that right was. Cottingham responded in a typically confident fashion; he said, 'Yes, I don't have to say anything.'

Denning stated the second right that anything he said could be used against him in court. The detective asked, 'Do you understand that right?' Cottingham said 'Yes,' and Denning asked him what that right meant to him. Cottingham explained, 'Anything we discussed could subsequently be used against me in court.' Denning told Cottingham he had the right to talk to a lawyer before any questions were asked of him and he could have a lawyer present during any questioning. Denning asked if he understood that right, and he replied 'Yes.' When asked what that right meant to him, Cottingham said, 'If I wanted to, I could have a lawyer present while being questioned.'

Not surprisingly, Cottingham asked as though he were anticipating the next right, 'What happens when a person cannot afford to hire a lawyer?' Denning told him, 'If you cannot afford a lawyer, one would be appointed for you if you so desire before questioning.' Denning then asked, 'What does that right mean to you?' Cottingham said that a public defender could be appointed for him if he needed one. Denning went on to explain that Cottingham had the right to stop answering questions at any time, and asked him if he understood that right. He said 'Yes,' and Denning asked what that meant to him. Cottingham said, 'If I wanted to stop answering questions, I could.' Again repeating himself cautiously, Denning asked him if he understood all the rights he had just explained, and Cottingham said yes.

Denning then asked the big question, 'Are you willing to speak to us and answer questions?' Cottingham said that he would and didn't need a lawyer at this time because he had 'nothing to hide.' Cottingham had already prepared himself for the inevitable, that he would get caught and needed an alibi. He said, 'The girl was in the motel room with me voluntarily, and I agreed to pay her one hundred and eighty dollars to go there with me to do anything that I wanted her to do.'

The investigators began with a reasonably safe question. They asked Cottingham to explain what he was doing between Wednesday, May 21, 1980, until his arrest on Thursday, May 22. He said that on May 21 he appeared at the Bergen County Courthouse in the morning for a divorce hearing. When investigators interview a serial killer, it's always important to look for obvious stresses in that person's life. In Cottingham's case, the thought of the divorce proceeding may have been what pushed him over the edge to engage a prostitute and seek to punish her for selling sex. That day it was Leslie O'Dell's turn.

Cottingham went on to say that the hearing was postponed, and he left the courthouse at 1:00 P.M. That information would be the only data that police investigators could corroborate. From the courthouse, Cottingham told police, he drove to New York City and went to a movie theater 'somewhere' in the Times Square area to see *Friday the 13th*. After the movie, he went to a restaurant and had dinner and a couple of drinks. He went to work from 3:00 P.M. to 11:00 P.M. Investigators asked Cottingham for the names of the restaurant and movie theater, but he said he could not recall. He said that after dinner he went to another bar. He threw out the name 'Blarney Stone,' the name of a bar in the Times Square area, and also another bar just a block away from Penn Station. When the cops asked him for the location of the bar he went to, he said he did not remember. 'They are all over the city.'

At that point in his statement, Cottingham believed he had the police where he wanted them. He could tell them anything he wanted just as long as he gave them nothing they could corroborate. He could have a problem remembering, he could be vague, he could tell them an out-and-out lie if he wanted, as long as he was sure they couldn't confront him with it. Cottingham was in control, adhering to the one steadfast rule that practiced serial killers abide by: say nothing the police will be able to corroborate. Accordingly, Cottingham did not say what theater he went to or remember exactly what restaurant he ate at, because he knew investigators could check his story out and use any inaccuracies to challenge not only his alibi but the entire aura of credibility and bravado he believed he was exuding.

Then Cottingham's statement jumped to 2:30 A.M. on the morning of the twenty-second. Cottingham said he stopped his New Jersey-registered Chevrolet Caprice somewhere along East Twenty-fifth Street between Lexington and Park Avenue South. He specifically avoided mentioning to police what happened between 11:00 P.M. and 2:30 A.M., but said he was driving in the area. He referred to his contact with Leslie O'Dell as 'the girl who was with him in the motel,' not by name. She approached him and engaged him in a conversation to solicit for sex. She agreed to accompany him to a motel in New Jersey, and Cottingham emphasized that she agreed to 'perform whatever sexual acts I desired for one hundred and eighty dollars.' At this point, Cottingham kept true to form for most serial killers. That is, he was cooperative – in his mind – and more than willing to deny any wrongdoing on his part. It's not unusual for a killer like Cottingham to rationalize the crime he was being investigated for by blaming the victim. She agreed to have sex with him, he told police, and wanted it.

At about 3:30 A.M., they stopped at a diner on Route 46, which, he said, was in Little Ferry on the right-hand side of the road. When asked about what he ate, he said 'cheeseburger and fries,' never mentioning what she had. He claimed that at about 4:30 A.M., he signed into the Quality Inn Motel on Route 17 in Hasbrouck Heights using the name 'Caruthers.' After he was registered, he let the 'female subject' in via a side door. In the case of most serial killers, they frequently depersonalize their victims by referring to them as objects, things, or 'female subjects,' as Ted Bundy did. He was asked why he signed in under an assumed name. He said it was just a name that he made up, and never answered the detective's question. At this point in the interview, Investigator Denning made note that 'when questioned about details as to location and places that he frequents, et cetera, Cottingham was evasive and consistently said "I cannot recall" or "I don't remember." '

The next segment of the interview focused on the activities that took place in room 117. The detectives were now on delicate ground. Talking about the actual sex acts they engaged in causes most killers to clam up because they'll be worried about their reputations. One thing is for sure: if a killer does talk, his arrogance will take over. During the five years I spent questioning Ted Bundy in Florida about his life and cases, one thing I learned from him was that the killer will look to reward the investigators for knowing what's going on, understanding the dynamics of the situation. So investigators must display this in some way. And that's exactly what happened in the Cottingham interview when the detectives confronted him with his use of handcuffs and other implements, which he knew they knew about.

He said, 'The girl disrobed and gave me a blow job.' Then he said he sodomized her and had normal intercourse. Telling police that he felt that the girl was responsible for what happened, he said with much bravado, 'At no time during this period did she object to any of these sexual acts.' When detectives questioned him further regarding the handcuffs found on the victim's ankles and articles found in his possession at arrest, he said, 'I just started playing the game. I used them as a means of sexual gratification.'

Cottingham defended his actions by saying that initially the handcuffs were placed on the girl's wrists after she performed fellatio on him. Then he sodomized her, after which he took another pair of handcuffs and handcuffed her ankles. He then removed the handcuffs from her wrists. The curious detectives asked him why he did this. He claimed, 'It was to keep her from running away if she became panicky.'

'Why did you have a knife and display it to the girl?' the detectives asked him.

Almost believing he had a right to play his game, he said, 'I pointed the knife towards her and told her not to make any noise.'

The detectives next inquired about why he had the handcuffs, knife, and other articles in his possession. 'The handcuffs and other paraphernalia were just something I kept on hand,' Cottingham said, being vague and avoiding any admission that might make him seem culpable. Cottingham, like most sexually sadistic serial killers, needed implements he had confidence in and that worked best for him in the past, so he carried his sexual assault and murder kit around with him wherever he went. In Cottingham's case, it was primarily the handcuffs he treasured because bondage 'fascinated' him, he told the police.

In another game he played with his sexual partner, Cottingham admitted to police, he took a toy gun out of his bag and put it in a position near the girl. He then would walk away so that she would have ample opportunity to grab the gun. He claimed the girl did in fact pick up the gun, aim it at him, and pull the trigger. After she realized that it was a toy gun, she became hysterical and started screaming. He was asked why he did that. He responded, 'It was just one of the games that I liked to play, and I wanted to see how it feels to have someone under control.'

At this point in the interview, detectives established Cottingham's familiarity with the body recovery sites and victim contact areas. Cottingham said he had lived at 29 Vreeland Street, Lodi, New Jersey, for five or six years, and wouldn't be specific as to when he moved there. Because he knew that detectives would eventually find out, Cottingham said he formerly resided in the Ledgewood Terrace Apartments, building 470, Little Ferry, New Jersey. When asked if he had any friends still residing there, he said no, but his wife might still be friends with some of the women who currently lived there.

Serial killers know their victims' neighborhoods better than the police, better even than people who've lived there their entire lives. Consequently, serial killers know each and every victim pickup site in the same way an animal knows how to find a watering hole or a favorite patch of pasture. Detectives asked about the bars he frequented in New York City, also obvious pickup sites for hookers, but Cottingham said he didn't go to any place in particular. Investigator Denning asked Cottingham if he had ever been to Flanagan's. Not only did Cottingham say that he had, but he gave its specific location on First Avenue and Sixty-seventh Street.

Because investigators had not collected evidence that would have connected Cottingham to each victim who had been previously assaulted or murdered, he totally denied any knowledge of them. He was shown a photograph of Susan Geiger, and he said he didn't know who she was. Denning explained to Cottingham that Geiger was abducted, raped, and held against her will at the Airport Motel in South Hackensack in October 1978. Cottingham repeated that he did not know her and claimed he couldn't remember ever having been to the Airport Hotel. Denning strongly accused Cottingham of this crime, but Cottingham repeatedly denied any knowledge and insisted that he had never been to the Airport Motel.

Cottingham was shown a photograph of Michael and Mary Ann Carr. He said he didn't know either person. Denning asked if he had ever rented or stayed in a room at the Quality Inn prior to that day. Cottingham's response was no. Cottingham was asked the same about the Stagecoach Inn, Jade East Motel, or the Congress Inn, and he also responded with no. Unfortunately, it would not be until later that investigators would find Cottingham's handwriting on motel registration cards under assumed names, so they couldn't confront him about that at the time of the interview.

Realizing they were not getting anywhere with this line of questioning, the detectives then asked Cottingham how often he would solicit the services of a prostitute. He said once or twice a week. To preserve his reputation and legitimize his frequenting of prostitutes, Cottingham said he had friends who were prostitutes, but declined to name them. Cottingham even claimed to have saved a prostitute's life, acting as though he was a protector and adopting the attitude of a hero.

Next, Cottingham was questioned about his previous arrests. He recalled being arrested for shoplifting in Paramus, New Jersey, only because he knew that the investigators were aware of this arrest. He was asked about other crimes. He said if he had knowledge of any other crimes of this nature, he would be crazy to tell them. He also said, 'I know you are doing your job, but I know what you are trying to do. You are trying to trick me and you're being nice to me because you want me to admit to things that I didn't do. Aren't you guys going to beat me like they do in New York?' At this point, Cottingham was in the driver's seat in the interview. Detectives were limited because they didn't know what evidence would hold up against Cottingham. He knew they didn't know anything; otherwise, they would have confronted him with it right then and there, just as they had with the names of other hotels in the area.

Cottingham could consistently deny any involvement in the crimes the New Jersey police were questioning him about because he knew the detectives had no evidence of other crimes they thought he committed and were only on a fishing expedition. He could sit there as long as he wanted and wouldn't have to budge so long as he believed the cards weren't stacked against him. Cottingham was cooperative and responded to all the detectives' questions, but denied any involvement in other crimes. They were relentless but he was immovable. After all, he considered himself a clever perpetrator and wanted investigators to appreciate his greatness. He was trying to deal with an image he was projecting which was, in his perception, greater than he. And after this interrogation was over, Cottingham went back to his jail cell not having admitted to any murders or assaults.

Evidence against Cottingham began to build in early June. Investigator Ronald Deramo learned from Mr. Van Atta, of the FBI's latent fingerprint section, that the print taken from the handcuffs seized into evidence from the room where Valerie Street was found matched the left thumb impression of Richard Cottingham.

June 9, 1980, investigators took Barbara Lucas,

Cottingham's girlfriend during this time, to the Quality Inn where she recognized it as a place she had been to with Cottingham at least two times before. On previous occasions, Cottingham checked in, parked the car in back, and entered through the southwest corner door just as the suspect had done with other victims who had lived through his assaults. On May 30, Lucas gave detectives information that she had also been to Flanagan's Tavern numerous times with Richard. She told them that the vehicle he drove was maroon T-bird.

Police interviewed Bruce Huff, Cottingham's coworker at Empire State Blue Cross Blue Shield, located at 622 Third Avenue in New York City. Huff said that it was frequently Cottingham's style to approach prostitutes, flash large amounts of money, and promise to pay them after their activity with him. His favorite places were the corner of Fifth Avenue and Thirty-second Street right near the Empire State Building. Cottingham spoke of how good it felt to be able to beat the prostitutes at their own game – taking money – and he revealed to Bruce that upon meeting a strange girl he would drop 'black beauties,' a depressant drug, into the girl's drink if she appeared not to be consuming enough alcohol. Several workers said they observed Cottingham regularly leave work between 8:00 and 8:30 P.M. and not return. The police saw that as a pattern whenever he went looking for victims.

Like most sociopathic serial killers, crossing other people's boundaries provided Richard Cottingham with some kind of a consistent thrill. He was a petty thief in the workplace, stealing keys that opened coworkers' desks and file cabinets. One time a worker noticed his meal tickets missing from his center desk drawer, along with a calculator. On May 29, 1980, a search warrant was executed at the Cottingham house in Lodi, New Jersey. Mrs. Janet Cottingham stated that she was curious about what was in the trunk of his T-bird, inoperable in the garage sometime around December 1979. She found a black bag containing handcuffs and a bottle of VO liquor, a wig, and a little black strap tapered at both ends, looking very much like an arm restraint.

In the search of Cottingham's house, detectives found several keys. One key was to an apartment of a coworker in Flushing, Queens, who had reported a Honeywell Pentax 35mm camera stolen from him over six to seven years before. It was discovered in the search of Cottingham's belongings, and the coworker identified the camera and its serial number.

The search of Cottingham's home became a virtual treasure trove of evidence linking him to many crimes. Found in Cottingham's possessions was a miniature tan toy koala bear just like the one Valerie Street usually carried with her. It was positively identified by her sister. In addition, a pair of earrings found in Cottingham's 'chamber of horrors' were identified as belonging to Street. The treasure hunt wasn't finished. A crucial piece of evidence was found when the police searching Cottingham's residence located the key to Mary Ann Carr's apartment, which was just like finding Cinderella's slipper for the detectives. Butterfly earrings belonging to Deedah Godzari and a heart-shaped pendant belonging to Ann Reyner were also discovered.

The ME, Dr. Napolitano, provided another piece of circumstantial evidence in the case. He was shown a mouth gag – item number fifteen from evidence found in Cottingham's residence – and asked if it could have caused the bruises on the neck of Valerie Street. He said the gag could have caused those marks.

At Barbara Lucas's apartment, police investigators recovered a Nikon camera, a black case, and two Nikon lenses. Paul Chinn, a fellow coworker of Cottingham's, positively identified them as items stolen from him sometime between Friday, September 2 and Sunday, September 4, 1977.

Further evidence was uncovered, and with it Investigator Denning continued to weave the circumstantial web around Cottingham even tighter. On May 22, 1980, Denning discovered that Richard Cottingham filled out a registration card and signed into the Quality Inn Motel using the name Jack Caruthers. He compared that card with the one filled out by the person who registered in room 28 of the Airport Motel on October 11, 1978, the date of the rape and abduction of Susan Geiger. The name on that card was John Anderson. The printing and handwriting on the two cards were remarkably similar. In addition, both cards listed Ford automobiles and the first two letters of the license number as 'VX.'

Denning reviewed additional motel registration cards that were retained in the Mary Ann Carr murder case, which included cards from the Quality Inn Motel, the Stagecoach Motel, the Airport Motel, the Jade East Motel, and the Congress Inn. He found a card from the Stagecoach Motel dated December 15, 1977, and filled out in the name of J. Boyle. This card was compared to the other two cards and it was also found to bear a handwriting similar to the previous registration cards in the other abduction and murder cases. In particular, the number *4* that was printed in the space for license plate number on the Stagecoach Motel card seemed virtually identical to the number *4* printed in the space for street on the Airport Motel card.

In the investigation of the fire at the Travel Lodge Motor Inn in New York City on December 2, 1979, where the bodies of Deedah Godzari and Jane Doe were found murdered, a motel clerk turned over the registration cards to NYPD detectives for room 417. The card listed the arrival date as November 29, 1979, and the departure date as December 2, 1979. The card was filled out in the name of Mr. Carl Wilson of Anderson Road, Merlin, New Jersey. Denning compared this card to the cards from the Quality Inn Motel, Airport Motel, and

Stagecoach Motel, and the handwriting was similar. The letters *M R* printed on the Traveler Inn card in the space for name bore a strong similarity to the letters *M R* printed in the space for name on the Quality Inn registration. The writing for the abbreviation of New Jersey, *NJ* on all four cards, was very similar. All of the similarities in the handwriting samples on hotel registrations that Denning noticed were later confirmed by a handwriting expert.

On August 30, 1980, the Bergen County grand jury returned a twenty-one-count indictment against Cottingham. He was ultimately convicted of the seven murders and assaults in New Jersey and New York.

The Killer's Signature

The killer's method of operation from his first known victim, Street, through his last, O'Dell, remained constant in regard to his approach to them and situationally changed in the places he disposed of their bodies. Here, the key to understanding the concept of MO was that the killer modified and changed the disposal sites if his preferred one didn't work or was unavailable. Otherwise he stayed with a particular method if it worked. Nearly all victims were taken to a motel or were killed in areas the killer was familiar with. The changes in body disposal were dependent on the killer's need for detachment and location at the time of the murder. Dead victims in motels in New York City stayed in New York. Those victims who made it to New Jersey with him were found in New Jersey. Whatever was convenient for the killer was where they ended up.

This killer's MO was extensively refined and stylized as he continued killing. In practically every circumstance, the killer did something to clean up the crime scene after him. He took jewelry, purses, and clothing from his victims. In New York, the motel fires could even have been interpreted as an effort to cover up physical evidence of the crimes. The killer also may have tried to prevent identification in the New York murders by removing the heads and hands of his victims at one scene, but he really didn't need to worry. After his two New York City mutilations, Cottingham didn't have to fear that the identification of the victims would lead police to him. None of his other crimes had put authorities on his trail. Like serial killers near the end of their arc of violence, part of Cottingham believed he was completely invisible and could commit rapes and murders at will. Another part of him remained obsessively paranoid about leaving evidence at the crime scene. Therefore, in the arson murders, where the act of setting the fires was the last act of the killer at the crime scene, the setting of the fire may not have been some sexually perverted paraphilia with fire that some offenders possess. It might simply have been Cottingham's attempt to lead Manhattan detectives down a blind alley.

Removal of the implements he had brought with him to commit the crimes was an indicator that this killer was highly organized. Sometimes he was careless, as he was when he left the handcuffs on Valerie Street, and ultimately, when he failed to maintain control of O'Dell, which led to his arrest. But for the most part, he dissociated himself from the death scene and body location by taking special care to organize the crime scene to minimize any evidence he would have added.

If we assume that the modus operandi of a killer is only a combination of those actions necessary to commit a murder, then in his cases Cottingham went over and beyond the act of murder. It was obvious that murder alone wasn't on his mind, because his actions went beyond killing and were the core of the signature that he left at five murder and three vicious sexual assault crime scenes. Each crime was characterized by prolonged, bizarre, and ritualistic assaults on the victim. Without hesitation, this killer was methodical, demonstrating his love for torture through his ritualistic acts.

From 1977 through 1980, throughout the northeastern United States there were no murderers or rapists that matched the sexually sadistic intensity of Richard Cottingham. The specific features of his signature involved his perceived luxury of having ultimate control over each woman for as long as he wanted. He also needed the victims to be alive to suffer through his torture so he, 'the master,' as he referred to himself to O'Dell, would be sexually satisfied.

The initial symbol of this killer's signature was his need for bondage. Bondage is the ritualized practice of compression and incapacitation of a person with the use of ropes, chains, handcuffs, suffocation, drowning, and a number of improvised methods conditional only to the limits of the killer's imagination. The act of bondage has an almost built-in guarantee of control by rendering a victim motionless to the degree of restraint provided by the implements. When used as a learning step within the sadomasochistic complex, the specialized uses of each restraint give a lustful pleasure in the administration or receipt of resistance. During the entrapment phase or conning of the victims, Cottingham used Tuinal in a drink to weaken and subsequently incapacitate them. That was a form of bondage known as chemical restraint. Cottingham needed absolute control. However, once the victims were isolated and secure, he awoke them for an active resistance to a variety of distress tortures. There were some victims he murdered with his own hands and others he simply left for dead. But even those who lived would be of no consequence to Cottingham, because he believed the drug he administered would cause some form of amnesia.

In the Cottingham murder cases, each victim either had handcuffs in place when found or had deep ligature marks around her wrists and ankles, signifying ample restraint. Bondage in combination with other torturous acts enhanced Cottingham's sexual arousal with his victims. In addition, although they were not identified by surviving victims, leather slave collars, another form of bondage, were found in Cottingham's murder kit.

As a part of the bondage routine, a killer such as Cottingham uses different efforts to asphyxiate his victim. Forensics revealing the use of tape as a gag, cloth as a gag, manual strangulation, and ligature strangulation were present on most victims. The repeated use of these devices was employed to prevent screaming and to torture the victim by depriving her of her natural instinct to call out for help. By doing so, the killer heightened the victim's dependency and dread by mute isolation. Cottingham's sadistic intent, like that of other, similar killers, was to instrument ritualistically a deprivation which has sensory and emotional feedback to the victim. This process enhanced the victim's responses.

Another implement used in these cases was a belt, a tool for recreational strangulation. This activity allowed the killer the tactile stimulation of squeezing the victim into symbolic or real death. For the sadist, the process of strangulation feeds his ego by signifying that his power is so great he can control life and death. Hence, Cottingham controlled his victim's consciousness as he repeatedly strangled, resuscitated, and again compressed the victim back into what he perceived as a state of nothingness. Hands, like the belt, were a form of manual strangulation that gave Cottingham a direct sense of unfettered power, dominance, and supreme control.

At the core of Cottingham's signature, as we evaluated it, was his upholding of discipline over his victims in its crudest and Neanderthal-like form. He used hands and belts to punish the victims for being whores or sexually promiscuous. He repeatedly beat them with fists and belts as a function of degradation. In the process of reducing them from humans to mutilated garbage, he punished them for their 'imagined' filth by beating them as a form of corporal discipline. Concurrent with complementary deviancies, the pummeling of the victims produced direct evidence of power through blood, bruising, and body markings.

To instill a deeper sense of discipline in his victims, Richard Cottingham made the victims lick his body, kiss his feet, and call him master. These acts are designed to enforce resignation, humility, and submission. Burning the victims' breasts, pubic, and anal regions was a threat of punishment done to create dread and victim anxiety as well as to desecrate their most sexual parts, what physically and externally made them women. If the victim pleaded for safety, this fed Cottingham's sense of power that she had become 'broken.' However, if she resisted or verbally assaulted him, he viewed that as a challenge and increased the aggression.

The sadistic Cottingham in these cases denied the human identity of his victims. Having converted the 'whores' into nonhuman refuse in his mind, he consistently refused at the crime, or later, to have any personal identification with the victims. They were no longer human from the moment he sprang his trap; they became objects after he had discarded them, and he then viewed them with detachment and withdrawal.

The fact that the killer made no attempt to conceal his victims, but to leave them as garbage in places where he knew they would eventually be found is a significant part of the signature. The living victims, with the exception of his last victim, O'Dell, were discarded. Reducing them from the vibrant participant in the killer's original approach to the position of mindless slave, unable to resist, was Cottingham's goal. The near-death state of his living victims or the death of some others made no difference. The actual fact that some lived through the episode was of little consequence in Cottingham's mind, because his need – as in the cases of other signature sexual predators – to consummate the death of the victim was not necessary. He was not a necrophile but a brutalizer and torturer who left his victims, whether living or dead, like garbage on the floor of a room, underneath sheets, or in a parking lot.

On two occasions, as he was experimenting with the complete removal of evidence, Cottingham tried to burn 'his' garbage in hotel rooms. In his eyes, this seemed like an efficient way to combine the thrill of eliminating all evidence, thus controlling the police, and incinerating refuse, thus controlling the garbage. In other cases, he just discarded victims as empty carcasses. Not only did he leave them in places to be found, but the killer was always careful to dispose of his victims in such a way so he could get away and avoid detection. The locations were considered neutral for this killer. His concept was that he was not associated with those places; therefore, his identity would never be discovered. He was invisible as well as invincible.

Another factor in Cottingham's signature was the constant battering in localized areas of the body while each victim was alive. Each victim was made to feel the terror of the unmistakable edge of a sharpened knife. The blows, abrasions, and scrapes caused by a knife to the chest and abdominal areas, the savage biting of each victim on the breasts, and the burning sustained by each victim were examples of his terrorism.

The sheer number of injuries inflicted on each victim showed the killer's need for severe torture and terror as a factor in his signature. The number of injuries Cottingham gave each victim indicated that he was unrelenting in applying traumatic pressure to the psyches of his victims. There wasn't just one or two injuries sustained by each victim, but many.

Acts of picquerism – jabbing, stabbing, cutting, and gouging through the use of a knife or other sharp-pointed instrument for the purpose of sexual gratification – strike terror in living victims. Knives are fearsome and unyielding, and their phallic nature as a weapon supersedes any harm the predator can inflict with his penis. Knives are therefore sexual weapons psychologically as well as weapons of combat. Accordingly, Cottingham consistently threatened victims with the knife and teased them with superficial cuts on the victim's sacral, sternum, and breasts to the deeper rendering of the flesh. In the latter, the satisfaction came from cutting, tearing, and biting the flesh. Cottingham gained additional satisfaction from the sensory stimulation of penetration, wounding, and blood loss. This was consistent with victim pain and terror. The cutting also was a satiation of the power to cut apart and dehumanize the victim into isolated parts and ultimate destruction.

In this series of cases, the last evidence of picquerism was the harvesting of body parts: heads, hands, and breasts. While taking body parts may have been simply an element of the organized cleanup, the question remains, why only the New York victims? One practical reason quite possibly was that Cottingham forgot his cuff keys and therefore could not remove the cuffs from the dead victims' wrists. Accordingly, he had to cut off the victims' hands to reclaim his handcuffs still on their wrists and sever their necks to remove the neck collars. As ghoulish as that sounds, the needs of the killer are paramount, not our uninformed perception of his actions. Again, when considering the Hotel Seville case along with the threats Cottingham made in the O'Dell case, he removed only the breasts and placed them on the headboard of the bed. Why?

Perhaps, given the killer's penchant for picquerism, if those particular victims offended him by resisting in any way, the added pathological punishment was administered to overpower the threat and the sense of identity the victims had tried to maintain in the face of Cottingham's violence. Cottingham needed to show his superiority even after he had killed the young women. Hence, harvesting the bodies by cutting off parts and burning the victims' remains indicated a specialized aggression toward these particular women. The flourish of picquerism in these victims was a signal that he was evolving from being satisfied by bondage alone along the violence continuum to a higher level of need: the stabbing, gouging, and cutting of picquerism.

Another important feature of this killer's signature was the absence of ejaculate on the victims' bodies. This killer was a highly sophisticated sadist whose whole method of satisfaction and gratification orbited around control. Therefore, the absence of ejaculate on the victim was to be expected. Cottingham enjoyed the process of accomplishing the power of control over his victim so much that he saved his sexual expression for later or ejaculated into a towel while he contemplated what he was doing. That explains why he took souvenirs, so he could masturbate and satisfy himself sexually at a later time. And that's also why he could have an apparent normal sexual relationship with a woman he didn't kill or torture, because he had all his little trinkets or trophies, such as the jewelry and clothing of his victims, around him. Unbeknownst to his wife, girlfriends, or other willing sex partners, his fantasy life was driven much beyond what was happening at the moment with that particular partner. In fact, Cottingham would probably say that his fantasies, even during sex in his normal relationships, were always driven by the images of sexual domination of victims and the torture and bondage he inflicted. Even though to his sex partner he appeared normal, his sexual satisfaction was driven by an intensely perverted sexual fantasy interpretation.

Contrary to expectation in most murders, the sadist is excited by the process of killing, not the death. In fact, the death may be only an incidental by-product or an organized act of postcrime efficiency. As for Cottingham's cases, the deaths appeared to be an artifact of his satisfaction. That is, the process of destruction of the victims was the key issue for him. If, for instance, a victim actually died before his act was satisfied, he would have continued to act out verbally and physically until his needs were met. Remember, these actions were for his satisfaction, not for the elimination of his victims.

The condition and placement of the bodies also relates to the level of sexual satisfaction Cottingham was seeking. Thinking along traditional homicide investigation lines, the way Cottingham dumped the bodies appeared to be strictly functional to the organized offender. Lead the police astray, throw them different leads, make sure police in different jurisdictions didn't relate the homicides to each other so as to form a series as the basis of a multiagency task force. However, Cottingham wasn't really thinking along these lines. When he left a badly mutilated victim abandoned to die alone, it was a strong indicator that this was a conceptual extension of the violence that Cottingham had inflicted on the victim. The victim, once vibrant and sexual, then reduced to pleading, agony, and submission, would become a stinking mass of dead meat. And all of it would happen in public. Albeit an act of cruel irony, it would extend the violence past the actual memory of torture and bondage and satisfy Cottingham's internal need for displaying cleverness and superiority.

Sometimes we are able to figure out a lot about the killer by the absence of evidence. In these cases, the killer used a religiously tinged motivational structure called the Madonna complex, in which if the victim displays any signs of overt aggressive sexuality, she's impure and needs to be tortured so as to extinguish her sexuality; to select victims, justify aggression, and dispose of these women as trash. Although this rationale is a common one for murders of prostitutes, the killers often try to redeem the victim to purity through the punishment process.

However, in these cases, there is not evidence to suggest that he attempted to redeem them, only punish. Although one could look at the arson behaviors as a possible attempt at purification, the point would not be supported with the collateral evidence. In fact, the arson appeared to be an act of aggression, for destruction or damnation, rather than an attempt to purify these women from what Cottingham saw as their illicit ways.

Finally, as with many sadists, Cottingham acknowledged that he liked to play a trick or joke on the victims to demean them even further. In many instances, he would place a plastic revolver within their reach to provide them with false hope. If they tried to use it against him, he watched their terror when they realized it was only part of the torture game. Again, although cruel jokes display the luxury aspects of the murder in the sadist, Cottingham inadvertently signed his signature by the repetitive use of the plastic toy gun. That is, only he used that specific gimmick repeatedly.

Cottingham's internal stresses governed whether he would repeat his crimes on a sporadic or episodic schedule. These assaults and murders were sporadic over a three-year period. His reliving each crime was conditional to his satisfaction and developed his motivation for further domination. This is why the chronology of his crimes appeared to wax and wane. But inside, his motivation was always persistent because his ego was the major driver of his personality.

Cottingham was described as a killer with a Jekyll and Hyde personality. Assistant District Attorney of New York, Miles Malman told the jury that Cottingham had a 'perverted, twisted lust in his mind' that caused him to kill the three women. It was much, much more, of course, but some investigators doubt whether even a rational jury could have comprehended the complex deviance that motivates a predator such as Cottingham.

Cottingham did not drug his final victim, Leslie O'Dell,

although he certainly had the opportunity, and that was part of his undoing. Perhaps his sexual need required that his victim be completely awake and aware, forcing him to maintain greater control over a struggling victim and pushing him right against the envelope of discovery. Perhaps he wanted to experiment with a fully conscious victim to see if the thrill was greater. But the experiment ultimately failed because the fully conscious O'Dell was not about to submit without a struggle, and her screams brought hotel personnel to the scene. How could Cottingham not have seen this? Sometimes sadistic killers delude themselves into thinking that they are really as invincible as they portray themselves to be, when in reality, they're weaker and frailer than their victims. Cottingham failed to see the obvious, didn't reckon on the strength and resilience of his streetwise victim, and wound up in the hands of the police who responded to a call about a screaming woman. The cops discovered a nude prostitute who had been sexually tortured and bound with handcuffs. Cottingham was apprehended fleeing from the motel, his visions of invincibility and power in tatters. Cottingham's house was searched in Lodi, New Jersey, and authorities found his 'trophy room,' filled with souvenirs from his victims. Only his bravado was left, and even that didn't last very long.

So vivid was Cottingham's signature after numerous murders that a New Jersey prosecutor convinced the court that his 'modus operandi in the cases was so unique and novel that it was only personal to Cottingham.' Cottingham's need to torture and mutilate women sexually and brutally set him apart from other killers of his ilk, and the prosecutor who so correctly argued that what he called Cottingham's MO was uniquely personal had, in effect, argued for an existence of a killer's signature. Of course, the calling card that Cottingham left was personal; he was acting out his extreme behavior disorder from crime to crime. He knew he was sick. He readily admitted to police interrogators when asked about his crimes, 'I have a problem with women.'

Years after Cottingham had been put away, as I tried to figure out what could drive the sexually sadistic serial killer subtype, I kept asking myself what it was that ultimately intrigued me about the Cottingham cases. Partly it was the level of sadistic torture that Cottingham acted out on his victims. He didn't kill them and desecrate their bodies; he forced them to experience pain and humiliation before he killed them. Then he desecrated their bodies. It was as if the living torture drove him into the frenzy necessary to mutilate the corpses the way he did. Like a multistage rocket arcing toward escape velocity, Cottingham used each phase of the crime to propel himself to the next stage. While all serial killers go through different phases during their crime, nowhere before had it been so obvious to me how the phases interacted with each other. Cottingham didn't just walk from one phase to the next; the sexual energy he derived from each act motivated him to perform the next act in the psycho-drama.

It worked like this: the lure and pickup were essentially low energy. He was cruising, trolling, like a virus chemically polling receptors on a cell for a match that would allow entrance, Cottingham was looking for a woman who fit his profile. Maybe she was a street-walker – plenty of them along Third Avenue below Thirty-fourth Street – or maybe she was just a bit too friendly at the bar. No matter, they were all working girls, and once the conversation was struck up and he conned her into taking that drink, she was his. So he bounced along the bar, casually pinging the likeliest looking victims, looking for the conversational hook that would tell him this girl deserved the fate he had in store for her. I can even see him working himself up with anticipation: 'Are you the one? No? Are you?' But he kept it under control. Too much frenzy in your eyes, and you look like Ted Bundy at Lake Sammamish when one of the living victims he'd bounced off said he was just too focused and threatening for a casual drive to get a sailboat.

Once he had his victim in a conversation at the bar, it took only a moment to slip in the little dose of a hypnotic drug that would send her staggering into his control. The recent Rohypnol sex video case that just broke out in Los Angeles in 1996 is part of the very same pattern of gaining control of a victim by rendering her semiconscious, wielding that control sexually, and then commemorating it by taking a token to reinvigorate the sexual thrill. It's all part of a sexual pattern into which the most violent offenders such as Cottingham fit very easily.

With his victim drugged and almost asleep, Cottingham was thoroughly aroused. The thrill of the capture moved him to the next stage of isolating her under his control. So he transported her, letting the thrill of control work itself up on the short drive through the Lincoln Tunnel, to a motel in one of the New Jersey river towns such as Hackensack, where he slipped her into a room he rented. Or he drove her right across town to the Midtown Motel in Manhattan, gliding west along Thirty-fourth or Forty-second Street past the drug dealers in Bryant Park, through changing traffic lights, around an occasional taxi, and looking over the few people courageous enough to be on the street at that hour. Cottingham was all alone with his victim in his private bubble. He was empowered like the hunter with his new trophy. Each sound the victim made, each furtive attempt to fight the drug only aroused Cottingham further. He was moving along an arc of violence where each phase thrilled him enough to enter the next phase.

Once safely ensconced in the room, the torture began, and it was important that the victim be awakened during moments of pain and humiliation but be unable to resist. The more Cottingham tortured his victims, the more he pushed the envelope of sexual thrill, taking him as far as it could. When the energy of the torture phase was fully expended, he murdered the victim, taking her over the line to where he could expend anger on the mutilation of the body. But during the course of the murder and bloody dismemberment, he crossed the midpoint of the arc, no longer torturing the victim but punishing the victim for allowing herself to get picked up, raped, and tortured. Cottingham became the scourge, eradicating the very thing that aroused him in the first place.

Then Cottingham took his trophies, his souvenirs, which in a very private place would arouse him during the dark phase of a serial killer's pattern when he went underground to digest emotionally the enormity of what he had done. His trophies from this and previous crimes invigorated him as well, sustaining him for the next time when the need to troll came upon him. He was also invigorated by the newspaper headlines describing the shocked hotel maids and clerks who discovered the headless body, the hopeless police as they groped around for clues, the hand-wringing columnists as they worked themselves into a fury, and the reports on the six o'clock news from a familiar face trying desperately to scoop another familiar face with a detail no one else had. What will plucky Michelle Marsh say, or even Diane Dimond? How about smiling Sue Simmons on *Live at Five?* They were all his victims. He owned them all from the privacy of his solitary apartment. Cottingham was making them report his crimes, all these working girls, making them talk about what he did to other working girls. The hatred he felt for all women was transformed into acts of unbelievable sexual violence and then relived every morning and every night: all part of an arc of violence transporting through each crime to the next. And when energy diminished to a level where emotionally and physically his low-burn anger needed to be satisfied, he went out again into the night, searching for a new victim.

Once I could see the relationships among the phases and the way they worked to drive energy into frenzy, and frenzy into an almost chaotic state of destruction, I could see how and why the killer left an unmistakable signature at the crime scene. The frenzy was fueled by an anger-driven need for sexual gratification, the same motivator that drives serial rapists. Was there a greater similarity between the crimes here than most people realized? We know that many serial killers begin as cat burglars and then rapists, but can we actually track a killer's career by examining a characteristic signature arc not just from crime to crime, but from stage to stage along the criminal's life career? And if so, what does that tell us about the nature of crime-scene signature?

I knew I was onto something here. Cottingham's crimes showed me that he had left a clear signature, a pattern that reflected the reverse imprint of his own unique array of character flaws. Women somehow abused, intimidated, or threatened him; he took it out on them. The greater the fury he expended, the greater the next level of violence had to be. It had the mark of an addictive behavior which needs to be satisfied. Yet each crime bore a clear resemblance to the one before. One could almost predict the next level of violence as he escalated. So I knew that a signature killer couldn't control his signature, because his array of character flaws was controlling him. The monster was inside – the *entity*, Ted Bundy had called it – and identified itself at the crime scenes.

I was driven. Like my personal hero Sherlock Holmes, I'm an obsessive categorizer and cataloger. Everything has to have its place. And with the DMV computer terminal and software we'd jury-rigged to trap tip sheet information in the Ted cases, I could catalog and categorize anything. I had a tool, and with the information I was gleaning from these old serial murder cases, I had data to categorize. Somewhere in cases that would soon unfold and among the cracked, yellowing pages of thermal-copied police records, the truth was in there and I would find it.

I researched old serial rape cases and matched the arcs of violence with serial killer cases. Then, as I began to discover a pattern, another case crossed my path which would highlight exactly what I was looking for. It was the case of Virginia's South Side rapist, a real-life version of a Patricia Cornwell novel.

CHAPTER 4

The Anger-Retaliation Signature

Timothy Spencer, the South Side Rapist

Anybody who investigates sex crimes knows that even the most minor of sex offenses directed against a victim is driven by the offender's anger and his needs to express it through control. This is Sex Crimes 101. So when I looked at the perplexing problem of solving the nature of signature murders, all of which were so overtly and explicitly sexual they were actually pornographic, I tried to find an existing psychological model that I could work with. Maybe by applying a behavioral model, I said to myself, I might find a key somewhere. And sure enough, the anger-driven rape-offender model seemed to fit. So I began applying it to known signature murder cases and was truly surprised at how well it fit. The anger-driven sex-crimes model not only fit signature crimes, it was as if the signature killer and the anger-driven sexual offender were on the same continuum of violence. Was I looking at an evolutionary model here? And if so, what did it say about the very dramatic rise in sex crimes over the past twenty years? Had I stumbled into the answer to why serial murders were on the increase?

THE ANGER-DRIVEN SEXUAL OFFENDER

Some offenders who commit sex crimes – whether they're crimes against women or men, adults or children – commit them out of anger. Anger either excites a sexual reaction and drives the crime, or it is the fuel for a retaliatory assailant seeking revenge upon some ultimate source of his anger but substituting each victim for that source. When we study rape crimes, we are many times able to figure out if a rapist is beginning a series by his behavior toward the victim. What he says, whether he robs his victims, and any unique characteristics of behavior that he exhibits can elucidate the attacker's mental state. Is the offender leaving a signature, acting out some scenario, because he is driven by some compulsion? The more violently an attacker assumes and maintains control, the more likely he is to escalate to murder. And the murders themselves will escalate with greater violence as the killer experiments with all the core components of signature murder to satisfy his ever-growing sexual needs. In this way, I know from the world of sex crimes that the anger-driven sexual offender is on a self-sustaining violence continuum from the moment he begins to violate someone else's space or person to wherever he eventually stops – voyeurism, burglary, rape, or murder.

Sometimes a potential offender will never cross the boundary into criminal behavior and he will be content to fantasize silently about potential victims while experimenting with furtive sorties into other people's spaces. He may quietly follow a woman or a child just to keep track of their movements, but never announce himself, never cross into the territory of the criminal stalker. He may watch his neighbor across a courtyard from behind a curtain, acting sociably polite when they meet Tuesday evenings while putting out garbage at the curb, but never intruding into her life otherwise. This kind of behavior is safe and the control a man like this gets from just watching is enough to sustain him through the day. But sometimes this isn't the case. Sometimes a person with such tendencies begins the process of escalating them into violence. When that violence leads to murder, he will become a signature killer.

In the world of signature killers, there are two basic categories of anger-driven crimes: the anger-retaliatory killer and the anger-excitation killer. Typically, a killer begins as a retaliatory type and may escalate to an excitation type as his crime series progresses. During the course of that crime series, the killer evolves according to the nature of his anger. He leaves a signature which represents one or more of the core components of sadism, control, humiliation, progression of violence, posing, torture, overkill, necrophilia, and cannibalism.

ANGER-RETALIATION

Because some cases of serial rape start as retaliatory crimes, when I applied the anger-driven model to signature murder, it was the anger-retaliatory type of killer who seemed to be at the first point on the continuum. The source of anger and the figure symbolically receiving the retaliation of it becomes clear once you start looking into the killer's life and match what you find with the victim profile. I can't help considering cases such as Arthur Shawcross, who complained about his mother's coldness and murdered women who derided him, or Bobby Joe Long, who described sharing a bed with his mother well into his teens and murdering prostitutes and barflies in a district known for its strip bars in North Tampa, or John Gacy, who, although married, murdered lost boys who turned to him for solace as he'd once turned to his own father who, in turn, rejected any expressions of emotion.

The anger-retaliation homicide is typically characterized by a violent sexual assault and overkill in which the killer uses more than one weapon. Perceiving his victim to be the symbol of his frustration, the predator usually chooses an adult woman who is from his own age group or older. He rarely sexually molests little children. Often, a victim may never know the identity of this stalker and killer. Similarly, the killer probably has had only circumstantial familiarity with his victim. Their paths cross by chance and she becomes a victim only because the killer may be in the first phase of his murder cycle. In this phase, he trolls or stalks for victims, sometimes driving around or aimlessly walking for hours in areas he usually frequents when he's looking for targets. When he spots a potential victim, he moves in to set up the lure. Typically, he'll spot a woman who fits the referred victim type in his mind and will see where she lives, or a nearby secluded place where he could grab her without being noticed. Prostitute killers often choose victims of opportunity when they are trolling. Killers who pose as roofers, painters, service workers, or anyone else with occasion to go door to door searching for work may remember that a woman who lives in a particular house fits his target group and go back months later to pick her up. With this type of killer, the crime may look random, but it's not.

ANGER-RETALIATION VICTIM PROFILE

Who are the prototypical victims of anger-retaliation predators? Mostly, they are women whom the killers believe to be representative of the strong women who they see as responsible for the difficulties in their own lives. They are the women who represent the focus of the killers' anger: overcontrolling mothers; mothers who drove the father away; mothers who were prostitutes or were promiscuous, or who had a lot of boyfriends that displaced the father; mothers who systematically abused their children sexually or physically; or mothers who inspired fear and terror are at the center of this killer's victim profile. Anger-retaliatory killers generally don't kill their mothers, but they will kill other women whom they perceive to be like her. Female bosses or any woman in a dominant position can also fit the victim profile.

The predator builds up a justification for the killing process, for getting even against women like this. Most anger-retaliatory killers tend not to attack their primary source of frustration, although serial killers Henry Lee Lucas and Edmund Kemper and spree killer John List did just that. Most, like Arthur Shawcross and Florida serial killer Bobbie Joe Long, will pick substitutes as stand-ins for the sources of their homicidal fury.

Killers like these usually choose their victim for her convenience. She either lives or works in the area near where he lives, works, or travels, and he has ample opportunity to attack her. The killer next considers the age, vulnerability, attitude, and accessibility of the victim based on a prototypical target type he has fantasized about and may have already preselected from a pool of available victims. The frightening aspect about all this is that no one – not the victim, nor friends of the victim or acquaintances or family of the predator, nor the police – are aware this preselection process is under way.

The angry killer's final victim selection process actually begins after the perpetrator has been angered or challenged by a powerful woman, possibly one closely representing the source of his rage. When he cannot confront her, he substitutes a prescreened or target-type victim as the object of his rage. He may follow her home or to a secluded location where he will make his initial contact. Or he may simply put her on a waiting list in his mind reserved for future use.

Most serial killers, no matter what their category, still

woo their victims into the trap. That's part of the pattern and it's the way the killer isolates his victim in preparation for the assault. The most common anger-retaliation pattern is the prostitute killer who picks up his victim on a street corner, drives to a private place, begins the assault, and escalates the violence until he's completely sated immediate needs for retaliation.

This was the pattern Russian police in St. Petersburg and Rostov confronted when they were tracking Andrei Chikatilo, 'Citizen X,' the serial killer who preyed on adolescent boys and girls in railroad stations by luring them out of the crowded waiting rooms, taking them out into the nearby woods, molesting them, and committing such acts of brutality on their bodies that authorities were stymied.

Even if the signature killer drives to the crime scene with his victim, he often approaches the last two hundred feet on foot because he drives his own frenzy with each footfall, physically stalking and hunting his prey and confronting her face-to-face. This varies according to the situation. When he's arrived at the crime scene, the killer sets up an obvious conflict with his victim. It could go something like this – offender confesses that he went up to a woman's house that he had painted before. She lets him in and said, 'Oh, yeah, I remember you, what can I help you with?' He answers, 'You know, when I was here I knew that you were looking at my ass and I knew you wanted me.'

She says, 'Well, I certainly was not interested in your ass.'

'Oh, yes, you were,' the killer replies, and that starts the deliberate verbal conflict with the victim as an anger trigger to attack. The anger-retaliation killer needs a specific event with each victim as a spur to the attack even if he has to set it up consciously.

THE ANGER-RETALIATION MURDER PATTERN

After interviewing a number of retaliatory sexual predators, I've come to believe that these killers don't actually see themselves as committing crimes, only administering revenge. Accordingly, they don't spend time binding and torturing the victim the way predators do who get sexually excited by the victim's pain. Instead, retaliatory killers like the power-assertive approach – a quick blow to the face or to the back of the head, immediately debilitating her. If an attacker is fueled by rage, many times his emotions are running so high at the point of attack that he can't even perform sexually, making him even angrier and more violent and resulting in an incomplete sexual assault. Nevertheless, the catharsis of what the predator's really after is beating a woman who substitutes for his real focus of anger. That's what he wants and that's what he does until his anger, which has been rising steadily through the beating and the homicide, is abated.

After the height of the intensity of the beating or assault, the killer's anger starts to cool. In his mind he has avenged the wrongs done by the disapproving female source. The killer begins to feel relief and validation at what he's done, and the 'legitimate' anger he experienced which triggered the revenge is assuaged. Thus, as an act of real and symbolic submission to his victim who has now – though dead – become his accuser, he tries to keep the victim's face away from him because he cannot look into her eyes. Therefore, when the killer has finished – and this is a hallmark for him – he will not leave a woman faceup or with her face exposed in any way. He will not walk away with her facing him. The killer always has to roll her on her side or drop her facedown, or if she's on her back, he'll cover her face with a cloth or something else so that the eyes of the victim, closed or open, will not challenge him alive or dead. In the killer's mind, once the anger has been satisfied he is no longer the righteous avenger and feels ashamed at what he's done to the victim. He realizes, as he completes the crime and momentarily vanquishes the anger that drove him, that his dead victim still has power to inflict shame and humiliation upon him, so he must erase these feelings by obscuring the victim's face. Some killers have even placed plastic bags or pillows over the head so the victim cannot watch him walk out. In his mind, he's just overcome his shame and guilt, both of which reduce him to weakness in his own mind, right before the eyes of a still-disapproving woman.

The anger-retaliation homicide is further characterized by what seems like the illogic of the killer. Most medical examiners scratch their heads at the number of fatal wounds the victim has. They ask why the killer has stayed there, sometimes after it's obvious that the victim has died, exposing himself to discovery by witnesses, while he continues the assault on a dead body. Whether it's a tremendous assault with a knife or whatever weapon of opportunity – a piece of sculpture, a fireplace poker, a brick or rock – that's handy, it doesn't matter as long as the killer can vent his rage by quenching his thirst for revenge. So he continues, even postmortem, until he's satisfied and the sexual dynamics are lessened.

I often find that blunt force trauma on the victim is a big issue in anger-retaliation signature murders even when the killer has stabbed or hacked his victim as well. This in influenced mainly by the weapon of opportunity such as fists, rocks, metal or wooden objects, the flat of a knife blade, or any sharp instrument or hand tool that can be used to beat as well as to cut. However, when we find evidence of stabbing as well as beating, it is likely the knife was either already part of the crime scene – it was in a kitchen drawer – and thus became a weapon of opportunity or was carried by an offender who always conceals a knife. When a victim has been strangled, it is most likely manual strangulation. If a ligature was used, the item, such as an electrical cord, garment, or twisted pillow case, was already at the scene. In other words, it's not the weapon that drives the crime, it's the premeditation in the killer's mind as a result of his chronic and seething anger. After the killer sets up the pretext conflict as a trigger and the initial assault on the victim has been completed, the killer may use any improvised weapon of opportunity found at the crime scene to pummel the victim until the killer's anger is satisfied.

Even though the anger-retaliation homicide is part of a sex crime signature, the killer's fury will probably have interfered with sex before death; thus, the expression of sexuality may be through postmortem, intentional exploratory mutilation of the body. Sometimes the dead victim is undressed and the killer takes souvenirs such as articles of clothing, hair clippings, and other personalized objects that he can identify with his victim in his private moments. If the killer does partake in this activity, his anger has not yet fully subsided and he is still in the process of the crime.

When all aspects of the killing are completed and the perpetrator has had his catharsis, he immediately feels a perverse sense of justification. He's expressed his rage; now it's over. 'She deserved to die,' he tells himself over and over again. 'I'm happy,' he repeats, because he's supposed to be happy at satisfying his revenge. Now he has a sense of calm, a sense of completion, a momentary sense of triumph over the disapproval he constantly feels from the real target of his rage that keeps on haunting him. This becomes a critical issue in how he thinks about the crime scene he is exiting, and so he doesn't clean up very well after himself, because it doesn't really cross his mind that he has to. Once he has covered the victim's face and no longer feels shame and humiliation in her eyes, his sense of wrong-doing in the killing vanishes and is replaced by the satisfaction of having avenged himself on someone who deserved it.

This rapid exchange of feelings the anger-retaliatory killer experiences explains the often bizarre contradictions investigators discover at this killer's crime scene. On the one hand, it's extraordinarily violent with blood spattered and running everywhere. The victim's repeated blunt force and stabbing wounds seem to indicate that the assailant wasn't satisfied with just killing, he was beating and hacking something inside himself that he could get to through the victim's body. Then, when the feeling has been satisfied, the crime abruptly stops. The killer, immediately awash in shame and guilt, covers the victim's face or turns her face away from him. The shame and guilt vanish and are replaced by righteous feelings of revenge and satisfaction. No need to cover up a crime when in his mind he's committed no crime, and the killer immediately leaves. What the police see when they discover the crime is the victim bludgeoned or hacked to pieces, even when the actual cause of death was strangulation; a bloody crime scene in utter chaos, but a victim's face so delicately covered or precisely turned away that the killer's handling of this one aspect looks like a paradox against the backdrop of the entire murder scene, particularly what he's done to the victim's body. But there's no mystery. This is what an anger-retaliation crime scene typically looks like.

The killer is on an emotional high while committing his violent acts, and so he has a tendency to leave a lot of evidence behind. When crime is disorganized, the death scene and body location scene are the same, and therefore loaded with clues. For example, the murder weapon may be left within twenty-five feet of the victim, often along with some of the killer's possessions. Alternatively, when the organized-type offender resists the tendency toward disorganization, he may only give superficial attention to cleanup, removal of weapons, and establishing an alibi.

In those instances when the killer has murdered the primary focus of his rage – his mother or his ex-wife or girlfriend – his sense of justification has a tendency to be even more profound. He truly has no sense of wrongdoing. He's killed her and he no longer feels haunted by her anger and disapproval. He's no longer pressured by her. Now he can afford to love her, so he develops the maudlin sentimental attitude that shapes his postcrime behavior. There is a great show of emotion and sadness. If not already in custody, the killer may even turn up at his mother's or ex-wife's funeral and display his grief with the rest of the family. If he ends up in prison, you'll find his family's pictures up on the wall of his cell and he'll actually worship the memory of the disapproving woman he murdered.

THE ANGER-RETALIATION SUSPECT PROFILE

So, who is the prototypical anger-retaliation signature killer and what kind of profile should I look for when I find an obvious victim of rage-driven overkill at a crime scene? There is no real defining age. The retaliatory type can be under thirty-five, but he can also be much older. Arthur Shawcross was forty-five when he committed the prostitute serial murders in Rochester. John List was over thirty-five as well. Usually, the victims are either the same age or older than the perpetrator, sometimes even much older if they're substitutes for his mother. But ages vary. Lucas was convicted for killing his mother, then years later he confessed to killing Kate Rich, an old woman, but murdered Ottis Toole's niece Becky Powell, who was much younger than he, when she refused to run away from Texas with him.

We can better identify him by personality type than by age or appearance. We can describe the retaliatory type as an explosive personality who is impulse-driven, quick-tempered, and self-centered. He is not reclusive, but sometimes he may have real trouble fitting into the crowd. Generally, his social relationships are superficial and limited to drinking buddies. He is a person no one really knows because he can put up a pretty good front even if it's only for the short term. Accordingly, you'll see him making acquaintances at his local bar, maybe even at work or at social gatherings. He likes sports and he has a high interest in playing anything that involves team contact such as football or pickup basketball, where contact rules are sometimes very relaxed. But he has no close friends, no one in whom he confides, because his closest companion is his constant anger that defines the way he sees the world.

The retaliatory killer is almost always in conflict within himself over his relationship with women. He often feels dependent on them and aggressively resistant to them at the same time, thus setting up the internal conflict. When his wishes are contested by women, he uses various forms of aggression to 'get even and degrade them.' We see this in the workplace, especially where there are women supervisors over blue-collar workers and the workers are hostile because these are not just their bosses whom they believe are treating them unfairly, but women. Typically, retaliatory killers transfer the need to retaliate *from* the workplace *to* victims of opportunity. But because anger retaliation is a sex crime, women supervisors or bosses can trigger the killer into action, who then transfers the focus of his violence onto an easier victim.

Historically, the retaliatory killer's marriage will have been ill-fated and he will usually be in some phase of estrangement. If he's estranged from a long-time girlfriend, there are similar feelings of possessiveness toward other women in general, especially if the guy's a voyeur or stalker who fantasizes about the women he's watching. If he has a relationship, there will have generally been a history of long-term recurring spousal abuse, which will not likely have been covered by criminal complaints, police interventions, and possibly even a series of arrests for domestic violence. Depending upon the community, investigators will either find a long paper trail of complaints or will get the same information from neighbors who might have reported loud and violent domestic disputes to the police. However, rather than dealing with general problems in the marriage, the retaliatory predator will often avoid confrontation and reconciliation by seeking extramarital liaisons. For the most part, these relationships are unsatisfactory because sexually, he is frustrated and may feel impotent. He may ultimately link anger with sexual competence.

Although he may use *Penthouse, Hustler*, or similar types of magazines for interest reading, this type of aggressor does not usually use explicitly pornographic materials for stimulation. These guys generally don't seek stimulation; they seek relief from anger and hostility. They look for an outlet from the primary source of rage and don't equate their sexual performance with the need for erotic materials. They claim a need for a woman who will understand them and won't be judgmental or hostile in her dealings with them. For a victim, this type of man selects a woman who attempts to force competence and responsibility upon him. In reaction to her behavior, he becomes angry and his feelings of violence escalate until he strikes out.

When his aggressive feelings toward women are linked with a lack of impulse control, the potential killer may develop a criminal history such as assault and battery, wife beating, felonious assault, and reckless driving. He is usually a school dropout who has not lived up to his potential. If he's joined the military, his unsettled behavior often results in a dishonorable discharge. And of course, consistent with these behaviors is free-floating anger. It is the cause of many conflicts with authority which result in job loss, confrontations with the juvenile justice and criminal justice system, and ultimately, if not stopped, homicide.

These anger-retaliatory types are walking time bombs who've displayed warning signs throughout their whole lives. Their unpredictable behaviors may have resulted in their being referred to mental health professionals and probably have worked with probation officers or social service caseworkers. What we sometimes find is a case history that's enormous, with different workers or law enforcement agencies having intervened at different points in their lives. But whether the anger retaliatory signature killer comes from a rural area, a blue-collar working-class neighborhood, or a middle-class family, unless his potential for violence is stopped early, he will ultimately become a predator of women. Just such a predator was a classic anger-retaliatory type who became known as the South Side rapist in Richmond, Virginia, a model for 'Mr. Nobody,' the type of criminal serial killer who would challenge Patricia Cornwell's fictional medical examiner, Dr. Kay Scarpetta.

THE SOUTH SIDE RAPIST

The South Side rapist case is notable not only because it dealt with the crimes, capture, trial, and conviction of a very cunning signature killer, but because it also marked one of the first cases in which a killer's identification was based on DNA evidence. This famous case began in Virginia in 1987, when police investigated the rape-murders of four women in Richmond and Arlington. Eventually, detectives arrested Timothy Spencer as the South Side rapist, and prosecutors cited as crucial evidence in that series the biological fluids recovered around each of those murder scenes.

In this death-penalty trial of recently released cat burglar Timothy Spencer, the prosecution introduced DNA evidence – DNA genetic 'fingerprinting' – to convince the jury that the man police had arrested was indeed the same one who had left seminal fluids on and in his victims and at the crime scenes. They introduced the DNA evidence again during the penalty phase to argue that the jury should impose the death penalty because statistics showed there was no chance they would later find it had been a case of mistaken identity. According to the state's experts, the chances were less than one in seven hundred million that someone other than Timothy Spencer had left the semen at each of the murder scenes.

Virginia prosecutors chose not to overeducate the jury in the arcane science of DNA typing because first, it was too new and confusing, and second, they wanted to focus on commonsense human pattern behaviors that the jury could understand. Thus, the signature aspects of the Spencer murders were used to set the stage for the conviction, while the DNA evidence was brought in afterward to help convince the jury that they had the right man and could feel confident about sentencing him to death. The strategy worked and helped establish both signature crime-based prosecutions and DNA matching as viable arguments for prosecuting attorneys.

In 1989, Spencer's convictions were upheld on appeal. The appellate review was a landmark decision to allow DNA evidence at trial because Spencer's murders were the first murder convictions in the nation in which the identity of the killer and the argument for imposition of the death penalty were based on DNA testimony. Spencer's conviction was such a legal milestone that it prompted Virginia state crime officials to open the first state DNA laboratory in the country.

However, buried in all the appeals and hidden by the headlines over the DNA controversy was the court's willingness to allow the prosecutor to interpret the crimes as having similar methods of operation, even though there was no expert testimony directly to the similarity of those crimes. My good friend, retired New York Police Homicide Lieutenant Commander Vernon Geberth, author of the bible on homicide investigation, *Practical Homicide Investigation: Tactics, Procedures, and Forensic Techniques*, recommended that I look into the Timothy Spencer cases because they were truly the work of a signature killer. Geberth highlighted the Spencer cases in his book, not so much as an example of their signature nature, but for the outstanding detective work of Detective Joseph Horgas. Horgas pursued his leads so thoroughly that he not only linked Spencer to his cases but also freed an innocent man who was sentenced to death for a 1984 murder that Spencer had probably committed but was not charged for.

What surprised me when I saw the appellate issues brought in on behalf of Timothy Spencer was that there were the murders very similar in modus operandi, as pointed out by the prosecuting authorities, but there also was clearly the underlying signature of the killer present at each of the scenes. In Virginia, crimes can be linked by similar MO and don't need to be related by a perfect signature. What I saw here, however, was a perfect example of a signature killer at work. The prosecutor was correct in his assumptions, and his reasoning was not flawed regarding the aspects of Spencer's MO. But a closer look at these crimes based on the signature aspects of each murder will conclusively link all four murders to the same rare signature killer. The fact that the DNA evidence confirmed the signature investigation and interpretation of the crimes is a happy circumstance; it was the rock-solid emphasis on the basics of human behavior, however, something a jury could understand without a degree in organic chemistry, that closed the door on Timothy Spencer. When the time came for the complexities of chemical and statistical interpretation, it served to reinforce a decision the jury had already made: that Spencer was guilty as charged.

Debbie Dudley Davis

On Saturday, September 19, 1987, between one and two in the morning, a southside Richmond resident noticed a strange automobile parked outside his home. It looked suspicious to him, but he let it go. When he awoke later at 6:30 that Saturday morning, the car was still there. When he went outside to take a closer look, he noted that the keys were in the ignition, and, incredibly, the engine was running. The home owner called the Richmond Bureau of Police to report this apparently abandoned automobile. The police ran a computer check with the Division of Motor Vehicles records and discovered that the automobile was registered to Debbie Dudley Davis at the address of an apartment only four blocks from where the car was left running. The police suspected something was wrong, because people usually don't leave their cars running all night, at least not blocks away from their home. They followed up by contacting the car's owner.

When they arrived at Davis's apartment at 9:35 A.M., the police received no answer at her front door. Suspecting perhaps a stolen car, maybe even violence, they entered the apartment and found Davis's body lying face-down width-wise across her bed. She was clad only in a pair of shorts. A black sock was tied in a knot around her neck as a ligature into which the killer had inserted a section of vacuum cleaner pipe. He seemed to have used the pipe as a ratchet-torque device in the strangulation, similar to the way one uses a stick to tighten a tourniquet to shut off blood flow around an open wound. The killer had tied his victim up with a shoestring. The shoestring traveled from the victim's left wrist, pulling it up the front of her chest, through the sock around her neck and down to her right wrist, where it was tied secure enough to hold her right wrist in the middle of her back at waist level. This was a strange type of bondage.

Dr. David Wiecking, the chief medical examiner of Richmond, determined that the cause of Davis's death was ligature strangulation which had been applied with 'very extreme pressure.' The ligature, when tightened down and 'twisted two or three times' with the vacuum cleaner pipe, had cut 'into the larynx, the voice box, and the muscles on the side of the neck.' The 'intense blood pressure congestion' in the victim's head due to the ligature had caused hemorrhage in one of her eyes. The victim also suffered bruising to her nose and mouth, as though she had her nose rubbed up against something. No defensive wounds were found on her hands or arms.

After the victim's blue cutoff shorts were removed at the postmortem examination, two 'characteristically Negroid' hairs were found when Davis's pubic area was combed. The medical examiner also determined that the posterior portion of the victim's vagina was bruised. Microscopic examination of smears made from the rectal and vaginal swabs obtained from Davis's body revealed the presence of sperm.

A careful crime-scene examination enabled police investigators to discover physical evidence that eventually would be connected to the killer. First of all, there were three semen stains on the comforter lying next to the victim on her bed. On top of the fitted bedsheet, police located four additional semen stains, all of which were processed as evidence.

The intruder had entered Davis's apartment by raising the screen in a kitchen window located approximately eight feet above the ground. Under the window was a rocking chair that had been stolen from the porch of a nearby apartment sometime between Friday afternoon and Saturday morning. Inside the kitchen, immediately beneath the window, was the kitchen sink and countertop. The area seemed virtually untouched by the killer, since none of the items around the sink or windowsill were disturbed upon entry. The only evidence of a struggle in Davis's apartment was the location of her eyeglasses and toothbrush, which were found on the floor of the hallway leading to her bedroom.

Dr. Susan Hellams

Two weeks after the murder of Debbie Davis, the killer struck again. This time, his victim was Dr. Susan Elizabeth Hellams, a resident in neurosurgery at the Medical College of Virginia. She was last seen alive about 10:50 in the evening of October 2, 1987, in the area of Ninth and Capitol Streets in the city of Richmond. According to coworkers, she was preparing to return to her Southside Richmond home located at 514 West Thirty-first Street. Dr. Hellams's husband, Marcel Sleg, returned to the couple's home between 1:30 and 1:40 on the morning of October 3. Knowing that his wife's shift had ended, he expected her to be home already, but after taking a shower, Sleg got worried. Maybe she was still held up at the hospital, he thought. He soon discovered otherwise when he opened their bedroom closet and found his wife's dead body faceup on the closet floor. The official police communications center recorded Sleg's telephone call for assistance at 1:56 A.M.

Later in the investigation, police discovered that on that same day as the Hellams murder, her killer, Timothy Spencer, resided at 1500 Porter Street in Richmond, a distance of approximately 1.8 miles from the Hellams's residence. Detectives clocked the distance and it took approximately seventeen minutes to walk that distance. The Linden Tower Offender Aid and Restoration of Richmond records showed that Spencer signed out of the home at 7:45 P.M. on October 2 and did not return until the following morning at 1:45. He had just walked out of the house literally minutes before Sleg returned to find his wife's body.

Susan Hellams's body was nude above the waist. Her

skirt and half-slip had been pulled up, and her underpants had been removed. She was wearing red socks and still had one red shoe on her left foot. The medical examiner observed a musky odor about her body, reminiscent of seminal fluids.

Around her neck, police found two different ligatures, a red belt and a blue cloth belt, that were tied to one another to make one long ligature. This is known as an 'overligature,' a handmade personalized strangulation device fabricated by the physically obsessive signature killer as one way to derive satisfaction from his relentless anger. Hellams's wrists were tied tightly together behind her back with a standard brown electrical extension cord. She also had a fine blue fabric-corded belt which the killer had twisted around her wrist as a second binding. A red belt secured the lower portion of Hellams's left leg at the knee and a loop of that still remaining would have accommodated the other ankle. It looked as though an opportunistic killer had used whatever ligature paraphernalia he was able to find in the clothing closet.

You would have thought the victim's house was secure from a quick look around, especially when you noted the six-foot-high fence which enclosed the entire backyard of the residence. However, there was a second-story porch immediately outside the victim's bedroom window which provided easy access to anyone able to scale the fence. Police concluded that this was the killer's point of entry. A large portion of the screen from the bedroom window had been cut and removed and was found on the floor of the porch, supporting the theory. Mr. Sleg remembered that the screen and window were intact when he had last left the house.

Dr. Marcella Fierto, executive medical examiner of the Central District, Commonwealth of Virginia, performed the autopsy on Susan Hellams and concluded that ligature strangulation officially caused Hellams's death. In the initial confrontation with the killer, Hellams sustained a fractured nose, a blunt force injury to the lower lip that caused bleeding and swelling, and various other contusions and abrasions about the face. 'Curva-linear marks' with 'black material embedded in the abrasion' were found on the back of the victim's right leg. In the opinion of the medical examiner, such marks were typical of a shoe-print pattern. She had been kicked or stomped by her killer.

The medical examiner also found body fluids on the victim's back and in the gluteal fold, right beneath the buttocks. An indication of sexual assault was also confirmed by the discovery of small mucosal tears in the anal ring. The medical examiner testified that these injuries are consistent with the anus having been penetrated 'by a hard object, such as a penis.'

The Commonwealth's expert serologist identified spermatozoa on the swabs taken from the victim's vagina, rectum, and perianal region. That same serologist also identified seminal fluid and spermatozoa on Hellams's skirt and slip. It looked as if the killer could not control his own ejaculation or had deliberately ejaculated onto the adjacent material. In the follow-up examination of a sample of Timothy Spencer's blood after his arrest, the analysis revealed that Spencer is a type O secretor, PGM type 1, PGM subtype 1+, and peptidase A type 1. Only thirteen percent of the population, including men, women, and children, have this particular combination of blood types. Hellams was determined to be a nonsecretor, PGM type 2–1, PGM subtype 2+1–, and peptidase A type 1. Marcel Sleg was found to be a nonsecretor, PGM type 2–1, and PGM subtype 2+1+.

The serologist identified type O secretions on the swabs taken by the medical examiner from the victim's perianal area. The serologist also identified type O secretions in the seminal fluid found on the victim's skirt and slip. The serologist testified that the identified secretions must have originated from a third party because both Hellams and

Sleg were nonsecretors. The expert further stated that the secretions in the seminal fluid found on the victim's skirt and slip were consistent with Spencer's type and inconsistent with Sleg's type. In addition, the secretions in the seminal fluid found on the perianal swabs were consistent with a combination of the blood types of Spencer and the victim and inconsistent with a combination of the blood types of the victim and her husband.

Later, Spencer's blood sample and a sample of the seminal fluid found on the victim's slip were subjected to a DNA printing procedure. The DNA printing procedure established that the DNA molecules extracted from Spencer's known blood sample matched the DNA molecules extracted from the seminal fluid found on the victim's slip. This became the basis of DNA analysis used to identify an assailant.

Diane Cho

Diane Cho was a fifteen-year-old girl of Korean descent who lived with her parents and brother in a Chesterfield County apartment complex. On the night of Saturday, November 21, 1987, at about eight o'clock, Diane had dinner at home with her family. After that, her parents gave Diane a haircut and she gave her brother one, too. Diane retired to her bedroom about 10:00 P.M.. Her parents heard her typing in her room about 11:30 P.M., but heard no sounds from her room thereafter. The parents slept in the bedroom next to Diane's and heard nothing throughout the night. Early the next morning, her parents left the apartment to go to work and assumed that Diane was still asleep.

Mr. and Mrs. Cho returned home about 2:00 P.M. that afternoon. They found Diane's body facedown on the bed, partially covered by a sheet. Her hands had been bound securely behind her back with a length of rope. Another rope was tied tightly around her neck with a slipknot. The end of that rope came over her back and was tied to her hands. Her body was nude and her mouth was covered with duct tape. A figure eight or infinity sign had been painted on her left hip with fingernail polish. She was dead as the result of ligature strangulation.

The medical examiner examined Diane's body at the crime scene and estimated the time of death at six to twelve hours earlier, probably while Mr. and Mrs. Cho were still in the house. As in the cases of Susan Hellams and Debbie Davis, there were no signs of struggle in the room and nothing was disturbed in the apartment except the screen covering the window in Diane's room. The window was unlocked and the screen was found on the ground outside. The screen frame had been broken and removed from the window by the intruder. In all instances of this series, including Cho, the intruder's MO matched that of a cat burglar who was skilled in gaining silent entrance to a premise.

Miss Cho's body was examined by Dr. Marcella Fierto, who had also examined Dr. Hellams. She found acute vaginal and anal injuries and two bruises on top of Miss Cho's head. Her vagina was lacerated and torn. The entire area of her hymen was torn. Did the killer know his victim was this young and a virgin? Miss Cho's anal ring showed some redness at the seven o'clock position, and there were smears of blood on the buttocks and genital area. Seminal fluid was found in the victim's vagina, and an unusually large amount of seminal fluid was found in three separate stains on a sheet taken from the victim's bed. Bloodstains were also found on the sheet, as well as a single 'Negroid' hair. Mr. and Mrs. Cho stated that no black persons had ever visited them in the apartment.

As a result of his being on probation from a prior prison sentence, Spencer was living in a halfway house on Porter Street, in Richmond, at the time of Diane Cho's murder. The halfway house was about six miles from the Cho's apartment. The record at the halfway house on the night of November 21, 1987, showed that Spencer had signed out and left at 7:15 P.M. He did not return until over twenty-four hours later, at 8:25 P.M. the next day. He was arrested on January 20, 1988, at the halfway house. At the time of the arrest, the police discovered, on the fabric covering the box spring under Spencer's mattress, a figure eight or infinity sign. The words 'I hope' were printed above this mark.

A serologist examined the known sample of Diane's blood, the known sample of Spencer's blood, secretions found on vaginal swabs taken from the victim, and the material taken from the stains on the bedsheet. The serologist made a comparative blood type and enzyme analysis of the blood samples, secretions, and stains. The victim was identified as a type A secretor, PGM type 2–1, PGM subtype 2+1+, and peptidase A type 1. Spencer was identified as a type O secretor, PGM type 1, PGM subtype 1+, and peptidase A type 1.

The expert testified that a bedsheet stain 'would probably be pure seminal fluid.' This sample corresponded to Spencer's blood type and enzyme grouping in all respects. Spencer belongs to a group comprising approximately thirteen percent of the population which could have been the source of this stain. The vaginal specimen and the other bedsheet stains were mixed with blood. They were consistent with a mixture of Spencer's blood type and enzyme grouping with that of the victim. In addition, a microscopic examination of the hair taken from the bed sheet revealed that it was 'microscopically similar' to a known sample of Spencer's underarm hair.

Before the police identified Spencer as the killer, all they knew was that there were three dead women sexually attacked in the same general area within a period of months by a killer who was able to gain entrance using basic cat burglar skills and who was so silent, he was able to kill while a victim's family members were right down the hall. Because this was a killer able to exploit resources at the crime scene, who killed his stranger victims quickly and quietly, and who seemed to take immediate sexual pleasure without having to move the victim to a different place, he seemed completely invisible. Therefore, typically in a series like this, there would be more victims until the police actually brought the invisible killer into custody. And that's exactly how the series progressed when Spencer attacked his next victim, Susan Tucker.

Susan Tucker

On the evening of Tuesday, December 1, 1987, the nude body of Susan Tucker was found lying facedown and crossways on the bed in the ransacked master bedroom of her Arlington town house. Susan Tucker was married but living alone. A slipknotted rope was tied around Tucker's neck; the free end of the knotted rope had been used to tie her hands behind her back. The medical examiner determined the cause of death to be strangulation by ligature, and she had been dead three to five days before her body was found.

When Tucker's body was discovered, a blue sleeping bag was partially draped over her buttocks, a brown blanket was underneath her, and her nightgown was on the bed. There were large semen stains on all three items. Crime laboratory experts determined that 'pubic hairs of Negroid origin' were found on the blanket, in the bathroom sink, and on the counter around the sink. 'Negroid' pubic hairs also were found on a washcloth that apparently had been taken from Tucker's bathroom and dropped on a bush a short distance from Tucker's home.

Spencer forcibly entered Tucker's town house using his cat burglar's skills to break a sliding basement window located under the balcony at the rear of the house. Each side of the window was measured by Detective Horgas at eighteen by fourteen inches. The window was secured by a wooden dowel rod, but once the window was broken the rod seemed to have been easily removed, allowing Spencer to slide the window. Detective Horgas found the rod outside the window. As one might expect from a crime scene with glass breakage, the police took samples of the glass to keep as standards to compare against glass fragments that might be located in the suspect's clothing, assuming, as is usually the case, that a transfer of materials took place at the crime scene.

THE ARREST OF TIMOTHY SPENCER

On January 20, 1988, Arlington County police arrested Spencer, a black male, in the city of Richmond on a warrant charging burglary. At the time of his arrest, police seized a camouflage jacket from Spencer. After advising him of his rights, a police officer asked Spencer to voluntarily give blood, hair, and saliva samples. Although the officer told Spencer he was charged with burglary, Spencer asked 'if this had anything to do with the rape.' When the officer informed him that the crime had occurred in Arlington, Spencer inquired, 'Does this have anything to do with the murder then?' These statements would later come to haunt Spencer, because they were admitted as evidence against him at trial, indicating Spencer's prior knowledge of these crimes.

It would later be discovered that Spencer had visited his mother's Arlington home over the Thanksgiving holiday, arriving Thanksgiving morning, November 26, and departing the following Sunday, November 29. Spencer's mother lived approximately seven blocks from Tucker's town house.

The medical examiner who performed the Tucker autopsy obtained oral, rectal, and vaginal swabs and a blood sample from her body. The vagina swab was taken by inserting the swab 'as high in the vaginal cavity as it will go'; the swab did not contact the external genitalia. The medical examiner's microscopic examination revealed 'four to eight' intact, nonmotile sperm in smears made from the vaginal swab. No sperm was observed in the smears made from the anal and oral swabs.

A forensic serologist who subsequently made smears from the swabs taken by the medical examiner found two sperm on the rectal smears but found no sperm on either the vaginal or oral smears. The serologist explained that she had to rehydrate the dry swabs before testing them. Consequently, the water diluted any seminal fluid present on the swabs, making the sperm more difficult to detect.

Forensic analysis established that the pubic hairs found on the washcloth, the blanket from Tucker's bed, and the bathroom sink were microscopically consistent 'in all identifiable characteristics' with known samples of Spencer's pubic hair. Forensic scientists also determined that glass fragments found in Spencer's camouflage jacket matched the optical properties of Tucker's broken basement window. Only two percent of glass examined at the state laboratory has the same optical properties.

Analysis of the semen stains found on Tucker's nightgown, the blanket, and the sleeping bag established that the stains were left by a 'secretor,' or a person whose blood characteristics are expressed in other bodily fluids. Analysis further determined that the individual had blood type O and enzyme groupings of PGM type 1, PGM subtype 1+, and peptidase A type 1. Analysis of Spencer's blood and saliva samples showed that they matched in all respects the secretions found at the crime scene. This particular combination of blood type and enzyme groupings is shared by approximately thirteen percent of the population. Spencer's blood sample and the semen collected from the nightgown and the sleeping bag also were subjected to DNA printing.

DNA, the name of which most people recognize from televised trials if not from basic science, is the abbreviation for deoxyribonucleic acid, the chemical compound that carries an individual's genetic information. The DNA printing technique was used to compare DNA molecules extracted from Spencer's blood with DNA molecules extracted from the semen found at the crime scene. The DNA printing test established that the genetic material in Spencer's blood sample had the same characteristics as the genetic material in the semen stains on the nightgown and the sleeping bag. Such characteristics would be present in one of every 135 million black individuals. There are approximately ten million adult black males in the United States.

CONNECTING SPENCER TO THE MURDERS

Debbie Davis worked in a bookstore in Cloverleaf Mall. Dr. Susan Hellams went shopping there and had negotiated checks on September 22, 1987, at the bookstore where Debbie Davis worked. Diane Cho and her best friend frequented the same mall, as well as a shopping center across from the mall where a drugstore is located. An open jar of Vaseline found at the Hellams crime scene had been purchased at that drugstore after June 15, 1987.

On the night of January 9, 1988, a detective observed Spencer standing around in Chesterfield Mall for about an hour. Diane Cho lived nearby and had often gone there. After leaving Chesterfield Mall, Spencer went to Cloverleaf Mall, where he remained inside for about half an hour. When he was arrested on January 20, Spencer falsely denied that he had ever been to either place.

At the time of Davis's murder, Spencer was living in a Richmond residence approximately 2.7 miles from

Davis's apartment. A walk between Davis's apartment and Spencer's residence takes about thirty-seven minutes. Spencer had left his residence at 7:30 P.M. on Friday, September 18, and had not returned until 12:30 A.M. on Saturday, September 19. Davis, who had a telephone conversation with her parents Friday evening, was last known to have been alive between 8:30 P.M. and 9:00 P.M. Friday.

Forensic analysis established that the two hairs combed from Davis's pubic area 'were consistent with' Spencer's underarm hair. Analysis of the semen stains found on Davis's comforter and bedsheet showed that the stains had been deposited by a secretor. Analysis of Spencer's blood and saliva samples established that Spencer, who is a secretor with blood type O, PGM type 1, PGM subtype 1+, and peptidase A type 1, was 'included in a group – comprising approximately thirteen percent of the population – that could have contributed the seminal fluid' found on Davis's comforter and bedsheet.

Spencer's blood sample and the semen collected from the comforter and the bedsheet were subjected to a DNA print identification which established that the DNA molecules extracted from Spencer's blood were identical to the DNA molecules extracted from the semen stains at the Davis crime scene. Spencer is a black male. The statistical likelihood of finding a duplication of Spencer's particular DNA pattern in the population of North American blacks is one in 705 million.

Spencer had been released from prison to a halfway house in Richmond on September 4, 1987, just two weeks before he raped and murdered Davis. Thus, he had to sign in and out of the house, establishing his presence in the house whenever he was there and his absence when he had signed out. Forensic evidence presented during the penalty phase established that Spencer also raped and murdered another Richmond woman in October 1987, and a woman in Arlington in late November 1987. Each of these victims had been strangled to death by strikingly similar methods. Spencer had been convicted of six prior burglaries, three as an adult and three as a juvenile. His past criminal record also disclosed that Spencer has been convicted of three counts of trespassing, sometimes a precursor to a cat burglar career.

In his defense, Spencer presented six character witnesses on his behalf who testified that he had been a shy, quiet, nonviolent person. He was a 'loner.' None of these witnesses could believe that he committed the crimes against Davis.

MODUS OPERANDI

The physical evidence in these four cases overwhelmingly linked Spencer positively to each murder. But in support of the Commonwealth prosecutor's contention, the prosecutor's closing argument described several points of similarity linking the cases together.

First, he said, each of the crimes occurred during a ninety-day period that Spencer was living in a Richmond halfway house following his release from the penitentiary, and each occurred when he had signed out of the halfway house overnight. The records showed that. The Arlington murder of Susan Tucker occurred while he was signed out to visit his mother in Arlington, again a point established by the records.

Second, each of the four victims was killed by ligature strangulation, a method which, while not entirely unique in and of itself, can be applied in a unique way in combination with other types of assault. This was the case in the Spencer signature.

Third, each of the four victims had been subjected to forcible rape and sodomy at the time of her murder.

Fourth, each of the four victims was overcome quickly, without an opportunity to struggle or call for help. None showed defensive injuries and there was no sign of a struggle. The evidence was consistent with the victims' being overcome while asleep. In no case was there evidence of injury by a weapon.

Fifth, in each case, entry to the victim's home was gained through a window either by cutting a screen or breaking glass.

Sixth, each of the victims was described as a white or Asian female of a 'stocky' body build.

Seventh, and very important, the type of ligature strangulation had a specific signature. Each victim was found strangled by a neck ligature and with her hands tied. In three of the four cases, the neck ligature was also tied to the bindings around the hands. This meant the killer had the ability to adapt materials found at the crime scene into a unique configuration in which the binding was also part of the strangulation process.

Eighth, all four victims were found in their bedrooms, indicating that the killer was preying on their defenselessness and inability to resist rather than luring them into a trap.

Ninth, the murderer had made an effort to hide or partially cover each body before leaving the scene, which we know is an indicator of a specific type of sexual crime.

Tenth, each of the killings occurred during a weekend, indicating something about the killer's travel pattern or the way he might have stalked his victims.

Eleventh, unusually large amounts of seminal fluid were found outside the body of each victim, indicating the killer's lack of control.

Twelfth, the source of the seminal fluid was in each case a secretor having Spencer's blood and enzyme types, a combination found in thirteen percent of the population.

Finally, in each of the four cases, the source of the seminal fluid was a person having either the same DNA print or the same DQ-alpha genotype as Spencer. As previously noted, the DQ-alpha genotype present in this case when combined with the blood type and enzyme characteristics, resulted in a combination found in less than one percent of the population. In the other three cases, where DNA printing could be used, the probability of the source being anyone other than Spencer was infinitesimally small.

THE SIGNATURE ASPECTS OF THE FOUR MURDERS AS ARGUED BY THE PROSECUTOR

In a hearing for the admission of evidence, Warren Von Schuch, Chief Deputy Commonwealth's Attorney, aptly described the signature components of the four murders to the court. He portrayed the signature of a killer as what the killer does at the scenes which is unique and unusual.

He addressed the court: 'In each one of these crimes, the defendant did something that was totally, absolutely unnecessary to the commission of the offense. It was purposely and methodically done, and it was done after the commission of the offense. The court will look at the photograph of Debbie Davis. You have heard the testimony that she was raped. Yet, when she was found after the rape had occurred and after she was strangled, her shorts were placed back on her, and her buttocks and genital area were covered. Part of her body was covered, after the offense.

'If the court will look at the case of Susan Tucker, you will find that after the sexual assault, after the homicide, a sleeping bag was deliberately placed over her buttocks covering the genital area, concealing part of the body. In the case of Diane Cho, after the sexual assault, after the strangulation, a sheet was placed over her body covering her buttocks area and the genital area.

'One victim, Dr. Susan Hellams, suffered significant

injuries. One victim, Dr. Susan Hellams, suffered substantial bruising on her back, on her leg, with pattern injuries. She suffered anal tears. She was, I submit to the court, based on the physical evidence, particularly the evidence about the type of strangulation, the petechia, showing that the strangulation was of a longer duration, a more tortuous, perhaps and on-off turning. It took longer for her to die, after being beaten the worst. After that, Dr. Hellams was concealed, totally, in a closet, totally unnecessary, totally willful, and subsequent to the commission of the crime.

'I cannot tell the court whether it was denial or shame, or whether it's streetwise trying to make the scene look as normal as possible. I don't know. But in each one of these cases, there was a deliberate effort to conceal the body, or part of the body, that was totally unnecessary; it was totally willful; and it was subsequent to the commission of the crime. That, I submit, is a signature in all four of these crimes that tells you something in the subconscious in each one of these cases.'

SPENCER'S SIGNATURE

Without much question, Timothy Spencer's murder scenes were classical signatures of the anger-retaliatory type of rape-murderer who kills in response to a perceived injury or threat to his self-image from a target victim. Even though we don't know the identity of Spencer's target, it seems clear that he felt thwarted by women who criticized and/or rejected him. Often, the target women in a retaliatory killer's background may have been a mother, wife, supervisor, or any woman who can situationally ignore or reject the potential killer. Given the foil backdrop for the motivational intent of the anger-retaliatory type of killer, it is common for the targeted victims to be in the same age range or older than the murderer. And also given the fact that the killer may be pathologically related to the intended target, it is quite common for this type of offender to search out substitute victims to act out his sexual aggressions.

It is so rare for a signature killer to attack the real woman who is aggravating him that the assault itself is usually classified as a domestic crime, crime of passion, or family crime, and many times it's solved within minutes after the event by the killer's on-the-spot confession. The signature killer who specifically cannot kill the target of his rage because of the power and dominance she holds over him must seek surrogate targets he has stalked or trapped or who cross his path completely by chance but who best meet the offending characteristics of the original target. By looking at the victim profile and knowing who the significant women were in a retaliatory-signature killer's background, you can sometimes figure out who the real target was. For instance, the victims in Spencer's murders were all overweight and within his age group, except the fifteen-year-old, Cho, who 'appeared' older than her actual age to anyone who did not know her.

Spencer's first three victims were all associated in some way with the Cloverleaf Mall. In the case of Dr. Susan Hellams, she negotiated checks on September 22, 1987, at the bookstore where Debbie Davis worked. The doctor was murdered on October 2, 1987. Hence, Timothy Spencer knew the area well. After he had identified Dr. Hellams as his victim, he took his time to track her routines and had several weeks to plan and select a strategy for entrance to her house and commit the rape-murder. This is typical of retaliatory-signature killers who position themselves within a readily available victim pool of surrogate targets. Whenever the killer feels compelled to assuage his growing anger, it is common for him to troll the streets for potential victims. In many instances, the preselection of future victims allows the killer to become familiar with their characteristics, habits, and routines. Although the victims may have only a casual knowledge of him at most, he knows much more about them because he has stalked them. This was clearly Timothy Spencer's pattern.

Whatever Spencer might have thought of himself, it was clear that he knew his skills as a breaking-and-entering artist could get him into any house. Spencer was *the* prototypical cat burglar who personified stealth. He was able to case a residence, identify its most vulnerable places, and use his breaking and entering techniques to gain entrance and take effective control of the crime scene. His skill was so considerable, Spencer could and did slip through a rear sliding window and assault his victim even in the presence of other members of the household without anyone's ever becoming aware of his presence. In fact, in the Diane Cho case, the killer was so effective at gaining immediate control over the girl that her family was unaware of the diabolical assault and murder committed even though they were in adjoining rooms. And because Diane did not display any defense-type wounds, it meant Spencer took her completely by surprise. Similarly, Spencer's ability to enter Debbie Davis's residence through an eight-foot-high kitchen window without disturbing items in his path demonstrated that he was a cat burglar extraordinaire who showed a preference for indoor crime scenes, where he believed he was comfortable and safe after he took control of the victim.

Timothy Spencer belonged to a killer type that often carries a knife for a threat and for symbolic reasons. Inasmuch as it was his intent to cause pain and suffering in retaliation against the perceived wrongs committed against himself, each of Spencer's victims was subjected to his fist and his penis, both used as percussive weapons of violence. Once the victim had been sexually assaulted and punished, Spencer ratcheted the torture to the bondage phase, where he methodically wound ligatures around the victim, twisting her limbs into contorted positions before he finally twisted the ligatures around her throat and strangled her.

In each of his murders, the use of ligatures and ropes exceeded the necessary violence to control the victims for rape-murder. The signature of pathological bondage became evident in the tying of hands with linkage to each victim's throat. In addition to the hand ligatures controlling the amount of pressure put on the throat, the vacuum cleaner pipe in the Davis case was a tool of refinement by which he could play and provide varying amounts of leverage on her neck. Therefore, while having sexual intercourse with his victims, he could regulate his tools of compression by twisting or pulling on the cords attached to their necks. Undoubtedly, the effect of this behavior probably caused the victims to gasp, pant, and rebel ineffectively against his assault. This reaction to the killer's taunts was sexually exciting for him, and because he was an ejaculator, Spencer became easy to identify once he left fluids for the crime labs to process for DNA and blood type. The consistent finding throughout all four murder scenes of the evidence of ejaculation demonstrated a truly rare signature in a series of murder cases.

Spencer followed the prototypical arc that we find in almost every signature crime beginning with the initial victim contact, moving to the overcoming of the victim's defenses, the assault, the killing phase, postmortem activities, and, finally, the positioning of the body. Spencer carefully positioned his victims as his final act at the crime scene, placing each body into a submissive posture, covering the sexualized body parts from immediate view, and closing their particular role in his search for payback and revenge. In each murder, once the killer was finished and his satisfaction complete, he exited the crime scene – just like any retaliatory killer – with a feeling of triumph and devoid of any guilt. Ultimately, from his point of view, they got what they deserved. His anger was sated for the time being, until he saw another potential victim that roused whatever it was that he was fighting. He went on the attack again, possibly hoping to quiet his demons, but never succeeding.

From the signature he left at the scene and the pattern from crime to crime, it was clear how Spencer had evolved in his use of bondage. Although he beat his victims, bondage was most important because it became a method of control and restraint, torture, and then strangulation. Bondage so became the direct relationship between Spencer and his victim that it was literally the threshold between life and death. Ultimately, for his triumphal act of murder Timothy Spencer chose ligature strangulation, because the omnipotence of applying percussive control over the victim made him feel powerful and sated his emotional needs. Likewise, within the same pathological continuum, he employed duct tape, evidence of which was left at the crime scenes, for practical and lustful needs. Although the violence levels with each victim changed situationally, the constant pathological index revealed consistent levels of sophistication within the bondage continuum. The infinity sign left on Diane Cho meant 'forever.' Here, with the sign of a young virgin, he marked the taking, keeping, and sealing of the victim.

Although the bondage continuum provided the primary and killing satisfactions for Spencer, these were also supported by behaviors of the domination-submission continuum. While acting out the trumped-up anger and grievances against each victim, Spencer energized himself by usurping power from the victim through repeated blows to the face and body. His victims all displayed a generalized beating, and one victim – obviously stomped – displayed impressions of shoe prints. Inasmuch as the domination of the offender caused submission by each of the victims, he could feel, smell, and touch the transition of power from each victim to himself. Akin to his need for control and punishment, he systematically degraded, humiliated, and incapacitated the victims. Again, while acting out his anger against the substitute victims, he used degradation and sexual assault for expressing contempt and hostility toward them.

Following each murder, Spencer laid three of the four victims crosswise on their beds, facedown in a defeated position. One exception, Dr. Hellams, was positioned in the bottom of a closet in a hidden and submissive position. Here, despite the satisfaction from the assault and killing practices, he refused to leave the crime scene until all signs or symbols of submission were in place. Of interest, it was noted that the killer redressed Debbie Davis in a pair of shorts, placed a sheet over the buttocks of Diane Cho, and left a blanket over the buttocks of Susan Tucker. As for Dr. Hellams in the closet, the doors provided nonvisual contact of the area. Although it may be easy to assume that the slayer had a moment of decency and covered his victims, this type of activity is inconsistent with the degradation process. Instead, it is much more likely that he covered them the way a lid on a trash can covers the refuse of the past. That is, sexually sadistic killers have left their victims as trash, similar to the conditions found at the body recovery sites of Richard Cottingham. But in Spencer's cases, he simply used the covering for an exit symbol from the scene. It was far from the motives of decency; he expressed symbolic and visual contempt for them in life and death. Like a used condom in the bedroom trash, the killer could exit the crime scene with satisfaction and a feeling of triumph.

The least apparent pathological signature expressed repeatedly at the Spencer's crime scenes was picquerism. Although police believe that Spencer carried a knife to each crime scene, it appears that his primary act of a penetrating weapon was with his penis. That is, although the penis was used for primary sexual satisfaction, the vaginal and anal tears indicate that he used his penis as a tool for penetrating pain and disfigurement. While he used his penis as a substitute wound-inflicting and penetrating object, the violence did provide blood and visual indicators of the assault. Given the repeat behaviors in each case, it appeared that he was on the beginning cusp of picquerism and would have progressed to stabbing and cutting if he had not been apprehended.

Timothy Spencer was rather enigmatic. Unlike George Russell in Seattle, whose life, as we'll see, was a well-documented narrative, or Jeffrey Dahmer, who tried to explain away in his confession most of his own crimes, Timothy Spencer was simply an angry killer who upon his release from prison simply 'went nova' and committed a brutal series of sexual murders. His case is closed. In 1994, after all his appeals had been denied, Timothy Wilson Spencer was executed by the Commonwealth of Virginia.

CHAPTER 5

The Picquerism Signature

Cleophus Prince

In the years after stories about the Green River killer – who operated in the rural King County area from 1982 to 1985 – splashed across the headlines, the task force office in Seattle continued to be deluged with inquiries about serial murders up and down the West Coast. Most of these inquiries came from the press, reporters pursuing stories about local killers who were related to the Green River murders only because they were serial crimes. Had the infamous Green River killer headed south to California? Was he up north in British Columbia? Inquiring minds at the tabloid newspapers wanted to know, so reporters dutifully followed up murder cases in jurisdictions from Boston to San Diego.

In many of these inquiries, about the only relevance between the cases was that a suspect was killing women. That was it! How was he killing them? Who were the women he was killing? It didn't matter. A guy who kills women is a guy who kills women, right? Some are strangled, some are stabbed, some are beaten to death. Don't serial killers change their MO and kill opportunistically? As far as many people are concerned, the most important aspect of the serial killer is the word *serial*. But to myself and the remaining members of the Green River Task Force, by the time the case was eight years old and Ted Bundy had been executed, the real issues of one serial murder case compared to another were those of signature: the core components of each and every crime scene. These were the psychological fingerprints that not only related the cases but showed us the direction the killer was heading along his continuum of violence.

After having successfully applied a rape-sexual offender model to the case study of signature murder, I could see that the general overlay fit. Signature killers were sexual offenders at the far end of the violence continuum who left their psychological imprints at crime scenes to gratify their sexual needs. But I could also see how you could use the rape model to categorize the *types* of signatures and, many times, what specific sets of actions the killer was using to satisfy himself. Much more than academic theorizing, this type of information helped me to distinguish between different types of signature killers on the loose, even in the same area, and to separate the signatures at the crime scene. Even more important, understanding what turned a killer on and what his expectations might have been at each crime in a series helped us include crimes in an investigation that were related even if the killer was deliberately trying to throw us off or had changed his MO because a situation presented him with new challenges or opportunities. So, in applying this level of specificity of signature to a particular series of crimes, I could see if the evidence at a crime scene told me whether a killer in Boston who crossed racial lines in his attacks on vulnerable young women was turned on by the same things that turned on the Green River killer. If you have a strong enough similarity, I thought, it might be worth allocating some of your limited task force resources and budget to chase down the lead. If they were different, you focused on something else unless another piece of evidence relating the crimes turned up. Operating this way, you had something to say when the question arose at a news conference about the one crime series starting up just as another had seemed to close down.

CONTROL: THE PRIMARY SIGNATURE COMPONENT

When you look at signature murder through the eyes of a serial sex crimes offender, you look at the single-most important issue in the offender's life: control. Signature killers, the largest subcategory of serial killers, are driven by a basic psychological motivation that compels them to act out the same crime over and over again in such a way that their patterns become obsessive. All signature murderers seek some form of sexual gratification and their crimes are expressions of the ways they satisfy that need. For example, inasmuch as most of the killers exert little or no control over their own existence or perceive themselves deep down inside as being life's losers and the victims of society, they gratify their sexual urges by demonstrating control over their murder victims. Control supplies the gratification, and events leading up to the ultimate moment of control supply the excitement of anticipation.

Almost all serial sex offenders, especially signature killers, need to demonstrate a degree of total control over the victim, whether she's living or dead. They have to; anger drives them to do it. When I see evidence that the control the killer has deliberately established over the victim was more important to him than the actual murder itself, that's one clear indicator to me that this guy's a signature killer whose goal is the power of conquest. He achieves his conquest by applying specific physical mechanisms of control. This is usually a specific series of actions signature killers use to assume and exert control, and then a set of potent ritualisms that reinforce their thrill of control long after the crime has been committed.

Control-type signature killers can revisit the thrill of control simply by driving by a murder site or body dump site undetected, hearing about their crime on the evening news, or watching how the police pursue the investigation. Sometimes they keep small souvenirs from the crime, if not from the victim, that recall the high of having achieved control. It is control which creates the thrill of a sexual orgasm and not the actual human contact with the victim. This is often misunderstood by most investigators and profilers who evaluate the nature of the killer's human contact with the victim as the essential aspect of the crime.

PRIMARY AND SECONDARY SEXUAL MECHANISMS AS A FUNCTION OF CONTROL

Once I applied the serial rape/sexual offender model to signature murder, I could also see clearly that there were two basic types of sexual mechanisms which offenders use as functions of control. There are primary sexual mechanisms, a specified set of actions, behaviors, and methods used in physical and mental – conscious or unconscious – tension or releases to produce an intended ejaculation and/or sexual climax such as sexual intercourse and oral copulation. In other words, whatever the killer does at a crime scene is for the purpose of reaching an orgasm right then and there. How do you know if the killer's purpose is to reach a climax at the crime scene? There's usually ejaculant all over the place, in or on the victim, and on whatever surfaces are adjacent to the body.

The secondary sexual mechanisms are an indirect, defused, and sometimes thwarted set of actions that substitute for primary sexual mechanisms. They produce aberrant delayed sexual releases through physical torture, bondage, or humiliation. These are some of the major things which turn on sexually delayed gratification, and we see them at crime scenes through such evidence of binding and the display of a body in a humiliating position. Here, rather than just a means to reach an orgasm, sexual dominance is used to achieve and prolong a sense of power. The signature killer won't achieve an orgasm on or in the victim; he waits until he's in a safe place, takes his souvenirs from the victim with him, and masturbates until his sexual energy is drained. His conditioned delayed response allows him control over his own orgasm as well as over the victim and allows him to sustain himself sexually for long periods of time between crimes.

How do we know we have secondary sexual mechanisms at work? They are there when we come upon the crime scene, where we see evidence of torture, bondage, and a body left deliberately in a conspicuously humiliating and subservient position. The victim may be spread-eagled or posed as if she'd been frozen in the midst of a sexual act, but there will be no ejaculant anywhere, and we assume that the killer took the entire package of energy with him and satisfied himself through secondary mechanisms. Needless to say, both mechanisms are pathologically deviant and very, very deadly.

You can see, therefore, that there can be very specific aspects of a killer's signature that are as unique as an individual fingerprint. Killers may be very similar, but a killer who deliberately grabs victims to reach a sexual orgasm through direct control both before and after the victim's death is one kind of killer. The killer who postpones and drives his energy upward with different behaviors which don't seem overtly sexual at first is another. But just when you think you've nailed a killer type down cold, you realize that the whole signature murder pattern is about progression and escalation. Killers aren't static, they're completely dynamic as they grow into their criminal careers.

The most uncontrolled and violent ejaculating killer in crime one can progress to a controlled, almost restrained, methodical murderer by crime five, and the police will have dramatic physical evidence at each and every crime scene. What's most bizarre about these crime scenes is that you can see the history of the signature laid out before you almost by reading the bits of the evidence. Measure the decreasing amount of ejaculant trace, analyze the different types of trauma the victim suffered, examine the rope burn or binding marks on her wrists or ankles to see how she struggled, or take note of how much of the crime scene was torn up by a victim's struggles. It's all there. Whether the killer is a retaliatory type or one looking for excitation, you can see the progression of the killer's state of mind through the sexual mechanisms he brings to the crime. And from an evaluation of all these mechanisms and dynamic progression of the killer, you can tell almost with certainty whether a killer has migrated from one jurisdiction to another or whether it's an entirely different killer. So when reporters tell you, as they did us six years ago, that the Green River killer had moved to San Diego, where he changed his MO and was killing women in their apartments, we knew from what the crime-scene signature evidence told us that they were probably wrong. But the San Diego murders were nonetheless brutal and sadistic. I remember them well.

THE CASE OF THE CLAIREMONT KILLER

In 1990, about thirty-five years after Harvey Glatman left the dry, bleached bones of his victims as his signature across the San Diego desert, another serial killer set to work in the county and struck terror into the community for almost a whole year. Cleophus Prince, or the 'Clairemont killer,' as he was dubbed by the local San Diego media, stabbed six women to death. These murders instigated what was described as the largest police manhunt in San Diego's history. No other murder spree gripped the city so severely, captivating the media and the neighborhoods where the murders took place. All of southern California was held in thrall to the phantom killer who could slip through walls and elude police dragnets only to strike again weeks later.

The homicides fit an eerie pattern, a trademark at first known only to the killer. Unlike the bondage and strangulation murders of Richard Cottingham and the bludgeoning and posing of murder victims by Morris Frampton before him, this killer's signature was different. The Clairemont killer enjoyed an often unrecognized form of sexual satisfaction called 'picquerism,' which is sexual pleasure gained by stabbing, cutting, or slicing of another person. The killer with this particular form of sexual deviation uses secondary mechanisms for satiating his sexualized power needs by penetrating and rendering flesh. That is, the specific focus and intent of picquerism is to instrument power and deviant sexual satisfactions by the process of penetration, be it by cutting, stabbing, slicing, or biting, or with sniper activity, or by cutting animals and/or fleshlike materials. The killer finds the bloodletting, odors, and victim screams harmonic and simply supplementary aspects of the primary purpose. As you might expect, the results of this type of crime are particularly gruesome.

The frightening part about the Clairemont killer for San Diego citizens was that the murders were committed exclusively indoors. This threat alone caused many women to fear for their lives while they should have been in their most secure place – their own homes. The killer seemed to be able to strike through locked doors and closed windows. No one was safe. Women were afraid to go to bed at night for fear of hearing the noise of the killer slipping through the door. They were afraid to shower because the sound of running water might mask the entry of a killer whose intent was to slice, carve, dig, and gouge, and let the blood drain from his victim. Truly, San Diego became a community gripped in terror, the flames of which were fanned nightly by the relentless evening news. The horror story began on January 12, 1990, when pretty Tiffany Schultz was found murdered in the bedroom of her Clairemont apartment.

THE MURDER OF TIFFANY PAIGE SCHULTZ

In typical fashion, the investigation into the series of murders attributed to the Clairemont killer began with a routine call to patrol officers to investigate a 911 report of a woman down. The caller had found his girlfriend in the bedroom, covered with blood. Officers arrived at 3107 Cowley Way at the Canyon Ridge Condominiums in the Clairemont area of San Diego at 9:01 P.M., having received the boyfriend's report. Their car was flagged down as it approached the apartments and directed to unit 202. A passerby told the officers that there were two 'guys' upstairs and a 'dead girl' in the bedroom. The police headed upstairs, ready for anything.

After walking up a short flight of fourteen stairs, the officers stopped at the threshold of the front door of the second-story apartment, observed that the front door was wide open, and overheard a male screaming and crying. In plain view, they could see the victim, a white female in her early twenties, lying on the tan carpet of the northwest bedroom in a supine position with her legs spread apart and her arms out on each side and bent at the elbow as though the killer had posed her in that fashion. The only clothing she was wearing was a black bikini bathing-suit bottom. From a cursory examination of the body, the officers saw right away that the victim had been stabbed multiple times in the upper-right quadrant of her chest. The wounds were obvious and encompassed an area three to four inches in diameter.

Bloodstains were scattered about the victim's body, floor, and walls. By her right hand was a rollerblade boot, and a tennis racket was near her left elbow, items, they eventually learned, that were common to the apartment.

Inside the victim's residence, investigators meticulously gathered over one hundred pieces of physical evidence. Unfortunately, none of the evidence would immediately lead police to the killer. Investigators also conducted an exterior search of the surrounding area. On the north side of the building, below a balcony, two shoe impressions were found on the ground about five feet from the building, possibly belonging to the killer. That would be all the police would have to go on for the immediate present as they pursued leads into the victim's background and the people she might have come in contact with.

Their investigation revealed that Tiffany Schultz was a twenty-year-old white female, five feet eight inches tall and 126 pounds, with light brown hair. She was an English major at San Diego State and moonlighted for extra bucks as a nude dancer at Le Girls. A maintenance worker at the apartment complex where Tiffany lived reported having seen her sunbathing on her porch at about noon on the day her body was discovered. They had a brief conversation. Schultz told the worker that she and her boyfriend had been fighting the night before until 11:30 P.M., because he was unhappy with her working at the club. The worker was the last person to see Schultz alive.

At autopsy, investigators from Homicide Team Four were informed by Dr. Christopher Swalwell, Deputy Medical Examiner of San Diego County, that the victim had been stabbed over fifty times. It was a gruesome attack by one of the most vicious predators the ME had ever seen. The postmortem examination revealed three localized areas of brutalization. Six severe stab wounds were concentrated on her right anterior neck with one fatal wound that completely transacted the superior right jugular vein just below the level of her jaw and caused extensive bleeding. The maximum depth of those wounds was two inches deep, well into the unprotected tissue.

On her right breast area, over twenty stab wounds were located in a small 5½ by 3¾-inch horizontal grouping. Those wounds were fourteen and three-quarters inches from the top of her head and one to four inches right of her anterior midline. At least nine of those wounds perforated her lung, any one of which could have been fatal. One stab wound actually exited the right back of the victim, which was a ghoulish indicator of just how powerful and well aimed the killer's blows were. The depth of that stab was calculated at six and three-quarters inches. The other stab wounds which penetrated the back were estimated at six to six and a half inches in maximum depth.

On the victim's upper left chest area, there was a 4½ by 2¾-inch grouping of ten stab wounds. Nine of those penetrations were through her left lung. The maximum depth of those stab wounds was a minimum of six inches. Ten other stab wounds on the front of her body were from 3 to 6½ inches in depth.

Beyond the stab wound evidence, blood analyses revealed that Schultz did not have any drugs or alcohol in her system. Shortly after the initial investigation, detectives arrested Schultz's boyfriend for her murder and then released him after a few days, convinced he did not kill her. That left the homicidal predator still on the loose.

Janene Marie Weinhold

Only a few blocks from the murder scene of Tiffany Schultz and just over a month after her death, a second vicious stabbing attack on a pretty coed stunned the local residents. Janene Marie Weinhold, a twenty-one-year-old white female and a political science major at the

University of California at San Diego in nearby La Jolla, was supposed to pick up her roommate, Shirley Erickson, from work on February 16, 1990. Weinhold didn't show up, so Erickson went to her sister's dormitory room and both returned to the apartment that Weinhold and Erickson shared together in the Buena Vista complex.

The complex formed a city block of apartments bordered by Dakota Drive on the north, Knapp Street on the south, Waco Street on the east, and Clairemont Drive on the west. The front door of apartment number four, Weinhold's second-story residence, faced predominately north even though it was located on the east side of Clairemont Drive.

Erickson and her sister arrived at the apartment at about 8:20 P.M. Since Erickson did not have her keys they summoned a maintenance man to unlock the front door and let them inside. Immediately upon entering, Erickson saw several items on the floor and felt something was wrong. She walked through the apartment calling Weinhold's name. When Shirley passed by her own room, she noticed her door slightly ajar and Weinhold's leg in view on the floor. Shirley screamed upon seeing the violent scene of her roommate's murder. The maintenance man came to her assistance. Shirley then called 911 from the apartment.

When police investigators arrived at 3301 Clairemont Drive number four, they saw red matter that appeared to be blood outside of the front door and on the door-jamb. They also noted a basket of wet laundry left by the front door, draped over a chair and on the sofa. As police processed the kitchen area of the crime scene, it appeared to them as if the killer had interrupted Weinhold as she was making cookies. There were fresh-baked cookies on a plate and also laid out on the counter. Cookie dough was in a bowl and burned cookies were found in a small toaster oven on top of their microwave oven. Police discovered the murder weapon lying widthwise in the kitchen sink, a bloody knife with a nine-inch blade and five-inch wooden handle. It appeared out of place, as though it was intentionally set there for the police to find.

Inside Erickson's bedroom, Janene Weinhold was lying on her back, posed with her arms splayed out from her shoulders and her legs spread slightly apart. She was clad only in a black brassiere. Her head was slightly under the bed. Just above her head and on the bedcover were bloodstains of medium-velocity spatter, caused by the repeated stabbing motion of the knife entering and being pulled out of the victim's body while she lay there. The blood then whipped off the knife and onto the bedspread, leaving a definite spatter pattern.

Officers observed that the victim was stabbed in the chest numerous times with the blade penetrating right through her bra on more than a few blows. Under her left arm was a pair of light green pants with black panties twisted within the legs. It appeared as if the killer pulled both off at the same time, much like clothing evidence found in forcible rape cases. There was an electrical cord near Weinhold's head, but it had not been used. Robbery definitely wasn't the motive, since Weinhold's purse, containing money, was found in a front room. Again, the local police investigative team was meticulous in its search for clues, with technicians and criminalists carefully lifting any fibers or prints they could find, especially some strands of human hair from Weinhold's left hand. In all, over sixty-four pieces of physical evidence were collected from the crime scene. Once again, as in the Schultz murder, police did not discover any evidence at the scene that would lead directly to the identity of Weinhold's attacker.

Weinhold's autopsy was performed the next day by Dr. John Eisele of the San Diego Coroner's Office. Several regions of Weinhold's body sustained multiple groupings of stab wounds. In the cold, dispassionate language of forensic medicine, the autopsy report read that over the upper-inner quadrant of the right breast centered fifty inches above her the heel and two inches to the right of midline – the middle line running lengthwise down the center of her body – 'there is an area with at least eight separate and overlapping stab wounds. The area measures 3 × 2 inches from top to bottom.' Extending over the left breast, centered about fifty inches from her heel and two and a half inches to the left of midline, 'there is a group of eight stab wounds. These are in an area that measure 3½ to 2½ inches.' Over the left pectoral region centered fifty-three inches above the heel and five inches to the left of midline, there was a group of three stab wounds. The medical examiner had described an intense, close-knit group of deep stab thrusts running up and down both the right and left sides of Weinhold's body. Several obvious defense stab wounds were found on Weinhold's hands and arms. Smears and swabs from the vagina, anus, and mouth were retained for cytological and chemical examination. The results of that analysis found 'large numbers of tailless and occasional intact spermatozoa present' in the vagina and 'rare tailless spermatozoa' were found on the anal smear. In other words, whoever this aggressive, seemingly mobile rapist-murderer was, he was almost impotent because his sperm lacked flagellating tails and were thus incapable of propelling themselves anywhere. They died in place. But they were so rare, the police hoped that if a suspect were ever identified, this evidence could be linked directly to him.

The summary of anatomic diagnoses was strikingly similar to the Schultz homicide. 'Multiple stab wounds of the chest' were the cause of death. The maximum depth of the wounds was seven inches, and the minimum width of deep wounds was three-quarters inches. If this were the same killer, the police knew they had a monster on their hands who was able to move in and out of the apartment complexes with relative ease.

Holly Suzanne Tarr

Several days into a southwestern California April, the killer of Tiffany Schultz and Janene Weinhold struck again. On Tuesday, April 3, 1990, the sound of police sirens and the sight of red and blue flashing lights once again stirred up the neighborhood of 3410 Cowley Way. This location was only a stone's throw away from 3107 Cowley Way, where Tiffany Schultz's murder had taken place just three months earlier.

Police had been summoned to apartment 3, 3410 Cowley, after receiving a radio call of an assault with a deadly weapon. One officer confronted the maintenance man in the front room of apartment 3 who directed the officer to the bedroom, where the officer found a neighbor lady kneeling over a body and holding a white towel to the victim's chest. The officer pulled the towel off her chest and saw a one-inch cut above the victim's left breast. The victim was clad only in a pink bra and white panties.

Witnesses were contacted and officers learned that the handyman for the apartments had been called after a woman was heard screaming in apartment 3. The handyman went to the door and found it locked. He used his master key to unlock the front door but found that the chain lock was in place when he opened the door. He forced the door open, popping the chain, and was confronted by a hooded knife-wielding man whom the maintenance worker described as a black or Hispanic male with what appeared to be a white bag over his head. The bag was later identified as a white T-shirt. The unidentified assailant bolted past the handyman and ran toward Dakota Avenue.

Prior to processing Holly Tarr's apartment for evidence, detectives were directed to the north end of the complex. There, the bright, sunny spring day served only to dramatize the contrast between the white T-shirt with vivid red stains lying on the freshly manicured green grass between a sidewalk and the apartment building. Not far from the T-shirt, another citizen discovered a knife covered with blood on the grass about ten feet from the sidewalk. It, too, was a grotesque sight because its blade revealed the telltale pattern of blood one finds when it has been withdrawn from the deep tissue of a murder victim's body. The knife was similar in type and size to the one found in the kitchen sink at Janene Weinhold's crime scene. Both the knife and the T-shirt were located along the route the killer used to flee the murder scene. The knife was subsequently identified as belonging to Richard Tarr, the victim's brother, who lived in apartment 3.

The dumping and leaving of evidence by killers along their escape routes is a common enough occurrence that investigating officers would be remiss were they not to have searched those possible routes. The location of the T-shirt and knife in this case and the two shoe impressions found outside Tiffany Schultz's apartment reaffirmed that searching along the murderer's possible routes of arrival and escape can be beneficial to the investigation.

The crime scene was on the second story of a two-story complex that houses four apartment units at the Buena Vista Garden Apartments. The police diagram depicts very few bloodstains other than those on the victim. A serologist from the San Diego Police Department located small stains on the door leading to the bedroom and on the steps leading up to the apartment. Otherwise, the apartment was blood-free.

Holly Suzanne Tarr, an eighteen-year-old white female, five feet three inches tall and weighing 128 pounds, was in town visiting her brother. Upon investigation, police detectives concluded that Holly was stalked from a nearby swimming pool to the apartment. On the hallway floor leading to the bathroom, a yellow and black two-piece bathing suit she had been wearing was found lying near a white terry-cloth-type robe, black shorts, and a white T-shirt. It appeared as though the killer interrupted Holly while she was changing her clothes.

The postmortem examination results on Holly Tarr were not as lengthy as the first two victims and corroborated what police detectives and witnesses observed at the scene. Tarr sustained a single stab wound to the left chest, perforating her heart. The depth of that one stab wound reached seven inches. Tarr could not have fought her assailant much, because she did not have the recognizable marks of defense-type wounds. Her vaginal, oral, and anal smears were negative for spermatozoa, unlike the autopsy findings in the Janene Weinhold murder. One reason for the dissimilarity could be that the killer was interrupted. But as we will see in the signature analyses of these cases, the actual evidence of rape is not a necessary ingredient for the killer's satisfactions.

Elissa Naomi Keller

The residents of the Clairemont area were not relieved when the news reported that the killer, obviously now on a serial spree, had struck in a different neighborhood of San Diego on May 21, 1990. The first officers arrived at 5225 Trojan Avenue, apartment 21 at 11:47 P.M. They were summoned to that location regarding a possible death. What they found was the fourth victim of the Clairemont Killer.

While en route, a police communications operator advised the responding officers that the victim's daughter came home to find her mother covered with blood on the bedroom floor. Upon arrival, officers discovered the front door wide open and an eighteen-year-old female sitting on the living-room couch sobbing and still holding the telephone from which she had made the 911 call. Two officers stayed with thc young woman, whom they learned was the victim's daughter, while two went to the southeast bedroom where they saw Elissa Keller, a thirty-eight-year-old white female, lying on her back, head to the north and feet to the south, parallel to a bed. A checkered blanket covered her body. The responding officer focused his flashlight beam directly into the victim's eyes, and seeing no pupilary reflex and not picking up a pulse or breathing, noted that she was probably dead. Later, as the officer removed the blanket, he could see clearly two severe stab wounds on the victim's chest. This confirmed that officers knew they were faced with 187 PC of the California Penal Code: homicide.

Keller's daughter told officers that at about 11:30 P.M., she decided to return home. When she unlocked the front door with her key, she noticed the dead bolt was also unlocked, uncommon for this late at night. She walked inside and smelled a funny odor that didn't smell like her home. Walking through the apartment to her bedroom, she saw, in the dim light shining through her window, some of her belongings scattered all over her bed. Then she turned on her lights and noticed blood spots all over the top of her bed. She looked down and saw her mother's feet and a blood-soaked bedsheet covering her mother's face. She then ran out of the bedroom and called police.

Investigation revealed that most of the stabbing to the victim occurred on top of her daughter's bed. The light pink bedspread was covered with patches of deep bloodstains on those portions nearest the door. An electric hair curler, comb, and other articles were also on the bed. It was unknown if any were used in the murder.

Elissa Keller was lying directly below the bed, clad only in a white tank-top shirt soaked with blood, giving the impression that the shirt was red. Her legs were slightly spread. It was evident that the killer moved and manipulated her body, because her legs, arms, face, and chest were covered in blood. Precariously lying on the victim's right abdominal area were two earring-type hooks. Did the killer leave these because he forgot to take them as mementos? Detectives thought probably so.

Detectives followed the path of the killer after the murder. They discovered several bloodstains in the bathroom which clearly outlined the trail the killer left as he fled the scene. There was a stain on the floor, another on a tissue container located on the counter, another inside the sink, and a final one located on a hair discovered on the floor. Outside the apartment, a bloodstain was recovered from a stairway railing leading away from the victim's residence. Although these were not large stains, they indicated the flight of the killer as he left the murder scene dripping with blood.

The autopsy findings of a discrete grouping of stab wounds in Elissa Keller's homicide case were similar to the findings of the Schultz and Weinhold murders. Within a five-by-two-inch area of the mid to left upper chest and slightly above her left nipple, there was a grouping of nine stab wounds. One stab wound perforated through the descending aorta and ended near the spine. The stab wounds penetrated deeply, with the deepest measuring six and a half inches. Unlike Holly Tarr, Keller was able to put up a fight. She had contusions on her arms as well as multiple superficial cut wounds to her forearms and hands. Now, police investigators had the usual cadre of boyfriends of Keller to pursue as possible suspects in her murder. But like all the others, those known to the victims turned out to be eliminated from suspicion.

Pamela and Amber Clark

With the discovery of two bodies on September 13, 1990, the city of San Diego's mood became more fearful and apprehensive. By then, homicide experts declared that serial murders were in progress and more murders were inevitable unless the killer was stopped. One couldn't miss the headlines in San Diego newspapers: 'Eerie Serial Killings Have San Diego Women on Edge.'

September 13th was a typical late-summer San Diego day, sunny, clear and eighty-five degrees. A warm ocean breeze was blowing across the bay from the navy yard. Joseph Lazzaro, Pamela Clark's husband, left for work at 8:15 A.M. By 11:00 that morning, Pamela had not yet shown up for work at Joe's doctor's office, where Joe was supposed to meet her. Joe became concerned and called Vickie Kempf, a family friend. He asked her to drive over to his house to make sure everything was okay. When Kempf arrived at 5890 Honors Drive, she found the front door unlocked and slightly ajar. Kempf pushed the door open and immediately observed Pamela Clark lying on the entryway floor. She gently touched one of Pamela's feet. It was cold and confirmed in Kempf's mind that Pamela was probably already dead. Kempf went to the kitchen, grabbed the cordless phone, and called 911.

At the time, Detective R. Thill was busy investigating other murders in San Diego when he received a call at 1:30 P.M. to proceed to the scene because the modus operandi at the Clark residence was strikingly similar to the other Clairemont murders. The single-story, four-bedroom, and two-bath house sat at the southwest corner of Honors Drive and Fried Avenue in the community of Universal City. The yard was protected by a wooden fence five feet high on the north and six feet high on the west and south sides. It was a secure, private residence.

Thill meticulously examined the premises and located the killer's apparent exit point, the east window of the dining room. Slightly to the west of the patio was a bent window screen, which had come from the dining room, lying on the ground. The sliding glass window of the dining room was slightly ajar. Underneath and outside the window on the ground was a wooden stick, the length of which verified that it was commonly used to secure the sliding glass window from the inside. At the rear of the house was a sliding glass door facing west. That door and its screen were partially open, but the drapes were pulled shut. Unless one jumped the fence, there was no escape through the backyard. It was entirely enclosed by fencing. The front door to the house had a deadbolt lock and a doorknob lock, neither of which was activated.

Right where the linoleum-covered entry way met the carpeted hallway was where Pamela Clark, a forty-eight-year-old white female, was savagely stabbed. She lay nude on her back, her legs slightly spread, with her knees about three inches apart. Her buttocks and upper torso were on the carpet with her arms spread out at ninety-degree angles to her body. Her hair was wet and it looked as if she had just gotten out of the shower. Concentrated mostly above her left breast were numerous stab wounds. They appeared in much the same fashion as those on the previous victims of the Clairemont killer. Blood spatters from those wounds were located on her neck, chest, abdomen, and legs.

At autopsy, it was discovered that Pamela had suffered eleven stab wounds to the chest and four to the right thigh. On the upper portion of her left breast, the eleven stab wounds were clustered in an area that measured 3½ by 4½ inches transversely. Five stab wounds penetrated her heart and two entered her left lung. Four of her stab wounds were so deep, from seven to ten inches, that they penetrated right through her back. She sustained one defense cut on her left index finger. Just to the south of Pamela's head was a wooden-handled knife with a blade that was ten and a half inches long. This was the third murder scene where the killer had left the murder weapon.

As detectives made their way down the hallway, they recovered bloodstains on the hallway carpet and walls. At the south end of the hallway lay the body of Amber

Clark, Pamela's eighteen-year-old daughter, a student at Mesa College, where her instructor had already noted her absent from her 11 A.M. class. Dressed differently from her mother, Amber was wearing light-colored coverall-type shorts and a white blouse. Her blouse, bra, and the bib portion of her coveralls had been pulled down, exposing her breasts. Again, there were what appeared to be stab wounds in her chest area.

At autopsy, it was found that Amber had eleven stab wounds to her upper left chest, like her mother. Four inches below her left shoulder and above her breast were nine stab wounds clustered together. The entry wounds on the outer surface of her body varied from three-quarters to seven-eighths inches in length. Her heart suffered two penetrating stab wounds and her left lung suffered eight perforating stab wounds. In addition, one penetrating stab wound found the lateral tip of the left lobe of her liver. Six of the penetrating stab wounds to her chest were seven to eight inches in depth. So vicious were two of the stabs that they penetrated through her back. Her left arm was parallel to her body, but her right arm was bent at the elbow with her forearm and hand resting on her right side and breast. She had a superficial laceration on her right thumb, which was described as a defense wound.

There were bloodstains on the bathroom walls, floor, and tub and on a towel on the floor next to the bathtub, as if one of the victims was confronted by the killer in the bathroom area. There was a damp towel in the bathroom sink. Lying on the floor of the bathroom was a broken knife blade. The rest of the knife was found in the northern most top drawer of the cabinets in the dining room. Detectives surmised that the killer rearmed himself. Processing the house for physical evidence took place over a four-day period, but the police found no information leading directly to the Clairemont killer.

SIGNATURE ANALYSIS

In glancing over the case materials provided by the San Diego District Attorney's Office, I found that the killer's modus operandi remained fairly consistent throughout the six murders. The first three victims were killed in the Clairemont area; then he changed areas and moved to the Universal City neighborhood in east San Diego, not a great distance to travel for an accomplished serial killer. This killer demonstrated that he was an experienced daytime burglar, as he attacked most of his victims between ten o'clock in the morning and two o'clock in the afternoon and entered through open or unlocked doors. He showed a preference for a knife as a weapon. He attacked white female victims indoors and, more specifically, in their own homes. Initially, the killer attacked a cluster of victims in close proximity to each other. In fact, those murders took place surreptitiously in second-story apartments; then he changed to a house as he became more and more confident in entering any type of residence.

These victims were not victims of chance, but victims of choice. They were stalked. As Ted Bundy once told me, the victim does not know the killer, but the killer knows the victim. The killer had to know who his victims were, because they had to match his preferred victim type, and most of all, he had to have knowledge, at least for the first four, that they were home alone. To attack women in their own homes in broad daylight assumes a level of intelligence and daring far beyond the normal criminal mind. There is too much risk of being seen, as was the case at the site of the Holly Tarr murder, where the killer was interrupted during his act. But that one interruption did not deter him.

Despite minor changes in the killer's modus operandi, his psychological imprint, or signature, was clearly detectable. First of all, each victim was posed in a sexually degrading position, intentionally left that way so the discovery of the bodies would startle the people who found them. The victims were not concealed or hidden away, but placed in locations where they would be easily discovered. The positioning of each of the victims reflected the cruel reality of the killer, his total mastery over their bodies. All were stretched out prone on their backs, completely nude or in partial underclothing with either a bra, panties, or both left on. They were all positioned in a supine way with the backs of their heads against the floor. The pleasure for the killer was demonstrating each victim's vulnerability. He showed it by leaving them openly displayed, some with legs spread and others with their arms left out perpendicular to their sides or over their heads. He did far more than was necessary simply to commit the murders.

The core of the killer's signature in this series was revealed by a unique form of sexual expression: the manner in which he ritualistically stabbed each of his victims. This killer showed the violence of eroticized power displayed through picquerism and the supporting secondary deviances. Both the killer's past and future could be seen in this dynamic signature. In preparation for the murders, despite the ability to perform 'normal' primary sexual acts with a consenting adult, this picquer emerged from a learning experience in deviancy in which secondary mechanisms came into prominence only to be absorbed and faded. Again, the killer's primary goal is satisfaction through eroticized power expressed as violence, not an ejaculation with fantasized love. In other words, the killer was not there to rape the women he killed. Rather, he became stimulated through the violence he inflicted and any sexual satisfaction occurred after he left the murder scene. Functionally, there is no direct sexual expression for this control-type, concept-driven killer whose obvious primary deviancy is picquerism. However, this is a killer who had evolved from previous forms of deviancy in which he might have had direct sexual expression at a crime scene – that is, he ejaculated. He showed this by his display of residual or previous satisfactions of bondage through his arrangement of cords and submission/domination through the positioning of the victim. In other words, the experienced signature investigator got not only a picture of what the killer was doing as he worked out his arc of violence on the victim, but he received a snapshot of what used to turn him on directly and how that still appeared as a stratum of his signature. None of this was about the victim; it was all about what aroused the killer.

But there was more. I realized the killer was also showing the beginning work for his next stage of violence. In this process of translating sophisticated fantasies into reality, the killer acquired a sense of mastery and control over his victims and himself. The easier it became to stalk and identify his victim, enter the private property in broad daylight, isolate the victim, and spend as much time as necessary with her at the murder scene, the greater the violence he had to perform to satisfy himself afterward. Everything he accomplished, however, was only undone by the extinguishing factor of the learning curve that wasn't providing him enough satisfaction for his efforts. Therefore, by choice, he would 'feel driven' to move further across the violence continuum to a higher stage which could very well have been the harvesting of body parts. But he was caught before he could experiment.

Before the murders, the killer avoided his fears about confronting life's challenges by lapsing into an involved sexual fantasy in which he controlled his sexual partner, as a way to relieve the tensions that haunted him. But with the execution of each murder, the Clairemont killer moved beyond his ideations of violence and turned his fantasies into a reality by committing the violent acts he had only imagined. His violent ideas couldn't serve his demand for dominance and power anymore. He had to retreat into the translation of his fantasies into actual violence to satisfy his need for power. Thereafter, each murder became a forum for a greater performance and drive. Although his second victim had semen in her vagina and anus, this single event indicated that the Clairemont Killer was experimenting with a picqueristic augmentation which did not serve his needs because the penis could not replace the knife for satisfaction. Therefore, he discarded the possibly learned behaviors of the past – penile insertion during violence – for the direct and unfailing potency of the knife blade.

The Clairemont murders were typified by localized areas of brutalization or stabbing, especially to the left breast area of each victim. Inasmuch as the vagina is sexual, the killer may have chosen the breast for the compatibility between secondary sexual characteristics and his own secondary mechanisms, the sensuality of driving a blade through human tissue. In addition, he may have learned that the breast fat shifted when pushed aside by the knife blade and provided him a sensation of deeper penetration. Likely, the bounce and cushion of the breast simply maximized his interest and energy levels. Noting that his interest areas were exclusive to the breast and heart regions, the amount of violence is an indicator of efficiency of performance versus satisfaction of his needs. For when his needs superseded his level of performance, the number of victims increased, his timing increased, or his sexual deviancy increased.

Beginning with his first victim and carrying it through to subsequent victims, the killer specifically focused his stabbing to the chest area. Unlike murders in which the killer stabs in a haphazard fashion, these murders, from the first victim, Tiffany Schultz, through the last victims, the Clarks, were characterized by the symbolic thrashing and sexual exploitation of each victim's left breast area. There was no frenzied nature to the attack, a random infliction of wounds, or a slashing of the victims' throats. The killer's specific set of actions to the left breast area was something he couldn't change because it provided him too much satisfaction. Accordingly, he always left his victims with their left breasts obviously exposed so as to communicate to police a bizarre form of sadistic ridicule. He derided the police and his victim at the same time through the deliberate positioning of her corpse.

In addition to the location of the wounds, another part of this killer's primary signature was the position and depth of the wounds. In many sexually related murders with knives, it is noteworthy that the killer stabs to a depth normally perceived as an erect penis length. Anatomically, the physiologist indicated that the average length of an erect penis is six inches. Of course, biology and fantasy alter the statistical average.

The blades of the knives used by the killer in the murders measured between nine and ten and a half inches in length and made the killer more fearsome and unyielding in the eyes of each victim. This killer was obsessed with the stimulation of penetrating the victims. Unlike Richard Cottingham, the Clairemont killer did not tease with superficial cuts, but stabbed with deep penetration. In a fit of learned and unfettered aggression, the killer sank his chosen blade to extreme depths. The deepest wounds on each of the six victims ranged from six to nine inches, with some so deep that the killer rendered the flesh off their backs by stabbing from the front. The deep stabbing coupled with the clusters of ritualized entry wounds were evidence of a satiation of power to dehumanize the victims and control every moment of their ultimate destruction.

It was remarkable that hiding the murder weapon after each killing was not a priority with this killer. Some killers are careful to remove all weapons and implements used to commit their crimes. But in this series, the killer left knives at the scenes of three of the murders. Cleaning up the crime scene of murder weapons was not important for this killer. Even more remarkable was that in the last two murders, the killer broke one knife and replaced it with another, and left both at the scene. In a final act of bravado, the killer laid a knife about one foot from the head of Pamela Clark and in a position where it was pointing at her head, a sure sign of ceremonial dominance for all to see. However, since the killer left the victims displayed and posed for postoffense satisfaction, the leaving of weapons matched in kind. As in a rape case, it is like leaving a picture of his penis to document the offending weapon, the ultimate arrogance and sarcastic irony. In addition, consistent with display of his victims, the killer was sending a message to police, 'Catch me if you can, sucker.' Finally, from a practical point of view after the murder, the removal of knives produced only wanted risk of discovery from the crime scene to a hiding spot or home.

CATCHING THE CLAIREMONT KILLER

After the sixth murder, the trail of the killer was as cold as a day of ice fishing in Minnesota. As intense as the police investigation was, it led nowhere. Four months after the murders of Pamela and Amber Clark, the first positive lead materialized in February 1991. Geralynd Venverloth returned home from the Family Fitness Center where she worked. What she didn't realize was that she was followed home by a stalking killer. Heading toward her bathroom shower, she heard the noise of the knob on the front door jiggling back and forth. She peered through the peephole and saw a man wedging himself against the door while trying to pry the lock with something. Just before the man was able to force his way in,

Venverloth was able to lock the dead bolt. The man got away before police arrived.

Charla Lewis was a coworker of Venverloth at the Family Fitness Center. Much to Venverloth's surprise, one day she saw the same man she observed through the peephole drop off Lewis at the Fitness Center. Through Venverloth's keen observations, police investigators arrested Cleophus Prince for the charge of attempted burglary of Venverloth's apartment. Prince was released on his own recognizance because the police did not have the evidence to hold him for the murders.

The police quickly began to investigate the theory that the Clairemont killer stalked several victims who had come directly from workouts at various fitness centers. After these women arrived home, they were slain after showering or preparing to shower at the time of the attacks. The circumstantial evidence in the case against Cleophus Prince, Jr., a twenty-five-year-old black male, began to build.

First of all, at the initial search of Prince's 1982 Chevrolet Cavalier, detectives found several knives on the floorboard. When they searched his wallet, they found a card for an automatic teller machine. The card had a small defect on it, and police detectives believed the defect was caused by slipping the card in the locking devices on windows and doors, a common technique for entering homes used by wily burglars.

In tracing Prince's travels, investigators found out that Prince was discharged from the navy in January 1990 and moved into the Buena Vista Apartments in the Clairemont area of San Diego. Then, after he had already began his murderous rampage of three women in nearby apartments, Prince moved in May 1990 to eastern San Diego into an apartment with his girlfriend, Charla Lewis. It was within one block of the house occupied by Elissa Keller, Prince's fourth victim, who was found stabbed to death the next month. The murders near

Prince's primary place of residence showed once again that serial killers operate in the surroundings that they are familiar with. Prince was extremely familiar with his own neighborhoods.

In September 1990, Prince joined the same health club as Pamela Clark. Homicide detectives suspected that Prince watched Pamela Clark leave the health club, followed her, and broke into her home. At one point, police discovered that Prince had bragged to a friend that he wanted to kill a mother and daughter. Witnesses later told police that they observed Prince wearing Pamela Clark's wedding ring on a chain after the murder.

The most crucial evidence against Cleophus Prince was a DNA match between his genetic material and the semen found on the victim's clothing at the scene of the murder of Janene Weinhold, the only murder scene where detectives found evidence of sexual activity in the form of ejaculate. After his arrest in February 1991, Prince agreed to provide blood and saliva samples. The samples were sent to the now famous Cellmark Diagnostics in Maryland. In March 1991, Cellmark officials informed the San Diego police detectives that the DNA profile of Cleophus Prince matched the semen sample. DNA scientists testified that the chance of getting a match in a random sample is one in several million. But the ejaculant found at the Janene Weinhold murder begs the question: Why were there no signs of sexual assault on any of the victims besides Weinhold?

The answer is complicated, but it makes sense. Prince displayed his control over the scene by enjoying the entire process of the act, which may or may not have an overtly exhibited sexual assault. Our experience from the previous killers shows that the sexual experience can be delayed until a later time, and at any subsequent murder scene. In fact, the more control the killer exerts over the victim, the likelier it is that the killer's immediate interest in a sexual assault is replaced by his anger and need for overwhelming control. He exerts so much control that he's able to enjoy his sexual release much later when he is completely private.

Based on the DNA evidence, detectives obtained a search warrant for Prince's apartment. They soon discovered that Prince had fled to his hometown of Birmingham, Alabama. But while at the apartment, they turned up their first evidence linking Prince to Holly Tarr, Prince's third victim. It was an unusually styled fourteen-karat gold ring given to Charla Lewis by Prince. Like Richard Cottingham before him, Prince gave a trinket of his perverted accomplishments to a girlfriend. This time the ring was identified by Tarr's father as the one he had given her for her sixteenth birthday. Police investigators discovered from the manufacturer of the ring that just sixty-three similar rings were made in that style. None were ever distributed in California.

Detectives located Prince and he was arrested in Bimingham on March 3, 1991. At his family's home, they found another ring that belonged to Elissa Keller and the shoes that matched the shoe impressions found outside the residences of several stabbing victims.

Ultimately, investigators developed evidence that Prince was the perpetrator of six murders and twenty-one burglaries that followed the pattern of the murders. Deputy District Attorney Dan Lamborn, in his closing argument at trial, said, 'This was not just some burglar being caught by surprise. This was someone with a purpose, a sexually perverted purpose. He liked to see blood flowing from the breasts of women.' Cleophus Prince was convicted of special circumstances murder under California law and given the death penalty at the sentencing phase of his trial.

The Cleophus Prince case was instructive because it showed a pattern of progression from one point on the continuum to another. But what happens when a sadistic killer actually goes backward in time? That was the story of Shreveport's Nathaniel Code and how the local police had the killer right under their noses but didn't know what they were looking at until the killer, thinking he was invisible, made the most classic mistake any killer can make.

CHAPTER 6

The Psychological Imprint of a Sadist

Nathaniel Code

When I applied the rape model to signature murders, one particular thing I noticed about how sex crime offenders gradually escalate their level of violence was the degree to which they became more and more sadistic toward their victims. Sadism is generally a feature of sex crimes. This is principally because sex offenders are exerting control out of anger, and that anger usually manifests itself as a form of sadism, taking pleasure from the pain and suffering of the victim. Using that broad a definition, almost all signature killers who inflict terror upon living victims can be categorized as sadistic. How sadistic they are depends upon how much pain, suffering, torture, and terror they force their victims to endure and how the pleasure of seeing the suffering drives them to greater heights of sadism.

If Morris Frampton, my first real signature case, took pleasure from the fear his victims exhibited when he abducted them, then he was sadistic. If Harvey Glatman enjoyed the terror he inflicted upon his victims after he bound and gagged them, then there was a level of sadism there. Cottingham, as he aroused his victims back to consciousness with torture, certainly qualifies as a sadistic killer, as do Spencer and Prince. But sexual sadism takes on many forms, each with its own definition and signature, and many, I found, pointing to different types of assailants.

SEXUAL SADISM

Unlike any other form of sexuality or sexual crimes, including murders, the sadist's satisfaction comes from the acquisition of power over his victim along a learning curve that he extends from crime to crime. In this learning curve he actually teaches himself how to achieve greater sexual gratification from administering what Dr. Richard Walter, forensic psychologist at the Michigan State Penitentiary, called the 'three *D*'s' of sexual sadism: dread, dependency, and degradation. Each murder takes the form of a vicious psychodrama in which the killer acts out the same script over and over again, changing the scenery, changing the actors, and experimenting with what turns him on, satisfies him at the crime scene, and then continues to satisfy him through the coming weeks or months. But each drama, as if it were some bizarre form of a classical Greek tragedy, must be built upon the three *D*'s of terror. First, the sadist tries to inflict a sense of dread in his victim, getting a sexual thrill from his perception of the degree of the victim's terror. Next, he wants his victim to be dependent upon him just as he is dependent upon the victim's reactions. The greater the perceived dependency – and we see this as an element in many serial rape cases – the higher the sexual thrill. Finally, the signature killer often degrades his victim physically, emotionally, and spiritually. Breaking his victim, and this means breaking her will to resist, is integral to his sense of derived sexual satisfaction.

To the sadist there is no thrill in murder, only in the prolonged and process-driven destruction of the helpless victim. Unlike other sexual assailants and killers, the sexual sadist enjoys the luxury of the power of emasculation rather than the experience of an on-the-spot sexual climax or even the death of the victim. For the sexual sadist, immediate sexual climax may not be what he's looking for because the explosion of his violence and its effect on the victim is what turns him on. The victim's death is often the coincidental artifact resulting from the violence of the crime, prolonged until the killer's needs have been met. Since the sexual sadist attempts to translate fantasy into reality, the assault 'ain't over until he says so.' It can last even after the victim has died. This is why the killer sometimes continues to assault the victim's corpse. What does the killer achieve by doing this? The satisfaction of his needs and a feeling that he has gratified himself through triumph, not time or death, are the test of success for the sexual sadist. We can often see this from the types of sexual wounds inflicted on the victim prior to death or from the secluded and secure nature of the crime scene in which the killer spent a long, long time with the victim without any fear of discovery.

MULTIPLE-VICTIM SIGNATURE KILLERS

Most signature killers rarely attack two or more victims at the same time. However, in a small category all by themselves are signature killers who do derive an especially intense thrill and sense of satisfaction from exercising control over two or more victims at the same time. I admit that I've been shocked at some of these crimes, because the killers who derive joy from capturing multiple victims and seeing the terror of one victim at the pain and torture of the others are particularly depraved. As Ted Bundy once told me, for a killer to accomplish that, 'he must be very intense.' So paramount must be his lust for control that the obvious dangers in manipulating multiple victims at the same time are superseded by the thrill of the exercise of control and domination. Killers who engage in this sort of control ritual are few and far between. Even if a killer does get satisfaction from controlling multiple victims and cushioning one victim off the other, it's almost unheard of to find one who has done it on more than one occasion. But, all of this notwithstanding, there are signature killers who have successfully attacked multiple victims at the same time and completed the crime.

Because the act of controlling victims in one event becomes more difficult as the number of victims increases, the serial killer must plan for the incapacitation of two people rather than one. But the minute you begin talking about a multiple-victim killer, you think of the prototypical mass murderer, and that is a mistake. Throughout history, mass murder has been the province of a crazed, commando-style shooter or a depressed man who kills his family and then turns the gun on himself. This is the overwhelming line of events in mass murders. Mass murders are paradigmatically different from serial murders, even multiple-victim serial murders.

A small number of signature killers, especially predators such as Ted Bundy and Kenneth Bianchi, murdered two victims at once in their series of killings in addition to executing single victims at different times. Ted Bundy perfected his modus operandi, roamed the Chi Omega sorority house, and bludgeoned to death two coeds while they slept in their beds. Bianchi, on the other hand, lured two coed-aged females to a house that he was guarding in Bellingham, Washington, and strangled them. Bianchi and Bundy showed their victims not only their propensity for violence, but also an obvious capability to carry it out. In each case, both Bundy and Bianchi murdered their victims in the surroundings they were familiar with, not at some place they just accidentally happened to come across when the opportunity arose. For both killers this was important, because they liked to kill in places where they knew the terrain and where they would feel well rehearsed. That was part of their turn-on.

THE NATHANIEL CODE MURDERS

In Shreveport, Louisiana, there was a killer, Nathaniel Code, who was different. He began with a single-victim murder. Then he went on to attack multiple victims at the same location. Those murders occurred several years apart without any apparent attempted murders or sexual assaults occurring in between, which is very rare when it comes to serial killers. Code's attacks all occurred within a specific black neighborhood, targeted black victims, and, carried Code's signature. His mark was permanently etched at each of three separate but remarkably similar scenes.

The Deborah Ford Killing

Code's calling-card murders began with the homicide of Deborah Ford, a twenty-five-year-old single mother. The killer left an obvious signature that could not be disguised as he moved about in Ford's home. The victim's body was discovered on August 31, 1984, when her friend, Brenda Greggs, walked over to her home to use the telephone. At about eight o'clock in the morning, Greggs knocked on Ford's front door but got no answer. About thirty minutes later Greggs returned with her child and knocked on the front door again. This time the door cracked open and she could hear the stereo playing. When Greggs called out to Ford, thinking that she probably couldn't hear the knocking because of the music, there was no answer. She peeked into Ford's living room, a small space measuring only twelve by thirteen. As she craned her neck around the front door, Greggs was immediately stunned by a hideous sight. The interior was in complete disarray, and there, almost in the center of the room, lay Ford's motionless, cut-open body bleeding out into the carpet and clad in only a nightgown turned inside out. Greggs stared down at Ford lying there amidst the tan-and-gold flower design on the carpet, and almost couldn't believe the blank demeanor of death across her friend's face. But later, to an experienced investigator, her demeanor was anything but expressionless. Her body bore the telltale vestiges of the work of a sadistic killer: hands tied behind her back, with the bindings tied in a fashion resembling handcuffs.

Detectives from the Shreveport Police Department put together the following information from their investigation and traced Ford's last steps. Deborah Ford lived in the Cedar Grove area of Shreveport at 315 East Seventy-fourth Street. Her two daughters, nine-year-old Nikki and five-year-old Shawn, lived with her in a small shotgun-style, single-story home with white siding. The home had been broken into previously, and shortly after that time, Ford's father had nailed the back door shut and secured outside screens over all the windows, hoping to prevent future break-ins.

On the day before Ford's murder, Danny Ware, Shawn's father, went shopping with Ford and the two girls for school clothes. Shortly before 9:30 P.M., they returned to the Seventy-fourth Street address and spoke outside while Nikki went inside to get her favorite stuffed animal. Danny was taking the two girls to their grandmother's house for the night. As Nikki routed around her room for her toy animal, she noticed the bathroom window was open and secured it by placing a wooden stick vertically above the frame to keep it shut. Other than the nailed screen, the window had no locking device. Unfortunately, investigators would soon discover that the stick could be easily dislodged by jiggling the window until the stick slid to one side, allowing an intruder just enough leverage to get the window open and gain entrance to the house.

Detectives tracked Ford's activities by interviewing her neighbors and friends. Up until ten in the evening, Deborah spoke briefly to her neighbor Gussy Bell and Gussy's daughter Juanita Parks. For another hour, Michael Bell, Gussy Bell's brother, visited Ford in her home. Another friend, Gregory Bell, who would later become the number one suspect in Ford's murder, talked to Deborah three times between 8:00 P.M. and 12:30 A.M., the last time anyone knew that Deborah was alive. Pretty close to eight-thirty in the evening, witnesses heard Ford yell, 'Stay away from me. I don't want you here.'

In front of the Ford residence that morning, a small crowd had gathered. Years later, police would discover that Nathaniel Code, who lived in the neighborhood, was a member of that small crowd standing in the ninety-degree heat capturing the sensation of power over those around him and in the house. He was reveling in the experience of knowing all about the murder while nobody else was aware that he had any involvement. He freely talked to others about the murder, but was careful not to implicate himself.

Under the protection of darkness, sometime after twelve-thirty in the morning, and while Deborah was asleep on the living-room couch, Code pried the nailed screen loose from the bathroom window and removed it from the side of the house. The detectives found out from relatives and friends that Deborah usually slept in the living room on the couch. Carefully raising the window so as to make no noise, he hoped, the intruder used a piece of metal to hold the window open while he slid through. These were not the actions of a novice wannabe breaking and entering, but the practiced nighttime stealth of an experienced cat burglar.

At sometime during the murder of Deborah Ford, the killer went to the kitchen, where he cut a piece of electrical cord from the box fan. Did he cut the cord when he realized she was on the couch and would soon be awake, or was she waking up when he broke in through the window? Whatever the sequence, he attacked Deborah Ford on the couch; from what was revealed the next morning by the condition of the room, she did not go quietly. When Ford felt Code's attack, she tried to rise from the couch, and a quick struggle ensued in which furniture was turned over, cushions were disarranged, and a cup and ashtray were overturned. Ford defended herself as best she could by fighting back with her hands. The autopsy revealed defense bruises on her hands and arms.

The intruder eventually subdued Ford by stabbing her many times and tied her hands behind her back with the electrical cord he'd cut from the fan. The cord wasn't tied in a haphazard fashion, but in a way especially important to the killer. It was anchored firmly around her left wrist and then looped around her right wrist; the loose end was retied to the cord on her left wrist with a space in between her hands, resembling a perfect set of handcuffs in place. At some point in the struggle, probably after he initially stabbed her but before he tied her hands, Ford was gagged with her own clothing.

After she had been bound and was too weak to resist, Code dragged her limp and trussed-up body across the floor to the middle of the room, where he continued to stab her. Perhaps she futilely struggled against her bindings, but Code kept on stabbing, exhibiting an extreme form of dominance over her. By the end of the assault, Code had stabbed her nine times in the chest: two times on the left side, and seven times on the right side. Several of the chest wounds penetrated her lungs, and more than one of those wounds might have bled out and become fatal over time if the killer had stopped at that point. But he didn't.

Continuing, in what could only be described as a murderous fit of utter domination, Ford's killer moved her body to the middle of the living room, where he slit her throat six times, stabbing into the right of her neck and dragging the blade across her jugular vein, carotid artery, larynx, and esophagus to the left, where he yanked the blade out and started again. The wounds were so deep, they cut right through almost to her spinal column. Remarkably, even though Ford had sustained near-mortal chest injuries, she was still struggling against her aggressor when he slashed her throat. The killer left Ford's body propped on her left side.

Police investigators located several crucial pieces of physical evidence during their crime-scene search. The front of the house faced south. On the west side, detectives discovered that the killer forcibly entered the house through the bathroom window that Nikki had secured. Unbeknownst to him, he'd left a smudged partial footprint in the bathtub immediately beneath the window. Also, the killer knocked paint debris and dirt into the bathroom and outside the window, and detectives concluded he might have had that same trace evidence on his clothing. Investigators found the most critical evidence when they discovered recent latent handprints from someone who had opened the bathroom window from the outside. In total, investigators recovered three latent palm prints and a thumbprint on the bathroom window, windowsill, and inside wall below the window.

At the postmortem examination, Dr. George McCormick, the Caddo Parish coroner, determined that Deborah Ford eventually died from an accumulation of severe bleeding due to stabbing and cutting. Based on the direction of the cutting wounds on her neck, he said the killer was right-handed. He estimated that the entire attack lasted from fifteen to thirty minutes. He noted that Ford's vagina contained only a trace of seminal fluid and that the killer did not climax in the victim. More important, Dr. McCormick also told police that the murder was clearly a 'signature crime' and the work of a solo serial killer who would strike again. In his consultation with police, Dr. McCormick informed the police about four classical elements of Code's signature: the perpetrator's total control over the victim, the perpetrator's use of a knife to *both* stab and cut, the binding of the victim with an electrical cord, and the unique structure of the ligature used by the perpetrator.

Investigators hoped that the latent prints they discovered would soon lead them to the killer. They thought there was a good chance they'd already had the killer on file. You don't just pop out of thin air to do these crimes, they believed; you had to start somewhere. So they started searching the records. Their routine investigation included a profile from the FBI's Behavioral Sciences Unit. The FBI was leery of giving a formal profile, since they felt that the original autopsy report did not reflect an examination for rape. But the Behavioral Sciences Unit did give an abbreviated and unofficial profile. Three major characteristics of the killer were provided to the Shreveport detectives: (1) Normally, a killer like this was about thirty years old and would be living in the immediate area; (2) he most likely had previous bookings for rape or burglary; and (3) the killer might be overly helpful and interject himself into the investigation in some way. The last item makes perfect sense, because the signature of the killer is control and dominance through a continuum of escalating violence. If you don't find that he ejaculated all over the victim during the assault, you predict that he will try to extend his control over the victim and the crime as far as possible. If that means mixing in with the investigation so as to get a sexual thrill from all of the activity surrounding from the helpless victim under his domination, that's exactly what he would do.

Armed with their ME's report and the Behavioral Sciences Unit profile, investigators agreed that Ford's killer probably was from Shreveport and had a recorded criminal history. So, Sgt. C. R. Owens and his partner took on the industrious task of manually searching through inmate booking records of the identical fingerprint record that would match the latent thumbprint. Unfortunately, there was no Automated Fingerprint Identification System available to them as there are in some jurisdictions today. The system can search for a single fingerprint among millions of prints in a matter of seconds. After three weeks, they had searched by hand hundreds of cards for the previous ten years and hadn't located the killer's prints. The ten-year time span was recommended by the FBI, since the killer was about thirty years old. In retrospect, Sergeant Owens said he felt he should have gone further back in time. But his superiors stopped him from doing so, saying he had wasted enough time searching print cards. It would come to light later that had Owens gone back eight more months, he would have discovered local resident Nathaniel Robert Code in his ten-print card file. All three palm prints and the thumbprint recovered at the Ford residence were later identified as matching those of Nathaniel Code who, as the profilers predicted, had an extensive record for burglary and sex crimes. He was also standing just outside the crime scenes as the police hauled away the evidence. Sometimes, as I have very painfully found out, you have to go with your instincts even when the brass upstairs tells you to shut it down. How successful might Owens have been were he allowed to pursue the search for the missing prints he believed were in the card file? It is conceivable that he would have saved lives.

The Chaney Homicides

Only a few blocks from the site of Deborah Ford's murder was the home of Vivian Chaney. She lived at 213 East Seventy-second Street with her boyfriend Billy Joe Harris,

Jerry Culbert, Chaney's brother, and her three daughters, Carlitha Culbert, Tomika Chaney, and Marla Chaney. Vivian, Carlitha, and Jerry were sight impaired, and Tomika and Marla were mentally retarded. All were in a physical condition that relinquished control to other people and made them particularly tempting targets for a control-hungry serial killer.

On the night of July 18, 1985, about one year after the Ford murder and sometime between 11:30 P.M. and six the next morning, someone forced open the back door to the Chaney residence. Twenty-year-old Shirley Culbert discovered the crime when she banged on the door after having arrived from Alexandria, Louisiana, by bus and getting a cab from the bus depot to take her to her sister's house. Ms. Culbert knocked on the south-facing front door, found it locked, and made her way along the east side of the house to the back door. When she reached the rear porch of the house, she noticed that the back door was slightly cracked, and she opened it easily. She entered the kitchen and could peak into the middle bedroom, where she saw the legs of her brother stretched out on the bed. Jerry was wearing a blue robe and lying on the left side on the bed. She called out to him in the early morning, but seeing no movement, thought he was sound asleep, so she passed through the kitchen and entered the middle bedroom on the other side of the house, where she found her two nieces, Marla, age nine, and Tomika, age ten, asleep. She woke them up and went to the southeast bedroom, where she noticed Vivian's common-law husband lying in bed. He wasn't moving at all. She immediately knew something was wrong because she spotted a gaping hole in Billy Joe's throat. Frightened, she grabbed her two nieces and ran from the house.

Under considerable duress, Shirley reentered the house with the cab driver who was still waiting there. She conducted a room-to-room search and noticed that her brother had been shot or stabbed in the left side of the head. In the bathroom she discovered her sister, Vivian Chaney, lying over the edge of the tub with her face inside the tub and her hands bound behind her back. In the living room, she discovered her other niece, Carlitha, bound with her throat cut. Billy Joe Harris's throat was cut, too, and he was also bound. Shirley Culbert and the cab driver left the house after discovering the bodies of her family, and the cab driver immediately called the Shreveport Police Department.

Responding officers found Billy Joe Harris in the southeast corner bedroom. His feet and hands were bound behind his back by a telephone cord that was still connected to the wall. His right wrist was tied tightly and a loop was made for the left wrist in a handcuff ligature. The cord was continuous from his hands to feet, but he was not hog-tied. The phone cord itself was a long extension cord that had been cut midway between the receiver and the handset. Under the phone cord, police investigators discovered that Billy Joe's wrists and ankles were secured with his tennis shoelaces, and the electrical cord was placed over the laces. Harris was fully dressed in a black shirt, blue jeans, and a pair of dark socks. In a fit of overkill, the killer had shot Harris two times in the left side of the head through a pillow and twice in the chest. After being shot, Harris was still alive, so the killer cut his throat. Police felt that the killer placed a hat on Harris's head, because it was cocked slightly to the side just off his head where he was lying. In addition, the killer threw a sheet over Harris that partially covered the lower portion of his body.

Adjacent to the master bedroom where Billy Joe Harris was murdered, police discovered the remains of fifteen-year-old Carlitha Culbert, Vivian Chaney's daughter. She was lying facedown on the floor, wearing an orange pullover shirt and pink cut-off trousers, both of which had been turned inside out. At one time, she had been bound at the ankles by a shoelace, but apparently she had kicked that loose, perhaps during the struggle for her life. Her hands were bound in handcuff ligature fashion behind her back with a blue cord from a steam iron. The iron was found on the back porch, where police discovered the back door open. There was a swath of silver duct tape slapped across her mouth as though the killer had gagged her. No other pieces of duct tape or the original roll were found throughout the house. Carlitha's cause of death was severe cut wounds to the throat. So deep were the cuts that the coroner surmised that the killer had tried to remove her head with his cutting tool. Within the living room itself, there were no signs of a big struggle, just several record albums strewn about, indicating that the killer had probably knocked them over while murdering Carlitha.

Jerry Culbert, a black male who was legally blind, lay dead in another middle bedroom, dressed in a blue robe and spread on top of his waterbed. Unlike the others, Culbert was not bound or gagged. He had abrasions on his left arm as if he had struck it while falling, but detectives felt he was shot while sleeping. He had a single gunshot wound to the left temple from a twenty-two-caliber firearm. There was no sign of a struggle in Culbert's room.

In the bathroom, police discovered the body of Vivian Chaney, a thirty-six-year-old black female, dressed in an orange dress and draped facedown over the edge of the bathtub with her knees on the floor and head resting against the bottom of the tub. The telephone cord had bound her hands behind her back about one foot apart. The cord came around the front of her waist and then down between her legs to tie her ankles. The bonds would have allowed her a hobbling walk as if she were a prisoner in shackles. There was evidence that another ligature had been used around her neck to control her and lead her around. The cord extended down and was secured to her ankles. The back of Vivian's dress had a large amount of Carlitha's blood over the buttocks area and the lower hem, indicating that Vivian had sat in the pool of blood caused by the initial cutting of her daughter's neck. There was evidence of both manual and ligature strangulation on Vivian. She had been beaten violently about the head and died from a combination of strangulation and bathtub drowning.

Relatives later discovered several items missing from the house, including Henry Culbert's wallet, a jar of loose change, food stamps, a food stamp identification card, pictures of the girls, and a striped tote bag. No money was found in the house, although Vivian Chaney had cashed a check for over one hundred dollars the day before.

Despite the number and viciousness of the murders, Dr. McCormick testified that the crimes were still the work of only one person – a serial killer working alone, killing repetitively, but escalating the violence of his crimes. McCormick believed that this was the same serial killer who had murdered Deborah Ford and was now increasing the level and intensity of his violence. This guy probably lived in the neighborhood with his victims, the ME said, and predicted even further that the killer would be among the crowd gathered at the crime scene. He suggested that the police probably passed the killer right in front of them as they processed evidence, but had no way of picking him out from the crowd.

The Chaney murders suggested a logical progression to investigators who could picture the scene as the sole murderer moved among the victims. The teenage hostage, Carlitha, and a gun were used to control the adults. McCormick theorized that the killer threatened Carlitha's life to immobilize Vivian Chaney and Billy Joe Harris. Vivian Chaney was tied so she could walk; Carlitha's hands were already tied. After binding Billy Joe Harris, the killer shot him through a pillow to prevent disturbing the sleeping Jerry Culbert, who was himself shot without being awakened by the killer. The murderer next cut Carlitha's throat but did not kill her. He made Vivian Chaney sit down in her daughter's blood before taking Vivian to the bathroom and strangling and drowning her. When the killer returned to the living room, either Carlitha had moved or the murderer had moved her. He finished killing Carlitha by trying to decapitate her. At some point the killer, still in a blood fury, returned to the already dead Billy Joe Harris and stabbed him in the neck. Here was a killer so violent that he couldn't stop stabbing and hacking.

Investigative officers found pieces of duct tape consistent with the type used to gag Carlitha Chaney in the alley behind the Chaney house. Upon processing the crime scene, the police found three latent left palm prints on the bathtub over which Vivian Chaney's body was draped. McCormick theorized that the right-handed killer had used his dominant hand to hold her head under water while he steadied himself with his left hand. Testimony later established that the fresh prints had been left after the tub had last been cleaned.

THE WILLIAM CODE HOMICIDES

William T. Code, Nathaniel Code's seventy-three-year-old grandfather, lived at 641 West Sixty-sixth Street in Shreveport in the very same house where he had raised Nathaniel Code from childhood. On August 4, 1987, William Code was working in his yard with the two grandsons of a friend, Enamerteen Williams. The boys, eight-year-old Eric Williams and twelve-year-old Joe Robinson, were also going to spend the night with Mr. Code as they had done, with Mrs. Williams's permission, a number of times in the past. People saw the boys working with Mr. Code in his yard as late as 8:00 P.M.

The next morning when the boys didn't return home,

a concerned Mrs. Williams went over to William Code's residence that afternoon to see if anything was wrong, but hoping that they were all just having a good time. She found the doors locked, and steel burglar bars on the windows and doors kept her from gaining entrance. There was no sign of forced entry. Although no one answered her knocking, she heard music playing, which later was revealed to be the television, still on from the night before. Peering through the window, Mrs. Williams could see the bound foot of her grandson Joe. She returned home, called the police, and came back to the Code house with her brother, niece, and granddaughter. After using her own key to open the burglar bars on one of the windows, Mrs. Williams and her brother discovered the bodies of William Code and the two boys. All three victims were found in separate rooms.

Joe Robinson was found lying facedown on the living-room couch. He had been struck in the forehead with a blow severe enough to have dazed him so that he could no longer defend himself, at which point his assailant continued to beat him, bruising him on the shoulders beneath the skin and over both collarbones. Joe's ankles were tied with a white plastic cord, leaving a gap in between both ankles as if he were wearing ankle cuffs. A length of the same cord had been used to tie his hands together behind his back, with one end of the plastic cord tied to one wrist and the other tied to the other wrist, like handcuffs. A loose length of cord around his neck held a gag, and a doubled length of the cord was used to strangle him. The boy was wearing only a pair of underwear which had been turned inside out.

Eric Williams was found lying facedown between two twin beds in a small bedroom where he had been dragged off one of the beds. Plastic rope held a gag around his neck. His hands had been tied identically to the way Joe's were: in a handcuff ligature. One ankle was tied with this cord, but then it ran out. The killer then took electrical cord to finish binding the boy's ankles together. A second length of electrical cord was used to strangle the boy. There were no signs that a struggle took place. The boy was wearing a pair of underwear.

William Code was found lying facedown on his bed, dressed in a dressing gown. His ankles were bound with electrical cord, then the cord was brought up the front of his legs and tied to his wrists. His hands were tied behind his back with electrical cord in the handcuff ligature. A telephone cord around his neck held a gag in place. The autopsy showed that William Code had been struck a very heavy blow to the side of his head, which alone could have caused his death. Hemorrhages in his brain were consistent with being beaten about the head with a fist. He had been stabbed five times in the chest, seven times in the back, and once in a major artery of the right upper arm with a long knife. Several of these wounds would have been fatal, but William Code died of their cumulative effect. Pat Wojtkiewicz of the North Louisiana Crime Lab testified that medium-velocity blood spatter – that is, spatter from a beating or a stabbing – was found on the wall in William Code's bedroom where he was killed.

Blood spatter is an important indicator at a crime scene because it usually tells an investigator what type of weapon caused the injury. High-velocity blood spatter typically results from a gunshot wound, medium-velocity spatter comes from a stab wound or a blow from a blunt instrument, and low-velocity spatter is the result of dripping blood.

In the William Code homicide, Medical Examiner McCormick testified that one person was responsible for all the murders in the household that night. The two boys were tied in the same way, gagged in the same way, and killed in the same way. Materials from the house were used to tie William Code. McCormick testified the victims were probably killed in the order in which they were found: Joe first, then Eric, then Mr. Code. Since there was no sign of forced entry, Robinson probably let the murderer in the front door. Robinson was subdued by a strong blow to the head, then gagged, tied, and strangled. Williams, who was in the front bedroom, was probably surprised as he slept. There was no sign of a struggle. Williams was then tied and killed.

McCormick testified that the focus of the murders was William Code. There was no element of overkill in the two boys who were dispatched quickly, and no knife was used on them. By contrast, William Code was beaten repeatedly over the head and rolled front and back to be stabbed many more times than would have been necessary to kill him. McCormick theorized that this showed an emotional relationship between the victim and the murderer.

No money was found in the residence, although William Code had cashed checks totaling between four and six hundred dollars the day before he was murdered. A small-caliber pistol was missing from the house as well. Investigators found a knife and a set of keys in a storm drain approximately six hundred feet from the residence. The knife was similar to a set found in William Code's kitchen; the keys fit the victim's door.

THE STRANGE SIGNATURE OF NATHANIEL CODE

I examined the investigation files and the photographs which depicted the indescribable destruction that the killer had wrought in these three individual murder cases, separated only by the time that the killer had chosen to strike. For the law enforcement officers of Shreveport, the developments in these three separate homicide incidents came in a slower and infinitely more tragic form than most murder investigations they were accustomed to. In a perplexing sequence of events over three years, the killer adapted his modus operandi from a singular victim killing to multiple victims. In some respects, the killer's modus operandi remained constant, since he obviously felt comfortable breaking into occupied homes in his own neighborhood. He felt no need to change.

There was also a shift from an ultimately unsatisfying assault in the primary sexual continuum – the killer ejaculated at the first homicide – to the concentrated use of secondary sexual mechanisms to produce a pathological sense of power – the killer's anger was the focus of the assault, and not sexual satisfaction. But something was very odd here. There were almost yearlong hiatuses between the signature murders, and Code's victim pool would include men, women, children, and his own grandfather. Where was the sexual thrill in these crimes, and how could it encompass such a wide variety of victims?

Many signature killers achieve their sexual gratification through primary sexual mechanisms by physically raping each of their victims. Primary sexual mechanisms are directed, specified sets of actions, behaviors, and methods which bring the killer to a sexual climax. When they relieve tension in the killer, they may be either deliberate or conscious activities or unconscious activities which operate below the killer's level of awareness. Nevertheless, these activities leave their mark on the signature murder crime scene and are obvious to the trained investigator. Essentially, the signature reveals to the cop how the killer, through primary sexual mechanisms, got his rocks off.

Other killers satisfy themselves through the use of secondary sexual mechanisms and don't look for sexual gratification – an orgasm – at the crime scene, because they achieve satisfaction through such processes as acting out their anger. If they're going to have a climax over the release of sexual tension, they'll have it after the crime, using the emotions they experienced at the crime scene as a sexual stimulant during masturbation. This process is much more common than most people realize and can provide the fully matured sexual signature killer a much greater freedom to commit crimes and control the murder scene. Nathaniel Code's sexual satisfaction, for example, made its appearance indirectly and was defused. His major concentration was the substitution of sexual release through an expression of power exhibited through ritualistic binding and cutting of his victims. In other words, the process of carrying out his anger through torture and forced submission substituted for sexual gratification.

In Code's and other cases, the basic foundation for the signature became evident through the way the killer integrated levels of domination and submission, bondage as discipline, picquerism, and pathological sadism, also expressed as the humiliation of the victim, at the crime scene. The cases revealed that the basic foundation for the killer's expressed actions were grounded within a matrix of domination and submission. Dominate his victims and force them to submit: these were the basis of expressing his anger and became the core of his sexual release. Here, the drive for supremacy was evident in the forced dependency, degradation, torture, and humiliation of his victims. The more they suffered emotionally as well as physically, the greater the satisfaction Code experienced, and it completely replaced his need to have an on-the-spot orgasm. But this was an evolution from his first murder, the murder of Deborah Ford.

Following the experimental killing of Deborah Ford, the multiple/mass killings revealed his interest in controlling groups of people – that is, the strategy of managing the victims to become incapacitated by shoelaces (later with his own creations), and to use and manipulate victims so as to increase their own dependency upon him. More important, after initially wounding them, he chose to force Vivian Chaney to helplessly watch the torture of her fifteen-year-old daughter, and his grandfather to witness the killing of the twelve- and eight-year-old boys who had already been incapacitated. By so doing, he attenuated the dread of their own impending torture and death, feeding off their own terror to extend and express his own power. In the ritual of subjugation of the victims, he preened in his own ability to mastermind and effect dominance over them.

What we wouldn't realize until after Code was arrested and the record of his cat-burglar robberies between multiple murders was revealed, was that murder of Deborah Ford was probably not intended to be a murder at all, but a robbery. In the small neighborhood where Code and his victims lived, news of who had cashed a check or who had come into money was probably the stuff of common knowledge. Neighbors talk. News travels fast. If you're a burglar always on the look-out for easy pickings, you keep your ears open for who's supposed to have cash on hand or valuables worth turning over. Code was a break-in artist, and that's how he supported himself. His victims, as his very extensive police record revealed, were the people in his own neighborhood.

At least at the time of the first homicide, Code had probably never set out to murder anyone if he could avoid it. More than likely, Code received sexual satisfaction as a cat burglar who violated his victim's boundaries night after night, stalked in their territory, stole their cash and valuables, and sneaked away. His anonymity no doubt also provided him with a great deal of sexual satisfaction, and that's how he processed his obvious anger over the years. Casing houses, seeing who was home and who wasn't, finding out about the movements of his intended victims – all provided him with much the same satisfaction as a serial killer gets trolling through the neighborhood of his victim pool. That's why his murders were so widely spaced.

So what happened to Deborah Ford on the night of her murder? I'll speculate that Code heard that Ford had cashed some checks and had money lying around the house. He also might have known that her kids were going off with their father, leaving her alone in the house and probably easy pickings for a robbery. The fact that he went straight to the loose screen on the bathroom window, which he pulled right off, indicates that he knew something about the house. His use of the bathroom window is a very revealing sexual signature that has a lot to do with the predator's sense of being able to penetrate his victim's domain. Picture Code having pulled off the screen and fumbling with the window frame, into which Ford's daughter had inserted a stick of wood to keep it locked. But as Code fumbles with the window, the wood jiggles in the frame, makes noise, and falls over. Ford is sleeping on the bedroom couch. I'll bet that Code didn't know that. She awakens at the sound of the window opening and spies Code as he moves through the living room. The cat burglar is spotted and identified by a potential witness.

What flashed through Code's mind in that instant? He knew Ford, of course, and she knew him. The police also knew him. There was no clean getaway. He had spent so much time in jail, he certainly got pissed off at the thought that he would have to return. The witness had to die, and it had to be thorough so that Code wouldn't be caught. Is that when he went to the kitchen looking for a piece of electrical cord – readily available in the box fan – or did he attack her first, incapacitate her, then tie her up with cord in a fit of anger? From the self-defense bruises on her hands, it would seem that Code attacked Ford first. Then, when she was wounded and subdued, he retrieved the cord, and tied her up. As he completed his work he was overtaken by an anger that rose up as if in retaliation for having been witnessed. Ford's fate might have been sealed when she saw him in her living room, but the torture she received was the signature of an anger-driven killer who thought about raping his victim but couldn't complete it because the fury got in the way of his sexual drive and short-circuited it. That's the reason for the small amount of ejaculant on the victim.

Code had not planned to kill anyone on the night he broke into Deborah Ford's house. Unfortunately, Ford had to die because she saw her assailant, and that became an imprinting murder – the threshold Code crossed on his way to becoming a signature killer. The signature was there first; the killing came second. However, Ford was tortured because her assailant was so completely taken over by the anger at being spotted that his retaliation upon the victim was complete and all-consuming, and escalated right through the attack. I believe that even Code might have been surprised by what overtook him on the night of the murder. He was so surprised, I believe, that he chose only the safest house to rob for the next year. By the time he came upon the Vivian Chaney family, he had preplanned the murder because he was dealing with a house full of people who were either blind or otherwise impaired and could not defend themselves. They were an easy target for an anger-driven burglar who was not above killing his victims by torturing them and making them experience the domination of a person they might have held in little regard.

Importantly, another key signature of domination found at each Code crime scene was the fact that the victims' clothes had been turned inside out. Prior to cutting his victims, Code reversed the nightgown of Deborah Ford, the orange pullover shirt and pink cut-off trousers of Carlitha Culbert, and the undershorts of twelve-year-old Eric Williams. In each case, the act of the clothing reversal was a symbolic gesture that he was so powerful that he could turn each of his victims inside out. In addition, the victim's humiliation and vulnerability of being stripped and redressed only increased the perpetrator's arrogant sense of superior power at the scene.

Also consistent throughout all of the Code cases was the prominence of specialized victim restriction. In particular, the homemade and improvised handcuffs were distinctive and unique in each crime scene. The cords were first applied from left to right wrists with linkage between them. The handcuff style was efficient and tidy. Since the perpetrator moved at least one victim in each case, it was also an efficient method for grasping, and handling the transport of, the victim. An elaboration of handcuff skill was demonstrated in the repeated hobbling techniques used on Vivian Chaney, Billy Joe Harris, and William Code. With these victims, their hands were tied behind their backs into a position of submission and they were hobbled to allow for controlled and limited movement. Hence, they were able to move and experience the torture of the other victims. Inasmuch as the perpetrator was the only observer-participant in the Deborah Ford killing, it was unnecessary to hobble her. Additional signatures of bondage were the improvised gags fabricated from either clothing or tape, and bathtub water drowning.

Finally, ligature strangulation recurred throughout the cases as an adjunct and supportive mechanism for terrorizing and causing death. In particular, the ligature strangulation provided Code with a supplementary power surge at his ability to control life and death. In essence, for the perpetrator, strangulation is simply a joy toy of the gods.

Although victims Jerry Culbert, Joe Robinson, and Eric Williams were not cut or stabbed with a knife, one or more victims in each crime scene did experience pre- and perimortem stabbing, cutting, and slashing of the flesh. Of note, all cut and stab wounds were above the victims' waists. In addition, going well beyond the level of violence necessary to kill his victims, Code wounded them, cut their flesh to make them bleed, stimulated blood flow with body movement, and then cut their throats. Also, the excessive amount of stabbing and cutting of deep-muscle structure went far beyond what was necessary and sufficient to cause death. For the perpetrator, his consistent and repetitive behaviors indicated the satisfaction he gained through picquerism. Here, he enjoyed penetrating and ripping human flesh and tissue. A gun was only utilitarian. Even though the shooting of a gun at times can be an implement of picquerism when the shooter uses it to cut holes in the skin and underlying tissue and not specifically to kill, the Code cases indicated that it served only as a functional tool to cause the death of a certain person whose role in the overall event was minimal to the killer.

Considering the interrelated harmonics of the pathological levels in each of these murder scenes, the synergistic effect is one of sadism pure and simple. That is, sexual sadism is the pleasure and satisfaction derived from killing unsuspecting victims in different ways. This isn't just murder; it's sustained and orchestrated torture. The matrix is one of dread, dependency, degradation, and death.

In his last act before he fled into the night, the perpetrator signed his signature card at each crime scene by staging in a meaningful pose at least one body at each of the three crime scenes. In the Deborah Ford murder, he left her propped up on her left side in a defeated position in the middle of her living room. She was openly displayed where anyone looking for her would be sure to find her. In the Chaney homicides, he positioned Vivian Chaney facedown over the edge of the bathtub in a defeated position. As for Billy Harris, the perpetrator covered his lower torso with a sheet and put a hat jauntily askew on his head. One could interpret Harris's staging as the final act of affection for a boyfriend the killer always wished for. But that fact was a private embrace known only to the killer, not to the victim, and certainly silent and unknown to those who were around both people. In the William Code murders, Nathaniel left his grandfather bound, facedown in a defeated position, dressed in a dressing gown. In all of these stagings, the perpetrator was sending a message of sarcastic irony and contempt against his conquered foe. In all likelihood, if the murderer had not been caught, the next probable emergent signature within the killer's learning curve of his picqueristic actions would have been the harvesting of body parts.

THE ARREST OF NATHANIEL CODE

Why did Nathaniel Code get caught? Upon beginning the investigation into the events at the William Code murder scene, Shreveport police investigators focused on the savage defilement of each victim and the methods with which they were struck down. Each victim was carefully inspected by responding officers. Some officers were detailed to process the crime scene; others were directed to complete a neighborhood canvass to search for witnesses and any evidence the killer may have discarded; and some were told to interview surviving family members.

Locating the killer's route of escape is an important aspect of any murder investigation because often, implements of the crime will be discovered along it. It was no different in this case. Officers were in the midst of a thorough search of the intersection of Wallace and West Sixty-sixth streets when, almost on cue, one officer walked over to a drainage culvert and discovered a set of keys. The keys were attached to a plastic key chain and a black and white teddy bear belonging to William Code. The Water Department arrived to remove the lid to the culvert. Officers recovered the keys; astonishingly, a hickory-handled kitchen knife, faded brown in color, was lying right next to the keys.

After only a short while, family members began to arrive at the crime scene, bringing with them the theory that all were killed by fellow family member Nathaniel Code. They all knew he was a strange bird who mooched off others when he didn't rob them. Family members also said that Nathaniel Code had grown up with his grandfather in that very house. This made him a natural focus of inquiry. Police also knew Code because he'd been in and out of jail most of his teenage and adult life. After the bodies were found, Nathaniel Code approached investigating officers and introduced himself as the victim's grandson, blatantly interjecting himself into the case as the FBI predicted he would.

Already alert to the possibility of Nathaniel Code's involvement, investigators became increasingly suspicious of Code, because he stated he had touched the vacuum, fan, humidifier, and phone while at his grandfather's house earlier in the morning, explaining away, just in case anybody asked, why his fingerprints were at the crime scene. These were the very items from which the electrical cord was cut to bind the victims. Code agreed to allow the police to seize the clothes and shoes he had worn the day before. Detectives Scooter Rushing and J. B. Smalls took on the task of the initial interview of Nathaniel Code in which he admitted that he last saw his grandfather, William Code, at two o'clock in the morning the day of the murders. Nathaniel claimed that he had begun receiving telephone calls from his grandfather as early as June. Nathaniel, perhaps setting up phantom suspects or false leads, told police that his grandfather complained that black males had been hanging around his residence. He stated that on occasion he would visit his grandfather and check the area around his home for suspicious persons. He gave the police a rationale for his being at the house. But because Nathaniel lived right across the street at 703 East

Seventy-third Street, the home of friends, he was again a focus of inquiry if only by virtue of proximity.

At approximately 11:00 P.M. on August 4, 1987, Nathaniel told police, his grandfather called while he was house-sitting for a friend at 300 East Seventy-third Street. This fact was refuted by others familiar with William Code. They felt that William was afraid of Nathaniel and would never have risked calling him. Friends knew that Nathaniel used to beat his grandmother when she was alive, and William Code didn't want him around. Also, Nathaniel could not make it clear to police how William Code knew his grandson was house-sitting nearby and why William complained only to Nathaniel and to no one else of people hanging around his residence. Nathaniel told him that he could not come to see him right away, but he would come when he left sometime after 12:30 A.M.

Nathaniel claimed he got on his bicycle and rode to his grandfather's house. He stated when he arrived the front porch light was on and he knocked on the door. Nathaniel said his grandfather let him in and began telling him that 'boys' were hanging around his house. According to Nathaniel, William cautioned him not to tell anyone else, because he was afraid that his relatives would think he was getting senile. Nathaniel claimed that he tried to reassure his grandfather that he was okay, and he would check the area for him. Code said he returned and was let back in. Nathaniel said he observed 'J. J.' and 'Eric' asleep in separate beds in one bedroom. After appeasing his grandfather, Nathaniel stated he left the residence and observed the front door get locked and the porch light turned off. Nathaniel claimed that this was the only time he had visited his grandfather in the last one and a half to two weeks, and that he was in the residence for a total of only ten minutes.

Detectives sensed that Nathaniel's statement was false and launched their investigation into his background.

They immediately ordered that Nathaniel's fingerprints be checked against those latent prints recovered from the Debra Ford scene. The point of entry into the Ford residence was determined to be the bathroom window. Fingerprints left on the window were consistent with someone entering the house from the outside and were inconsistent with someone standing in the bathroom and touching the window. The fingerprints had been left very recently. The fingerprints were matched to the defendant. Also, Code's finger and palm prints were matched to the latent palm prints found at the Chaney homicide. Later, bloodstain experts located a medium-velocity blood spatter on the tennis shoes worn by Code. Although the crime lab determined the blood to be human, there was an insufficient amount to do further typing.

Oscar Washington, a National Guard member, was jogging that morning at approximately 2:15 A.M. in the area where Henderson Street intersected with Seventy-second and Seventy-third Streets. As Washington jogged south on Henderson, he saw Nathaniel Code, whom he knew well. They spoke for a few minutes, with Code informing Washington that he was 'going to tend to some business.' Washington noticed Code had a little brown paper bag rolled up under his arm. Washington continued his run. Code headed north on Henderson, toward East Seventy-second Street.

About forty-five minutes later, Washington turned around and jogged north on Henderson Street. He again saw Code, this time between Seventy-third and Seventy-fourth Streets. Code, covered with blood, was heading south on Henderson. When Washington asked what happened, Code stated he and someone had 'got into it' and that 'he had come out on top' and had 'gotten even.' Code now carried a peppermint-striped bag. Code tried to sell Washington various things in the bag, including a knife Washington described as a dagger with a seven- to eight-inch blade, a handgun, credit cards, food stamps, and some marijuana. Washington noted the food stamps were smeared with blood.

Several days later, Washington again ran into Code. Code asked him, 'What did you see me do?' When Washington told Code he did not know what Code was talking about, Code gritted his teeth and balled his fists. Washington later testified at trial that Code had made the same gesture when Code saw Washington sworn in as a witness.

Although Washington heard about the Chaney homicides after they occurred, he did not know the details and did not immediately connect seeing Code that evening. But a neighbor, Ernest Demming, would later testify that he saw Code standing on the corner of Henderson and Seventy-second Street and staring at the Chaney house at 5:30 A.M. on July 19, 1985, before the bodies were discovered.

The police investigation built its circumstantial case against Nathaniel Code. It revealed that Nathaniel Code had been employed by a plumber from March 12 through the first week of July in 1985. A series of witnesses established that Code had never rented the Chaney residence at 213 East Seventy-second Street and had never done plumbing work in the house. Duct tape found in the nearby alley behind the Chaney residence, and the duct tape used to gag Carlitha Culbert were found to be chemically identical to duct tape later found in the search at Nathaniel Code's house. The pieces of tape either originated from exactly the same roll or from separate rolls made by the same company. It was professional-grade tape used only by plumbers and other professionals, unavailable at retail stores.

The two survivors of the Chaney murders did not testify. Both Maria and Tomika were examined by doctors prior to trial and found to be mildly mentally retarded. Tomika was interviewed several times by the police and by doctors. Thiopental sodium was administered in an effort to retrieve information about what she may have witnessed. She gave conflicting stories. The majority of the time, she stated one killer broke in the back door carrying a knife with holes in it and a rope. Tomika's drawing of the knife matched the description of a knife missing from Deborah Ford's house. She also gave other statements about the killer and 'ladies' breaking in that night and putting flies and spiders on the face of Billy Joe Harris.

Officers arriving on the scene found flies on Billy Joe Harris, and the coroner found evidence of postmortem roach bites on his face. Marla was generally withdrawn. By joint stipulation, the state and defense agreed not to call the girls as witnesses. Testimony regarding Tomika's differing statements and a videotape of Tomika's interview were admitted in evidence.

Donald Ray Johnson, William Code's neighbor, testified he saw Nathaniel Code exit William Code's residence sometime after 8:00 P.M. the night of the murders, which refuted the statement Nathaniel Code initially gave police detectives. Johnson saw Code shut the inner door and the iron bars, check to make sure they were locked, then walk out to a vehicle. Code drove down the street toward Johnson and stopped to say hello through the car window. Code introduced a female passenger in the car as his new wife, then the two drove off. Johnson thought the situation unusual because William Code always walked guests to the door to make sure the security doors were locked, and because he knew William Code would not allow Nathaniel Code into his house. Johnson had been present two weeks before, when William Code had refused to loan any more money to his grandson because Nathaniel Code had not paid him back the money he previously owed.

John Huckabee, an electrician who installed security lighting at the Code residence, testified about a conversation he had with William Code in which William Code stated he was afraid of his grandson and told of Nathaniel Code's attempt to borrow money from him in the past. William Code had refused to lend his grandson the money.

Police detectives obtained consent from Code's wife to search their residence. Among other items, police seized several cut electrical cords and professional-grade duct tape. Testimony was adduced that Nathaniel Code had approached several people seeking a loan just prior to the murders. The day before the bodies were found, Nathaniel Code had approached Shreveport narcotics officers and offered his services as a paid confidential informant. He indicated that he knew of persons who were dealing drugs and needed one hundred dollars to pay one of them.

The day the bodies were found, Nathaniel Code called his cousin Beatrice Holmes and invited her to his house. The two shared a gram of cocaine, which Code supplied, and then went to a liquor store where Code bought some beer. On the way home, he bought a second gram of cocaine from a dealer. Holmes and Code were snorting this cocaine when they were interrupted by a phone call informing them of William Code's death.

Holmes later testified that a grain of cocaine cost $150 at that time. The police found no money in the William Code house despite the fact he was known to have had between four and six hundred dollars in cash which, just prior to the murders, defendant Nathaniel Code had tried to borrow from his grandfather. Nathaniel Code had tried to borrow money from several persons, police learned, but was refused by all of them, including the victim William Code just before he was found murdered.

Why was Code eventually caught? Nathaniel Code violated the very first law of serial murder – the prime directive that governed the lives of Ted Bundy and Jeffrey Dahmer, the two most successful invisible serial killers of all time. Serial killers don't kill people who know them.

Serial killers know their victims but their victims don't know them. Kill a person with whom you have a relationship, especially a family member, and you might as well hang around your neck a neon sign that keeps flashing Suspect. Code, because he deluded himself into thinking that by this time he was not only completely invisible but invulnerable as well, made the cardinal mistake of murdering a family member. Once he did that he became an immediate suspect, because all family members of a murder victim are regarded by police as potential suspects. It's the first place they look in their investigation. Therefore, Nathaniel Code, who was on the outs with most of his family and who had tried unsuccessfully to borrow money from his grandfather right up to the day of the murder, became the sudden and obvious suspect in William Code's murder.

In the murder of William Code, I could readily see how the scenario might have played out. Nathaniel, needing money and unpopular with everyone around him, knew his grandfather had a few hundred dollars in the house. He knew the house, having grown up there, and knew where the old man probably kept his cash. It was also clear from what family members told police that Nathaniel had had no compunctions about beating his grandparents, so a threshold of violence had already been crossed. The stage was set. But what Nathaniel hadn't figured on was the presence of two small boys on the night he committed what he at first might have planned as a burglary. A desperate Nathaniel Code broke into his own childhood home and found two boys, images of him years earlier, perhaps, sleeping in a room he grew up in. Sadly, it makes a world of sense, given Code's signature of humiliation and torture, that he would force his grandfather to watch the murder of the little boys before he turned his rage on William Code and then fled into the night. This is why I suggested that the Nathaniel Code murders, which should have evolved into more difficult cases for the police to solve, fell backward in time with a signature killer committing a family murder – easily solved – because he was overpowered by his own rage at the crime scene.

But William Code was murdered by a killer who left an unmistakable signature. Not only were the ligatures almost exactly the same from crime to crime, but so was the violence perpetrated on the main victim and the way the killer seemed to manipulate the principal victim through the process of watching other victims die. So, if suspect Nathaniel Code, whom family members readily identified and placed right with the victim, looked good for the William Code murders, it was as if the police had hit the jackpot in solving the other signature murders in the series. What sealed it, of course, were the fingerprints that police processed at all the murder scenes. The suspect's prints matched. Of course, when the police ran Code's prints, they ultimately realized that they already had him on file from the previous times he'd been arrested. Where was his fingerprint file? Only eight months outside the cutoff date of ten years they'd arbitrarily imposed on themselves for the search. Just like Bundy, Dahmer, the Green River killer, the unknown signature killer was in their files all along and could have been picked up right after the first murder. But they never knew it.

CHAPTER 7

The Retaliation-to-Excitation Continuum

Steven Pennell

I found a very insidious aspect to the signature killer as the number of cases we could identify as signature murders seemed to abound right before our eyes. Like the rapist/sex offender, the signature killer's calling card appeared to evolve from crime to crime. While the core components such as necrophilia, torture, humiliation, bondage, or overkill remained present among crimes, certain components seem to jump out at you when you look at the crime scene. One focuses on bondage, while another killer gets turned on by torture or humiliation. Different killers emphasize different aspects of sadism. I soon realized that because the killer was truly a sex offender, he was committing crimes to get his rocks off, arouse him, and satisfy him sexually even if the satisfaction was so bizarre as to be ghoulish. Therefore, signature killers weren't just playing games with the police, they were playing games with themselves. As deviant as they were, they were nevertheless still experimenting sexually to see what types of violence and what kinds of victim reaction would turn them on. This is what made their signature dynamic instead of static.

The more cases you analyze, the more you also realize that you can just about see a timeline calling card imprinting itself from case to case. In each successive crime, the killer still incorporates aspects of the signature from the first cases, but his method is gradually evolving to encompass new things he wants to do. By looking at a crime scene carefully enough, you can actually track the entire history of the killer from crime one to the present. You can see what once turned him on, what he's abandoned, and what still turns him on. But worse, you can also predict where a killer will go along the psychopathological continuum. If he seems to be expending himself on overkill or if he is a necrophile, the chances are that he will be heading toward cannibalism because he's seeking greater satisfaction from the annihilation of his victim.

One specific direction I've noticed signature killers take as they mature, become successful at eluding police and abducting victims, and grow more careful in organizing each of their crimes scenes is that they seem to abandon evidence of retaliation upon their victims in favor of sexual excitation. This may seem like a paradox, given the amount of overkill and torture that most retaliatory killers inflict, but it's not. The difference between retaliation and excitation is in the way the killer converts his homicidal anger.

The retaliatory killer converts his anger to retaliation upon a symbolic victim who represents the ultimate target. The excitation converts his anger into sexual excitation and kills for the sexual thrill, not merely to execute revenge on the victim. Both types of crimes are anger-driven and control-governed, but it's the destination of the anger that helps define the killer's signature. How can a novice tell whether the crime scene belongs to an anger-retaliation or an anger-excitation killer? Usually, you can tell by what seems to have turned the killer on. If the killer turned the front of the body toward a wall so as to look away from him as he left the crime scene, then the killer was probably retaliatory. If the crime scene looks as though the killer spent time sexually manipulating the victim after death, then he was probably an excitation killer.

The Cottingham, Frampton, and Prince crime scenes were different from the anger-retaliatory crime scenes of Timothy Spencer. They were clearly anger-excitation crime scenes.

THE ANGER-EXCITATION REACTION

In an anger-excitation rape/homicide the signature calling card is usually sadism, and the sexual assault, either by itself or leading to homicide, is completely pre-planned. The rape is designed to inflict pain and terror on the victim, and during the commission of the crime, the predator's prolonged torture of the victim gratifies him, energizes his fantasy system, and temporarily satisfies his lust for control, domination, and mastery.

The killer's fantasy system is highly specialized. We can see this from the victim profile: Bundy chose all-American college coed types, Dahmer preyed on young gay men, the Green River killer picked streetwalkers and runaways. His lust whetted by his fantasy – both of the nature of his prey and the imminent process of the rape and murder – the predator first selects and then isolates his victim. He then springs his trap and escalates the violence of the sexual crime to incremental levels of ritualistic carnage. By stages, the killer approaches the victim and exploits his or her trust, simple naïveté, or sometimes outright greed. Bundy feigned an injury and asked for help; Dahmer offered his potential victims money to pose for him at his apartment-*cum*-photo studio; Gacy offered runaway boys the promise of a job with his company; maybe the Green River killer straight-out solicits hookers or offers runaways a ride, a drink, or a fix. But once the killer has his victims under his control, his torture and subsequent mutilation serve to appease his insatiable fantasy appetite. In other words, in the execution of the crimes, his excitement is heightened by the acting out of his researched scenario of eroticized anger and power, the playing out of the three *D*'s of sadism: dependency, degradation, and dread. This the killer does from encounter to encounter throughout the series, changing his MO perhaps, but leaving the same specific signature at every crime scene: victim profile, type of violence, and escalation of violence.

THE ANGER-EXCITATION HOMICIDAL PATTERN

The anger-excitation killer's homicidal pattern is characterized by a prolonged, bizarre, ritualistic assault on the victim. The killer has rehearsed the plan of action over and over again and often implements it with a well-equipped traveling murder kit or with tools gathered at the preselected murder scene. This thoughtful preplanning is also the mark of the organized murderer. The killer chooses a stranger who fits his needs in a sexually symbolic category – such as nurse, prostitute, child, student, or matriarch. The killer may be also attracted to victims who satisfy such fetishes as long hair, hair of a certain color, or hair of a certain style, or women who are particularly tall or particularly short. Some are attracted to specific clothing – especially short dresses or occupation-related uniforms – specific types of shoes, or specific cosmetics. Then there are killers who look for victims who display an outgoing demeanor or sexually aggressive personality, or victims who represent luxurious secondary sexual characteristics. This is a killer looking for sexual excitement based on anger but triggered by a fetish.

In his approach to his prey, this type of organized killer often displays a disarmingly charming manner that dispels the most immediate fears the victim would have facing a total stranger. The predator must isolate the victim quickly, usually by taking her away in his car, which, as in Bundy's case, might be specifically modified to entrap the victim once she's inside. If the predator is not already cruising in his car when he identifies his victim, he may make the contact on foot with the car close by for a quick abduction.

Once he's isolated the victim, the killer will begin to display vacillating mood shifts which confuse the victim, who will eventually become terrorized, activating the predator's fantasy system to its next phase. Now the killer implements his bondage/domination scenario, gradually building up its intensity and adding to it his various ritualistic components, including bondage devices and weapons, clothing or decoration, and specific scenarios involving dialogue, submission of the victim, and expressions of terror and fear. The killer is almost always methodical even though he demonstrates his passion for torture through specific acts of escalating violence. For example, in addition to antemortem cutting, the infliction of severe bruises or contusions, and attempts at various forms of incomplete strangulation, the victim's body may also reveal signs of washing, shaving, or burns. Each category of violence has a special sexual significance for the killer and either turns him on or prompts a reaction in the victim that will turn him on.

For the killer, the issue is always sex and sexual control as an expression of anger. The most complete control available to the serial killer is over a dead victim. The various stages of violence leading to the victim's death excite the killer but are only the means to an end rather than the end themselves. Therefore, although the killer may attempt sex with his victim just prior to the point of death or on the verge of unconsciousness, a signature which may indicate the vestiges of a rapist-turned-killer, the evidence of ejaculant in the body is not likely.

However, after the victim has been bludgeoned and manually strangled, the likelihood of the killer's post-mortem experimental sexual activity will increase.

In most cases, the signature murderer will sexually explore the victim's dead body, and we know this because the evidence of such exploration is revealed by specific localized areas of obvious and deliberate brutalization, lacerations of the skin, and foreign objects that have been inserted into the body's sexual orifices. In addition, a signature killer may leave his victim's body in a bizarre state of undress and in a posed position after possibly cutting off clothing parts. In some cases, the clothing could be a fetish item taken as a souvenir or ritualized totem to reinvigorate the killer between his crimes. Just as likely, in some case histories the killers will leave the clothing neatly folded alongside the body as if to demonstrate not only their control over the helpless victim, but a reverence for the act of undressing the victim carefully. In these cases, it is as if the killer has imparted some ritualistic significance to the garments that covered the victim's body.

The amount and level of sexual activity the killer has with his dead victim are very specific indicators of his signature. Depending upon the nature of the killer, his experimentation in one crime may lay the groundwork for possible style modification in the next crime. Within limits, these violent people can be creative, and their creativity can sometimes throw police completely off the track. For example, killers can experiment with different ways of dumping their victims. A flowing river or forest scavengers might hasten the job of decay, or, as in the Arthur Shawcross murders, the killer himself will carve up the corpse according to his feelings for the victim. No matter how much the experimentation varies, however, I believe that signature killers grow in their ability to master control over themselves and the crime scene.

The more sophisticated the sadist becomes, the less

likely you're going to find ejaculate or any overt sexual activity on the victim or at the crime scene. In an anger-excitation reaction-generated signature murder, the killer's supreme satisfaction is achieved not at the moment when the victim lies helpless under his control – as in many rape scenarios – but long after when the killer has disposed of the body and goes home alone with his thoughts and his trophies. He enjoys what he's doing, and he takes such items as clothing or body parts so that he can masturbate later and satisfy himself sexually as an experience separate from the homicide. This is another aspect of the killer's need for control and one of the keys to understanding the nature of anger excitation. The killer's sexual climax must be completely under his control, and for that to happen, the victim must be physically inert until the killer is the only one who exists in his universe. The killer needs only the thrill of the victim he controls, either the vivid memory of the event or the physical items he has taken, to stimulate his climax. It is exactly as if the signature killer is feeding emotionally and visually from the experience of exerting control and domination over a victim. The energy derived from the murder – itself only a means to this end – is reinvigorated by the trophies the killer has taken from his helpless victims. Because these items now have a special significance by virtue of their ability to stimulate sexual arousal, they become part of the killer's ritual, like primitive totems, and literally sustain him from kill to kill.

Thus, in a ghoulish version of a relativity theory of murder, the predator's primal anger – increased by his reduced social inhibitions and his proximity to and involvement with a constant victim pool – is expressed as an assertion of ante- and postmortem control over his victims. Either lower social inhibitions and/or a proximity to or involvement with a victim pool increases the control over his victims. This primal anger, increased exponentially by decreased inhibitions or greater proximity to a pool of victims, is converted into an ongoing series of sexual orgasms achieved as a result of that control and sustained from kill to kill by the items taken from his victims and coveted sexually in the privacy of the killer's own lair. In the killer's vision, the innocence of life in his victims in combination with his anger is transformed into pure sexual energy. This energy is the killer's life force which he lives to sustain.

Dependent upon his internal stresses, the level of his anger, and the availability of victims whose mere appearance can drive him into a frenzy, a killer will repeat his crime on a sporadic or episodic schedule. His motivation for further domination and exploration for new victims may wax and wane depending upon the satisfaction he's able to sustain by reliving his most recent crime, but his drive is always persistent. The predator has linked his satisfaction from the crimes directly to his ego and measures himself by the amount of the gratification he receives, the lengths he has gone to at the arc of each crime to achieve that gratification, and his ability to sustain it. This is why it is unsurprising that signature criminals are usually loners with only a thin mask of sociability that enables them to playact at life. At their very core, these people shun living human contact except for the times when they are stalking and killing their prey.

Signature killers also reinvigorate themselves by returning to the sites of their dumping grounds and spending time with their victims' bodies. These corpses, too, have become totems – objects invested with a ritualistic magical pull on the killer – because they carry the power to restimulate the predator. Depending on how organized he is, the killer can move the body one, two, or three times after the initial kill. Although the body can be buried in a shallow grave, it could also be dumped in a location considered neutral for the perpetrator, especially if the site is so secluded the killer believes it will never be discovered. In other instances, he may slaughter the body, butchering it like a meat cutter, and keep the pieces as a souvenir. This is certainly what Jeffrey Dahmer talked about when he made his confessions to police. I will never forget his descriptions of wearing the shoulder muscles of one of his victims as if they were a costume. He took the totem to chilling lengths.

The crime scene is of vital importance to the anger-excitation signature killer because it's the place where he can least afford to be careless. Accordingly, he takes special care in organizing the crime scene to minimize any additional evidence. Location is also of extreme importance. Except in the cases of Jeffrey Dahmer and John Gacy, who had human remains at their homes, the crime scene is usually very separate and distant from the killer's everyday activities. It is also far away from where he will eventually dump the bodies, a place the killer will return to from time to time to interject himself into the criminal investigation and gain a ritualistic thrill from being there. This will provide even greater excitement for the killer, because only he knows the secret the police are scouring for. Finally, when his crime has been completed, the killer will carefully repack his ropes, knives, and specialized tools of torture into his murder kit for safekeeping until the next time he needs them.

THE I–40 MURDERS

One of the prototypes of an anger-excitation signature killer is Steven Pennell. He had a job as a mechanical construction tradesman and sustained the ability to segment his life into a quiet half with his family and a violent half spent trolling for prostitute victims. Pennell, in his dark van cruising the Delaware interstates for victims, fit an almost too-perfect profile of the killer on the move.

Serial killers troll; they're always in motion, because that's how they come upon murder sites, victim pools, and body dump sites. Even those who operate in circumscribed areas, such as neighborhood killers Cleophus Prince or Nathaniel Code, are always on the move in a connect-the-dots life, and that's one of the signature hallmarks of their lifestyle. So it's no surprise that even tiny Delaware became a killing zone when Steven Pennell left his mark by torturing and killing several women seventeen years after Richard Cottingham had done similar things to his murder victims in New York and New Jersey.

The Steven Pennell case also marked the first time that John Douglas of the FBI's Behavioral Sciences Unit appeared as an expert about the signature aspects of a killer when he testified about the rarity of certain types of wounds to a female body. He talked about the brutality of the killer when he said that even though the infliction of various wounds upon each victim was different, the fact remains that the victims were alive when they received those wounds, and this was central to the killer's signature. The torturing of victims requires 'a very unique individual,' he testified, 'who wants to keep his victims alive during the assault.' Agent Douglas understood, as few people can, the very precise meaning of torturing live victims and what that says about a killer like Pennell. As in the cases of Frampton, Prince, Cottingham, and Code, the central theme in the Pennell cases was anger and power, not necessarily sexual assault. The absence of the primary mechanisms of sexual assault – satisfaction and gratification – was significant. It tells investigators that they are looking for a guy who's working through an arc of anger, not one who's looking to have an orgasm over a pleading victim.

Shirley Annette Ellis

The series of murders in Delaware began with the homicide of Shirley Ellis. On November 29, 1987, a desultory evening just a month after the worst stock market plunge in recent history, two teenagers were looking for a place to park at about 9:25 P.M. It was the Sunday after Thanksgiving, and as an east coast chill drove across Delaware Bay, the teenagers cruised onto a construction site off Albee Road, a pretty rough area and desolate after dark, which was located behind the Iron Industrial Park in Newark, Delaware. Instead of finding a place to park, they found the body of a defiled murder victim.

As they drove onto the site, they found the victim's body, openly observable to passers-by, approximately three to four feet off an unfinished roadway. Partially clad and left there in the open in a position that could only be interpreted as sexually degrading, the victim was lying on her back with her aqua blue pants pulled down all the way to her ankles, her blue denim jacket and shirt pulled open, and her white brassiere cut in front, leaving her breasts exposed.

Ligature strangulation marks were clearly visible on her neck, and the garroting evidence of binding was etched in dried blood and bruises into her wrists and ankles. In addition, the victim had a piece of black duct tape stuck in her hair. Had it been used to cover her mouth and stuck to the strands of hair when the killer ripped it off? Investigators quickly surmised that the victim had been killed elsewhere and dumped where she was found. It was also apparent that the victim had not been at the body discovery scene for any extended period of time, because there were no physical signs of a disturbance on the ground or in the area around the body. When a body has been at a dump site for any extended period, animals begin to pull at its decaying flesh as they consume it, body fluids leech into the surrounding soil, and all kinds of predators leave tracks in the bushes or weeds. Newly dumped bodies discovered only a couple of hours after they've been dropped look as though they're lying right on the surface of the ground and have not become a part of the microenvironment where they were found. This was the condition in which Shirley's body was found.

Shirley Annette Ellis, a white female born on July 7, 1964, was seen for the last time earlier in the evening of November 29, 1987, at 5:55 P.M. She was walking along US. Route 40 at the entrance to Brookmont Farms and heading towards Wilmington to visit a sick friend in the hospital. She was carrying a Thanksgiving platter of food for the friend. Shirley was a known prostitute and drug user who frequented the high-traffic Route 13 and Route 40 corridor, a key network of support roads near the dense Northeast interstates carrying traffic between New York City, Philadelphia, Baltimore, and Washington, D.C. She was a walker and hitchhiker, thumbing rides from whomever pulled up alongside, which is exactly what she was doing when last seen. Her body was found approximately four miles from where she was last seen and approximately three miles from where the killer, Steven Pennell, lived.

Under the supervision of Dr. Jonathan Arden of the Delaware State Medical Examiner's Office, an autopsy was performed on November 30, 1987, in Wilmington, Delaware. Dr. Arden's conclusions were that Shirley Ellis suffered nipple mutilation to one breast, she had been bound at the feet and ankles, and she had three distinctive cylindrical blows to the head – the signature of a hammer. There were no signs of sexual assault, but she had been tortured *prior* to death, which the ME was able to determine from the presence of antemortem injuries, which were a reddish blue and showed evidence of having bled. It seemed clear that the killer had been determined to inflict pain on a suffering, terrified victim rather than act out his rage on a dead victim. The cause of death was ruled to be blunt force trauma to the head as well as ligature strangulation.

Analysis of the Shirley Ellis Murder

Shirley Ellis's murder case contained several distinctive features that were rarely found in any murder investigation. When I examine murder cases and sift through evidence, I look for those characteristics of murder that are considered rare and unusual, over and beyond what the killer did to commit a routine murder. This way I can predict whether I think the killer might strike again. In addition, I look for the goal of the killer. In cases like these, it is the power of conquest, achieved through the actual physical mechanism of control expressed as a series of actions which exact and exert control, and potent ritualisms that reinforce the killer's thrill of mastery long after the crime has been committed.

This murder had three such unique and significant characteristics which together are not found in other murders and reflect the power of conquest. The first unique feature was that Ellis was bound by unknown devices before death and the binding implements were removed after the killer was finished. Obviously, the more terror the victim feels, the more heightened and intense is the killer's experience. The thing to remember about bondage is that it is also a form of control when it's an actual primary part of the crime, and not just a means to restrain victims from escaping or turning on their attackers. As a simple restraint to prevent escape, bondage is a secondary aspect of the crime. Besides the abrasion-type evidence of bondage present on Ellis's wrists and ankles, there were also ligature strangulation marks on her neck. The killer in the Ellis case restricted the movement of Ellis while she was living, as a part of the ritualistic operation of the crime. This was a display of the killer's need to control a living victim so as to build up the anticipation of becoming sexually gratified. Bondage killers also play out the tension of keeping the victim alive and in restraint. In this case also, the killer moved Ellis from bondage through torture and, finally, humiliation.

The second unique component of Ellis's murder was overkill. As the previous cases here have shown, overkill involves multiple causes of death, any one of which could have been the proximate reason for it. For instance, in the Ellis case, the ligature strangulation could have killed her as well as the three hammerlike blows she received to the top of her head. Undoubtedly, this type of overkill signified an organized effort which simply was necessary to satisfy the killer's angst. It didn't really matter to the assailant what actually killed his victim. His anger was too intense. It was so intense, actually, that the killer was almost robotic, acting out a sequence of demands regardless of whether the victim actually suffered from the coup de grâce in each mechanism of death. Nothing evidences the killer's hatred for his victim more than an overkill which progresses or escalates from crime to crime. We would expect that the next victim of the Ellis killer would demonstrate additional hatred characteristics.

The third significant characteristic of murder was the absence of ejaculate. Like Richard Cottingham before him, Ellis's killer was a highly sophisticated sadist whose entire method of gratification involved the process of control. Pennell enjoyed accomplishing the power of control over his victim so much that he saved his sexual expression for later. In addition, the presence of overkill meant that the violence was more important than the sexual gratification to Pennell and that the personality of the victim herself was not the important aspect of the crime. In fact, it was only her unfortunate fate to have been where she was at just the right time that made her a victim. It was the commission of excessively violent acts that drove the emotion of the killer. Through his actions, the killer might also be trying to kill a form of control over himself that he perceives the victim type as being able to exercise. The absence of ejaculate and the presence of pattern-type injuries around Ellis's upper right breast is significant. The sadistic biting of Ellis's breast satisfied the killer's increasing lust for domination, control, and possession as well as his almost feral need to inflict a physically disfiguring wound with an instrument as intimate as his lips, tongue, and teeth. He needed to taste the wound.

The most extraordinary finding about bondage, overkill, and the absence of sexual assault was that for all three factors to be present in the same murder is truly a rare phenomenon. I would almost certainly predict that if the same factors show up in another murder nearby, the murders would most likely be committed by the same person. The Delaware police would soon have another case.

Catherine DiMauro

Catherine Ann DiMauro, a white female born December 26, 1956, was last seen on June 28, 1988, at 11:30 P.M. She was dropped off by a friend at the entrance to her home at the Greenfield Manor Apartments after being picked up hitchhiking along U.S. Route 40 in the area of Route 896. It had been over seven months since the body of Shirley Ellis was discovered. Like Ellis, DiMauro's main mode of transportation was walking or hitchhiking, and she was known as a former lunch-wagon driver with a police record of prostitution arrests.

The next day at about 6:15 in the morning, workers arriving at the Fox Run home construction site located off of U.S. Route 40 at Route 72 found the body of DiMauro. It was lying on the edge of a dirt access road in plain view, just like the body of Shirley Ellis, openly displayed and in a position where she would quickly be found by any passersby. As in the Ellis case, it didn't appear that any type of assault took place at the body recovery site, because the killer's activities would have been recorded in the smooth dirt surface. DiMauro was simply left there in the open to decompose or wait to be found. However, because of the ideal smooth dirt surface, the tire impressions on the road were very clear to investigators and would come in handy later when it was time to match them to the tires on the suspect's vehicle. Investigators concluded that these had all the prima facie indicators of a series, because both bodies were dumped where they were found, and they were both killed elsewhere.

Unlike Shirley Ellis, DiMauro was completely nude, lying on her back. None of her clothing was found at the crime scene. Both arms were positioned at right angles to her sides and one leg was bent back at the knee. A watch was still secured to her left wrist. At first, it appeared to investigators that the killer had stripped the victim clean of any physical evidence. But like the black tape found in the hair of Shirley Ellis, a piece of gray duct tape was discovered in the hair of Catherine DiMauro. In addition, this time there were blue fibers covering her body from head to toe.

The autopsy report of DiMauro could have easily been construed as Ellis's, since they bore so many similarities. DiMauro suffered from abrasions around her hands and ankles as if she had been bound at one time, then the killer removed the bindings. The familiar signs of ligature strangulation were present about her neck. Exactly like Ellis, three distinctive cylindrical blows (hammerlike) were struck to DiMauro's head. The final diagnosis for DiMauro read like Ellis's: (1) strangulation (ligature mark of neck and petechiae of conjunctivae), (2) blunt head trauma (lacerations of the right temporal, parietal, and occipital scalp; depressed skull fracture with linear extension to the anterior base of the skull; subarachnoid hemorrhage, mild; and facial abrasions and contusions), (3) contusions and abrasions of the right breast and scattered contusions and abrasions of extremities and trunk, and (4) contusions of the buttocks. The investigators had a series on their hands, and they moved into action accordingly.

Police Take the Offensive

On July 1, 1988, the police went public by announcing that they had begun looking into similarities between the Ellis and DiMauro killings. Unbeknownst to the public and as consequence of the Ellis and DiMauro murders, the police began a decoy operation along a highway corridor which the victims and other prostitutes were known to frequent. As part of the operation, female police officers wearing hidden microphones were dressed as prostitutes and engaged in conversations with men who stopped for them. The officers were not permitted to enter the vehicles of these men, but if the occasion arose, they would reach inside any vehicles with blue carpets and remove carpet samples.

On August 28, 1988, the ongoing investigation along the Route 40 corridor was rocked with the disappearance of yet another prostitute, named Margaret Finner, an eighteen-year-old white female. Finner was standing along the roadway of Route 13 soliciting clients. She was last seen at 11:30 P.M. getting into a windowless blue van with rounded headlights heading southbound on U.S. Route 13. An eyewitness described the operator only as a white male. Finner was reported missing by her parents with whom she lived. This information was incorporated by police into their investigation and decoy operation. Finner was eventually found murdered, but prosecutors felt that there was insufficient evidence linking their eventual suspect, Steven Pennell, to the crime.

Then came a break in the case from the decoy operation. On September 14, 1988, almost a year after Ellis was discovered, Officer Renee Lano, working decoy along Route 40, saw a blue van cruise past her seven times as if it were stalking her. Officer Lano called in the tag number of the van and learned that it was registered to Steven Pennell. Thinking possibly that she had a strike on her line, Lano moved to a darker area of Route 40 in the hope of luring the stalking blue van into stopping. It worked. The driver stopped for her. From the front seat, a man motioned for Lano to enter the van. She approached but did not enter the vehicle. Instead, she spoke with the driver, later identified as Steven Pennell, engaging him a casual but distanced conversation. Her suspicions became aroused and she took a good look inside the van, thinking that she might be talking with either a suspect or someone who knew who the killer might be. That was when she became stunned at the bright blue carpeting covering the interior of the man's van. Was this blue carpet, now almost blinking at her from the van, the source of the same blue fibers found covering DiMauro's body? Could she be staring into the actual vehicle that whisked away three women from these very same streets? Without tipping off the driver, Lano surreptitiously reached inside the van and pulled at the carpet, removing some of the fibers from the carpet.

Kathleen Anne Meyer

Before any arrests could be made, there were still more victims. The disappearance of Kathleen Meyer, a white female born on March 24, 1962, led investigators to believe that she was probably a victim of the same killer who had murdered Ellis, DiMauro, and possibly Finner. Kathleen Meyer was last seen walking toward Route 40 from her residence on Saturday September 18, 1988, at 9:30 P.M., four days after Officer Lano had made contact with what she believed might be the suspect vehicle. Later that evening an off-duty Wilmington police officer observed a white female, possibly Meyer, enter Steven Pennell's blue Ford van (Delaware license number RV2059). The frustrating part for detectives was that Kathleen Meyers' body was not immediately found.

Michelle Gordon

While police investigators were getting the blue fibers taken from Pennell's van compared to fibers from the DiMauro crime scene, Michelle Ann Gordon, a twenty-two-year-old white female, disappeared and was last seen Monday, September 19, 1988, at approximately 8:30 P.M. She was loitering in the area of Bill's Friendly Tavern, located well within the Route 13 and Route 40 corridor. The area was widely reputed to be a prostitute pickup location. The victim was reputed to engage extensively in prostitution and was said to be heavily involved in cocaine use as well. Gordon mostly resided in motels within this corridor.

The next day, Tuesday, September 20, 1988, at 10:12 A.M., Michelle Gordon's body was discovered lying on the rock shoal of the Chesapeake and Delaware Canal banks, by a passing boater who observed it clearly from the water. The body recovery site was a tidal waterway which was accessible on both sides by a dirt road that twisted off the main streets to an area not frequented by anyone but fishermen and homeless people. This canal area was desolate, with no businesses or residences within earshot, and was easily within ten minutes travel time from where Steven Pennell and Michelle Gordon resided. The police determined that the scene where the victim was found was not the site of the murder. No evidence was located in this area.

Michelle Gordon was nude and facedown. Soft-tissue areas of her face were missing, which showed she was submerged in the water for a period of time. At the scene, detectives saw abrasions around the victim's wrists and ankles, indicating that she had been bound before death. The entire nipple of her left breast had been cut or bitten away. The buttocks showed extensive antemortem bruising with signs of a cylindrical instrument being used to cause those injuries. Superficial lacerations were seen on the rear of both legs; some began in the lower portion of the buttock and ran to the lower portion of the thigh.

On September 20, 1988, Dr. Jonathan Arden performed an autopsy on the victim. Although the classification of death was ruled a homicide, the actual mechanism of death was undetermined. However, cocaine use was listed as a contributing factor. Dr. Arden noted the following: (1) contusions of the buttocks, probably by a cylindrical object; (2) focal contusions of the anterior hip, lower back, left upper arm, and anterior right knee, and superficial abrasions and scratches of the right forearm and knee; (3) bandlike contusions of the wrists and ankles, consistent with binding; (4) the absence of a left nipple, probably cut postmortem; (5) intravenous drug use; (6) no evidence of sexual assault; and (7) superficial cuts of both buttocks down the thighs, in a linear fashion.

The medical examiner concluded that Gordon was the victim of a homicide, but because her body had been submerged in water, no determination could be made as to the exact cause of death. She was definitely ruled a victim of homicidal violence, though, and injuries inflicted on Gordon's body were very similar to those found on both Ellis and DiMauro.

On September 23, 1988, the Delaware State police and New Castle County police investigation grew into a serial-killer task force in response to three murders and one missing person's report. The very act of forming a task force immediately placed a drain on staffing and resources for those two agencies. Police administrators typically pull from areas where the street crime units will not be impacted. After the Gordon discovery, the police began twenty-four-hour surveillance of Steven Pennell, whose tags had come up during the search requested by Officer Lano on decoy detail. Even though the police had formed a major force to search for the killer, and the killer was well aware of it, Pennell was observed repeatedly cruising the same area of the highway corridor that was the site of the decoy operation. It was clear to police surveying Pennell that the killer's control had reached far beyond the victims and now included the police and media. Typically, this is when the killer is most vulnerable, because he's no longer invisible; he knows the police are trailing him and feels he can defeat them because he's exerting control. When the killer feels in control of the situation around him, he tends to make mistakes, and that's when his risk of getting caught is greatest.

On September 30, 1988, the police stopped Pennell for a traffic offense. A search of his van uncovered a bloodstain. Blue fibers and swatches of red cloth were taken from the van, all thought to be similar to the blue and red fibers found on the body of Catherine DiMauro. Search warrants were subsequently issued for Pennell's trailer, shed, vehicles, and person. Pursuant to these warrants, police seized a buck knife which was in the suspect's pocket, eight pairs of pliers, a bag of unused flexcuffs, and two rolls of duct tape.

Margaret Finner

On November, 12, 1988, at 10:30 A.M. the body of Margaret Finner was discovered by two hunters approximately three to four feet off the roadway which runs along the Chesapeake and Delaware Canal about one mile east of the St. Georges Bridge in South St. Georges.

Her remains were severely decomposed and they were mostly skeletonized from the thigh region up, including her skull. She was found nude, lying on her back, and although close to the road, was concealed by tall weeds. Dr. Jonathan Arden concluded that the victim died as a result of a homicide, but the cause of could not be determined. Owing to the similarities of the circumstances under which the victim was last seen and the area where she was last seen, Dr. Arden felt that this case was related to the other Pennell cases.

In the affidavit for probable cause to search Pennell's van, much of the offering of proof relied on Officer Lano's belief that probable cause exists if the facts would make a reasonably cautious person believe that the item in plain view is useful as evidence in a crime.

Officer Lano's information, which led her to believe that the blue fibers from the van's carpet might be useful as evidence, was extensive. She knew that a van matching Pennell's was used in at least one abduction, and that DiMauro's body was found covered in blue fibers which are most often found in carpet. In addition, the FBI had given the police a profile of the person they thought was responsible for the murders. The profile described the individual as a white male, between twenty-five and thirty-five years of age, probably in the construction or building trades, and residing in the general vicinity of the crimes. In their conversation at the van, Officer Lano elicited personal information from Pennell which coincided with the FBI profile.

APPEAL ATTACKS THE SIGNATURE TESTIMONY

Attorneys for Steven Pennell contended that Agent Douglas's testimony went beyond the scope of the trial court's ruling. The trial court permitted Agent Douglas to testify as to the 'signature' aspects of the crime, but would not allow the introduction of 'profile' evidence. Profile evidence is that which attempts to link the general characteristics of serial murderers to the specific characteristics of the defendant. Such evidence, Pennell's lawyers argued, does not advance the search for truth, while at the same time it can be extremely prejudicial to the defendant, who is in a sense being accused by a witness who was not present at any of the crimes.

Attorneys for Pennell argued that Douglas's testimony that the perpetrator was 'not youthful' impermissibly implicated Pennell, who then was thirty-two years old. Upon examining the context of the comment, however, members of the Supreme Court of Delaware were satisfied that Douglas's statement was not improper. Douglas noted the sophistication of the crimes, which tended to negate their commission by an inexperienced youth. Thus, he stated, 'We are not talking about, well, a youthful type of offender.' 'Youthful' was in reference to the criminal experience of the perpetrator rather than his age. Moreover, Douglas never gave an age range for the offender, and 'youthful' is open to numerous interpretations. Thus, under all of the circumstances the court was satisfied that Douglas did not impermissibly interject profile evidence into the case.

Douglas further testified that the victims were alive when they received their wounds, even though the infliction of those wounds was a little different on each. It is a very, very unique type of individual who wants to keep his victim alive during that type of prolonged and painful physical assault, Douglas said. He went on to say that the killer obviously was maintaining control over the crime scene and had no fear of detection. He also had his victim under such control that her screams of pain and terror didn't unnerve him. Quite the contrary, the typical signature killer's blows serve only to make him angrier until he works through his arc of fury. The suffering of the victim intensifies that experience and thus serves to drive the fury even further, until the anger crashes like a wave and abates.

The lack or absence of sexual assault is also hard to understand even though there is a clear reason behind what the killer is doing. The physical signature on the victim shows that the general themes driving the killer are anger and power, not the craving for on-the-spot sexual satisfaction. Anger and power were related physically by the assailant's removal of the victim's nipple, the scars from ligature marks, and the physical evidence of binding. The binding was also significant in that all four appendages were involved. Police also believed that the assailant quickly rendered his victim unconscious so he could tie them up without too much of a fight. What this also reveals is that there has to be some transportation involved from the pickup site to the murder site, and finally to the body recovery site.

At Pennell's trial, the signature testimony also concluded that the victim did not die swiftly. The defendant wanted to spend time with the victim, and therefore wanted to transport the victim to an area where he could spend as much time as he wished to do whatever he was inclined to. In addition, there was a degree of sophistication: mobility on the part of the offender, careful bindings on both wrists, and a special attention paid by the killer to the victim's breast where the wounds were fixated. This was not the signature of an unsophisticated or novice offender who was tentatively improvising his way through the crime. This was a veteran assailant who understood control, felt the need to exercise it, and knew exactly how to take it. Therefore, we were not talking about a youthful offender.

FBI Agent John Douglas summarized the signature aspects of breast-nipple mutilation as extremely unique. He said it was the subject's ritual that he had to do time and time again, because it was critical to his working out of the crime. The bindings went beyond binding for just transportation. They had a significance that imparts power to the killer and therefore had to be considered as a kind of ritual. The bindings served to excite the killer sexually; they became an archetypal moment of the crime which the killer had to complete before he actually began to assault the victim, leading to death. It was, he said, principally the aim of the assailant to manipulate, dominate, and control his victims.

A good signature investigator always learns to separate the signature – the part of the crime the killer does not control – from the modus operandi, the carrying out of the crime which is under the killer's control. In the Pennell murders, the dissimilarities in crimes were related to his modus operandi and not to his signature. The different dump sites did not reveal a concerted effort to conceal the bodies. Pennell understood that sooner or later these victims would be found. Thus, he dumped them in desolate areas where no one would see him with the victims. One cannot link whether the victim has been dressed or unclothed. That too, was catch-as-catch-can, because Pennell left them as he left them and not as he wanted them to be discovered. And the head trauma was different for each victim, too, because the specific forms of head trauma weren't part of the signature. Head trauma qua head trauma was important only because of the way the killer expressed his anger. Conversely, there was evidence of tools in each case, whether it was a pinching tool or hammer. The key areas to focus on for the signature are the extent and nature of the wounds, the use of bindings, and the prerequisite that the victim is alive when she received these injuries.

The postmortem cutting of the nipple with regard to the third victim was not part of the MO. That is part of the ritual, and the killer's focal area was the breast, which still made it unique even though with the third victim the injury was postmortem. The injuries to the nipple area for the first two, and the beating of the buttock area of the third one, were the focal areas.

At the trial, it was reported in the *Wilmington News-Journal* on November 1, 1991, that Judge Richard Gebelein ruled that the state had proved the statutory aggravating circumstances – one being that the murder of Gordon was 'outrageously and wantonly vile, horrible, and inhuman in that it involved torture . . .' – and that they outweighed any mitigating circumstances. Pennell showed no reaction as Gebelein read his decision. His mother sobbed uncontrollably. 'The evidence shows that in a coldly premeditated fashion, Defendant abducted Michelle Gordon,' Gebelein said. 'He held her in captivity alone and afraid. He bound her hand and foot. He tortured her. He murdered her, mutilated and disposed of her body.

'The victim . . . experienced terror, fear, pain, and hopelessness. . . . Her suffering and death call for retribution,' said Gebelein. 'In the case of Kathleen Meyer . . . we know only that she died at the hands of the defendant, and probably died in his van. Her death calls for retribution.

'The enormity of these two crimes, their cold-blooded premeditation, and their callous execution clearly outweigh any mitigating factors,' Gebelein said. Pennell was sentenced to the death penalty. Later, led past all the cameras and shouting reporters to a waiting prison van, Pennell only smiled.

THE PATHOLOGICAL APPROACH TO THE KILLER'S MODUS OPERANDI AND SIGNATURE

While preparing their murder kits for organized excursions into their fantasy life and murderous episodes of reality which they consider fun, most serial offenders keep their goals in mind and sort out what worked in the past and look for methods of improvement for the future. That is, after progressing through earlier phases of learning and discarding obsolete MO elements, the killer selects what is and is not critical to him at the crime scenes. In these Delaware cases, the focus for the operative pathologies which highlighted the killer's signature is reflected in the ascendancy and range of the cusp in the sadistic arc of violent behavior. Sometimes the signature was intermingled and codependent with MO factors. But the pathological features which adorned the killer's signature in each one of these murders were evident in the following intrinsic behavioral patterns: the arc of dominance–submission, the use of bondage as discipline, and the acts of picquerism.

A highly prevalent feature of the killer's signature in each of these cases was the killer's dominance-submission continuum over the victim. The ritual series of dominating actions necessary to incapacitate and render the victim submissive were precedent conditions and stimulants for the killer's perceived needs of potency and power. Once ritualized with signs and symbols, the sum effect is greater than the parts.

At the beginning of the Delaware series, the choice of prostitute victims may have been primarily a function of Pennell's MO factor of easy availability. However, as time progressed, the omission of any other types of victims indicated that he targeted a certain type of victim for his own internal satisfaction. In the world of predator and prey, the killer's interest is higher when he's doing combat with a worthy foe. In these murders, the notion of outwitting and maneuvering the purveyors of rental romance of the streets may have been the onset for Pennell's developing desire to ensnare, trap, and crush the victims. Hence, the killer's signature over time became more activated through the pathology of dominance and submission over prostitutes. This is important because it does not mean that prostitutes were easy prey merely because of their profession. It meant that the killer saw a special test in bringing women he perceived as strong and challenging to a state of true submission through terror and pain. He was not choosing them just because they were acting a role they'd gotten paid for. Pennell wanted the real thing and killed to get it.

Like the signature of Richard Cottingham before him, Steven Pennell's signature feature of dominance and submission over his victims fits a clear pattern compatible with the other deviant forms of violence he perpetrated against these victims, such as specialized torture, prolonged terror, and physical and emotional humiliation. In the killer's administration of pain, angst, and despair, his signature and MO dovetailed so that each supported the other. For example, the use of a hammerlike instrument in each case showed the effectiveness of his tool choice – which worked – and at the same time, the perpetrator benefited from the effect it created for the victim.

Eventually when three blows to a victim's head were no longer satisfactory, the killer changed his MO to include arms, back, knees, and pelvis. Again, while Pennell's signature for pain remained constant, his method of operation was expanded and modified. Considering the hammer attacks on each of the victims, it was significant to note the value of that to the killer. That is, while taped and bound, the victims were systematically pummeled with the weapon to cause a maximum amount of torturous pain. As a result, the victims reported back to the killer with muffled screams and moans. This was a stimulus/response reaction from the hammer blows to targeted areas of the body. After all this, despite the physical incapacitation of each victim, it was noteworthy that as the MO became more elaborate and dynamic, the killer struck those areas of the body that represented strength. Those areas were rich with bones and nerves which yielded a maximum amount of sensory stimulation.

Adjunctive in the killer's mind to the satisfaction he received from seeing the direct cause and effect of pain he was inflicting with each blow, the messages of resistance and submission were translated by each victim via visual, tactile, and auditory feedback. They visibly suffered, they shuddered and flinched at each blow, and they cried out in pain. For an anger-driven predator seeking retaliation on a surrogate victim, what the feedback represented was the central core of the killer's pathological satisfaction. In particular, it seemed that the strength of his attachment to sounds of torture were indicated in the case of Margaret Finner. It appeared that she died prematurely before his interests in screams and moans could sate his needs. Inasmuch as his needs could not be met with a quiet body, he discarded her and sought out a live victim less than three weeks later. Some serial killers choose to strike in a very short time after one murder because they are not satisfied in some way from the last kill. In my talks with Ted Bundy, he once told me that a short time between murders meant that the killer 'was very intense.'

The killer's interest in the response of moaning caused by acts of torture augmented with sensory supplements was a strong indication that the sound was also arousing him sexually. The more the victim moaned or cried, the more it indicated her submission to his dominance and the more it turned him on. Moaning is a common sexual fetish that men who frequent prostitutes demand, and most prostitutes go along with it. In ninety percent of the encounters, it's only acting. When the johns actually get violent to elicit groaning and cries of pain, it represents a criminally deviant sexual crime. Pennell elicited these responses through torture that he inflicted with specific tools. Eventually, the tools themselves had the power to arouse him sexually. Thus, they became ritualized. We saw this signature in the Michelle Gordon murder, where Pennell inflicted pain on her through the use of a tool while she was still alive.

We saw from the crime scenes and the analysis of the victims' wounds that Pennell's use of multiple forms of tactile aggression revealed his appetite for variant forms of domination. Especially with his last victim, Michelle Gordon, Pennell was no longer capable of sating his needs with simple percussion as he had done in the Ellis and DiMauro murders. Instead, his experimentation and developing signature thrust him forward into elaborate and intrusive forms of dependency, dread, and degradation. He bit or cut off the victim's nipple, attacked her entire body, and apparently spent a considerable amount of time with her keeping her alive while he tortured her.

Finally, the cycle of domination was complete when the victims succumbed to the ultimate submission. While alive, the barometer of the killer's effectiveness was how he humiliated the victims. In those circumstances, the killer enjoyed each aspect of sensory feedback he received from the suffering victim. He could see the results of his blow, he could smell or even taste blood, he could feel blows and the victim's response to them, and he could hear and get off on the sounds of pain and suffering the victim involuntarily uttered. Once dead, however, the victim offered Pennell new opportunities for enjoyment. His final act in the dominance-submission continuum was the disposal of each victim. Here, in each case he dumped them, almost tumbled them into a submission position, discarded like trash. Pennell engaged the victims on their own lifestyle terms, hitchhiking or hooking, and exercised domination over them, beating them at their own game by perpetrating in reality what they only playacted at feeling and then reducing them to garbage, shocking pieces of human remains left to rot as if they were animal roadkill.

Pennell also exercised control and satisfied himself

sexually through the compression and restraint of bondage. Bondage was an adjunct to his torture and sexual dominance-submission signatures and struck to the heart of control and power in these murders. To be totally bound eliminated any control by the victim and created a feeling of absolute power for the killer. The killer consistently used bondage mechanisms for victim control and personal perversity. Throughout the cases, he ritualistically secured wrists, ankles, and throats. After death, he removed the bonds and undoubtedly kept them as trophies of the kill. Again, the signature and MO ran along parallel lines within the killer's efforts at bondage. On the one hand, the restraints were necessary control devices; on the other hand, they demonstrated the pathological and sinister elements of physical conquest. Increasingly, while the killer viewed himself as virile and a superhuman beast, the bondage activities conveyed a real sense of control and a rush of superiority to Pennell over his victims as if the act of bondage itself were the objective correlative to the allegory of humiliating death that aroused his deepest sexual passions, Pennell's Grecian urn.

In particular, the strangulation of each victim was indicative of Pennell's direct need for playing on the tightrope of life and death. There was a direct and tactile feeling of giving or taking a life. In addition, the gagging and noises from the victims were important to these signature behaviors, and while eclipsing the head and brain center, the strangulation had a direct relationship to breathing, gasping, and recovery. Those activities were strong and a potent power thrust for Steven Pennell.

Also, consistent with a signature theory of strangulation, Pennell's duct tape served as a regulator of restraint. That is, if a victim was not verbal enough (moans and groans), the killer could temporarily loosen the tape to offer a pseudopromise of recovery – and manipulated the victim into begging for mercy and release. Equally, the tape could serve to mute the victim into an automaton who had been stripped of her identity. Thus, the killer fantasized superpower at turning prostitutes into nothingness. Under these circumstances, the tape became a tool of human obliteration and restraint by compression. As with the deviant sexual stimulation of the act of bondage itself, the auditory moans served as the tension/release mechanisms of that bondage. It was the soundtrack of the perverted satisfaction of the killer. The bondage described here was pathological and an important factor in the killer's signature. It's something he had to do with each of his victims.

From the bra cutting in the Ellis case, the inference of cutting and knives – picquerism – gained importance as a tool of torture and threat for subsequent victims. Eventually, the case of Michelle Gordon revealed how pathologically important picquerism had become to Pennell through his infliction of superficial cuts on both buttocks and down the thighs in a linear fashion. Also, there were added foreign-object penetrations in the form of hammer blows onto the buttocks. Picquerism is actually an advanced state of signature, because it requires that killers spend more time with their victims, experiment visually with a pattern or actually cover a body part with wounds, determine where on the victim's body they're most likely to find satisfaction through inflicting wounds, and penetrate the victim just enough to cause the wound and provide satisfactory sexual feedback without actually hacking up the victim in an overkill signature. As bizarre and gruesome as this sounds to most people, this is what signature means and how police have to evaluate it to investigate this type of homicide.

Most significantly, from the killer's first victim, Shirley Ellis, through his final murder, Michelle Gorton, Pennell bit and mutilated the victims on the breast. Again, the application of pain to a sensitive area by biting was a strong indicant signature for picquerism. In particular, by biting and mutilating the breast, the killer caused pain and sated his needs for cutting, penetration, and invasion.

As an outsider can see, Steven Pennell exhibited a clear signature and committed acts on his victims that were far and away more than necessary to commit the murders. The core of Pennell's intrinsic behavior could never change. If he had not been caught, undoubtedly the law enforcement authorities in Delaware would have investigated more victims. In his search for other victims, Detective Joe Swiski told me that Pennell's killings were unprecedented for the state of Delaware, and they immediately ended when Pennell was apprehended. On March 15, 1992, the *Wilmington News-Journal* reported 'Delaware Executes Pennell. No Last Words From Serial Killer.'

CHAPTER 8

The Bellevue Yuppie Murders

George Russell

For sexually sadistic killers such as Glatman, Heirens, and Frampton, sexual domination was the overriding reason for all their crimes. This is what signature killers are all about, whether they commit only one homicide or an extended series. They exist in a world of anger-driven sexual fantasy and emerge periodically into real life to thrive upon domination by controlling their victims through sexual degradation and mental humiliation. They may choose to become serial rapists and control their prey by drugging them and creating a living doll or somnambulistic zombie who is totally subservient to their wishes. Or as full-fledged serial killers they break and enter, burglarize and bludgeon their sleeping victims, and then fulfill their acts of fantasy with a helpless corpse. Whatever the case, the intended result is still the same: domination and control. The sadist's goal is to take away the victim's mind and then her life. The victim who has been rendered powerless and almost motionless doesn't have the energy or mental clarity to debate or resist. All their mental power is transferred to the killer. This was the very intention of the infamous Ted Bundy. He would be sure that his victims were in a vulnerable position, either alone and in a dark place or asleep in their beds, and then he would bludgeon and strangle them until they were totally within his power, mindless and silent corpses.

In the killer's fantasy, the victim has no identity; she is a possession.

Bundy once told me that he never killed anyone he was with for more than twenty minutes. In other words, his victims had to have already been extensions of his own fantasies and not real people. This is a critical piece of the picture to grasp if we are to have an understanding of what's going on here. It means that Bundy fantasized about a potential victim, whether it was Lynda Healy, whom he stalked through Seattle's U District before he broke into her apartment and killed her, or Janice Ott, with whom he had only shared a few minutes of conversation in which he tricked her into climbing into his car. To Bundy, these women existed only as his victim. Once the person had achieved some sort of foothold as a real person in Bundy's eyes, she was no longer his victim because her reality was greater than his fantasy. Bundy even suggested that it would have been a chink in his armor had he killed someone with whom he'd developed a meaningful relationship. He wanted to attack only those who didn't know him and to make sure they were unconscious or dead as soon after he met them as was possible. He was a necrophile who carried his victims over the threshold of death where he could exercise complete control over their corpses. That was the only relationship his fantasy allowed him.

Because dead girls tell no tales, Bundy's killing spree continued unabated in four states while police blindly groped after the missing women. But the very internal forces that made Ted so successful also pushed him to take greater and greater chances. While he started out that way, Bundy soon was not content merely to abduct a victim and secret her body away. Driven by a high-test mix of fear and anger, Bundy pushed himself into more daring moves. He didn't want to get caught, but his fear that his career could not go on forever forced him to challenge his skills and put him into high-risk situations again and again. For example, he was safe in Utah as long as he stayed camouflaged, but he tried to abduct Carol Da Ronch in broad daylight and gave police in two states one of the first leads they'd use to begin to unravel the mystery of Bundy's secret life. By the time his case was wrapped up and Bundy was in jail spending his final days talking to me and other investigators, he had become legend, especially among serial killer wanna-bes struggling with their own internal sexual demons. One of those wanna-bes was a young man living on Mercer Island, Washington, named George Russell. He crossed my path in a Seattle courtoom even as I was writing my own book on Ted Bundy.

THE *SIX DEGREES OF SEPARATION* MURDERS

Fifteen years after Bundy made headlines in the Northwest, a more contemporary Seattle killer emerged, one who also learned that live victims struggle too much and dead ones are much more obliging. His name was George W. Russell, and he cruised the yuppie singles bars at a time when the Seattle area was quickly becoming the center of the cyber universe. Russell struck in the midst of the yuppie singles scene. Mary Ann Pohlreich, another member of that same scene, was his first victim. The discovery of her defiled body on one warm Puget Sound morning on the second day of summer sent a shudder through the upscale town of Bellevue.

The Mary Ann Pohlreich Murder

It was June 23, 1990, just after 7:30 A.M., and the day had begun routinely for an employee of the McDonald's fast-food restaurant, located next door to the Black Angus Restaurant in Bellevue, Washington. Both eateries shared the same alley for their garbage in the parking lot behind the Black Angus. On his first trip to the Dumpster that morning, an employee made the startling discovery of a deceased woman lying there sprawled out in the alley. The young McDonald's employee gazed in silence at the woman's body, whose appearance was so grotesque it could have barely been replicated by a fictional monster like Ross Thomas's Hannibal Lecter. The young employee called the local Bellevue police.

The scene was riveting. Every police officer who arrived to secure the crime location stared at the single grim, motionless female stretched upon the pavement in an outlandishly bizarre position. The police had never seen anything like it before. Clearly, her body had been deliberately posed. And there was no question in anyone's mind that whoever committed this terrible atrocity hadn't worried about spending considerable time with her corpse. The body had been displayed in a busy area – the killer obviously wanted his work to be discovered quickly – nude and arranged to bear an unmistakable message of sexual degradation. The victim was left lying on her back, with her left foot crossed over the instep of her right ankle. Her head was turned to the left and a Frito-Lay dip container lid rested on top of her right eye. Her arms were bent at the elbow and crossed over her abdomen with her hands gently touching, one inside the other. In one hand, detectives found a startling piece of evidence: a Douglas fir cone. What did this clue represent? What kind of message was being sent, and to whom? Only the killer knew.

The victim's gold watch on her left wrist and her gold choker chain with a crescent-shaped white pendant around her neck were the only personal items left on the otherwise nude corpse. Noting that the especially aggressive predator had been meticulous in removing all of the victim's clothing, police figured that he was either too pressed for time to strip her of her jewelry or he didn't see any value in the pieces and deliberately left them as adornments to the body.

The surface of the garbage area, uncommonly clean, was a cement rectangle bordered by the asphalt pavement of the parking lot. A pile of debris was within three feet of the victim's head, and two brooms were leaning up against the wooden fence that enclosed the area on three sides. The body was discovered near the unfenced side. In front of the trash compactor, several bloodstains and chips of fingernail polish from the victim were found. It could be assumed from this evidence that the killer had initially taken the victim deep into the trash area, as if he were going to deposit her in the Dumpster, but then decided to display the body prominently back toward the opening, where it could be clearly seen.

The victim had wounds that indicated strangulation: severe blows to the right eye, nose, and mouth, and abrasions – received after death – to the right arm and right breast, and both hips, knees, and feet. Those postmortem injuries were produced when the killer dragged the body about twenty feet along the parking-lot surface inside the fenced garbage area. The injuries she had received before death looked like defense wounds, suggesting that she had put up a struggle when she was attacked.

The medical examiner had determined that death took place between 2:30 and 5:20 A.M. A late-night Black Angus worker who had dumped garbage at 3:15 A.M. said the body was not there at that time. Since the corpse was discovered within four to five hours after death, it was concluded that the woman was probably killed someplace else and brought to the Dumpster.

The autopsy examination revealed blunt impact injuries to the head that produced a fracture to the right base of the skull and similar injuries to the abdomen that caused a laceration of the liver. The medical examiner found the victim's stomach to be empty, and her toxicological screen showed a blood alcohol level of .14. The victim had been raped, her anus had been severely lacerated with a foreign object, and sperm was detected in her vagina. This guy had done a lot of work on this victim. And that led us to believe that unless he was caught, this wasn't going to be his final victim. From the amount of activity the killer had expended on this victim to inflict punishment, cause her death, and manipulate the body after death, it was clear to us that he had issues he was working out.

We surmised that through his experimentation at this crime scene the killer was laying the groundwork for possible style modification in the next crime. His MO could change, but his signature would only become enhanced in some way. Experience told us that when a killer spends more and more time rearranging bodies in successive murder scenes, that very act is indicative of a more intense need for the killer to display victims in poses that arouse him sexually, and is the core of his signature. The elapsed time a killer like this is with successive victims usually increases with each scene as do the number of postmortem activities – provided the killer is not interrupted.

This killer would be affected by his internal stresses, like every serial killer, and would no doubt repeat the crime on a sporadic or episodic schedule. Either a particular victim type would turn him on and set him into motion stalking her or tracking her movements, or an event would precipitate a sexual episode which he could satisfy only through his taking a victim. Conditional to the satisfaction received by reliving a former murder, his motivation for further domination and exploration might wax and wane. But it wouldn't go away. Our assumption was that the signature killer would strike again. The pressure was on us to discover as much as we could from the crime scene and launch an extensive investigation.

On June 27, 1990, the victim found behind the Black

Angus was positively identified through dental records as Mary Ann Pohlreich, who had been listed missing a day or so after her body was first discovered. Police routinely run a search of missing person reports when a Jane or John Doe turns up, and Mary Ann's identity was discovered after just such a search. Mary Ann Pohlreich was white, twenty-seven years old, five feet seven inches tall, 150 pounds, with light brown, shoulder-length, slightly curly hair, and blue-gray eyes. The young woman was last seen alive on Friday, June 22, 1990, at about 10 P.M. at Papagayo's Cantina, a popular yuppie singles bar and dance spot in Bellevue, the high-tech suburb of Seattle. Papagayo's is located about one mile northwest of the Black Angus Restaurant. Evidently, Mary Ann left the restaurant either with her killer or with the person who took her to her killer, because her 1984 Chevrolet Camaro sat undisturbed in Papagayo's parking lot and her purse, which contained her car keys, was found later in the lost-and-found property at Papagayo's.

Detectives surmised that Pohlreich had met someone, possibly a date, at Papagayo's. She left with him after 10 P.M., intending to return to retrieve her purse and car. She was assaulted and murdered at an unknown location nearby and dumped behind the Black Angus after 3:15 A.M. Evidence from the murder suggested that it had been a sexual confrontation gone bad. Judging by the number of defense wounds and the blunt-force injuries inflicted by the killer, Pohlreich put up quite a struggle prior to death. She probably left her mark on her killer, possibly inflicting bruises and contusions. Judging from her injuries, the killer most likely had to wash her blood from himself as well.

The rape-murderer rarely derives any specific sexual pleasure from the actual killing of the victim. Killing, in these cases, is usually only a means to an end, especially if the predator is a necrophile who enjoys primarily the control he wields over helpless bodies. The murder itself is usually a process in which the killer's thrill is found in exercising control over the victim both before and after death. In the Pohlreich case, it seemed the killer derived an especially great satisfaction from his postmortem sexually sadistic activities. He must have spent a considerable amount of time with the dead Mary Ann Pohlreich behind the Black Angus, because it was evident he took time to arrange her body carefully in its final pose, even though the macabre ritual greatly increased the risk that someone might see him with his victim. This after-death victim-offender contact demonstrated the killer's complete possessiveness and his ultimate degradation of the female victim, a modus operandi strongly reminiscent of Ted Bundy's. Pohlreich, therefore, was not killed by some common rape-murderer whom she spurned on a date, who got mad, beat her up, raped her, got scared, and then killed her. As tragic as a date rape or a date-rape-murder is, the Pohlreich murder had even more sinister overtones, because the obvious signature of the crime belonged to someone fitting the necrophilic profile of a serial killer.

The Pohlreich murder had three unique, significant characteristics that – when taken collectively – would signal even to the novice investigator that there was more here than straightforward rape-homicide.

First, posing a murder victim's body was very rare. In fewer than one percent of all murder cases have killers posed a victim's body. The deliberate act of posing involves positioning the body or its parts just as a photographer would arrange all aspects of a subject for a photo shoot. It takes time, much control over the actual crime scene where the body is positioned, and a prolonged level of intensity on the killer's part to sustain the mental and physical effort required for this task. In the most extreme case of posing I've ever seen, a deranged killer repositioned body parts that he'd mutilated and amputated back in their correct anatomical positions. There is hardly a stronger statement of domination than a killer exercising control over not just the victim, but the victim's individual limbs or other parts, as if he's just fabricated a human puzzle out of its individual pieces.

Posing is not to be confused with staging, because staging refers to manipulation of the scene around the body. For example, in 1974, convicted murderer Tony Fernandez brutally assaulted and killed his wife and staged the death scene. Fernandez placed her body behind the steering wheel of their motor home, which he had previously pushed over an embankment, thereby staging her murder to look like an accident. Both staging and posing require that the killer spend extensive time after his victim's death arranging things in a certain way and going beyond the actions necessary to perpetrate the murder.

The second unique component of Pohlreich's murder case was the disposal of her body. There are only three notable methods that a killer uses to dispose of a victim's body. In the most common method, employed by murderers fifty-eight percent of the time, the body is left in a position reflecting that the killer is unconcerned that the body be found. That usually occurs in domestic violence and argument murders, when the body is left in the spot where it fell at the moment of the assault or death. A second method of disposal, used ten percent of the time, is deliberate concealment of the body. Common methods of concealment include burying the body, placing the body in a crawl space of a house, or putting leaves or branches over the body in the woods, much like the Green River killer had done in Seattle, Washington. Leaving the body in a specific location where the body was guaranteed to be found, was the third method of disposal, which also is used ten percent of the time. A body left in this manner is commonly referred to as 'open and displayed,' which is how the body was found in the Pohlreich case.

The third significant characteristic of murder in the Pohlreich case was sexual insertion of a foreign object into a cavity of the body. The object can be found left inside the body, or the only evidence of existence that might remain is penetration injuries and surface abrasions. More common are killers who lacerate or cut out the vaginas of their victims, like Arthur Shawcross, in their fury either to obliterate or take away with them the sexuality of their victim. Insertion, however, is very rare and is found in only less than one percent of murder cases.

The most extraordinary observation about the posing, sexual insertion of a foreign object, and open display of the body in the same murder case is that they appear combined in less than one-tenth of one percent of all murders. And here they were, all three present simultaneously, in the murder of Mary Ann Pohlreich. To find all three of those crucial factors was indeed a remarkable and horrifying occurrence. This is a signature so distinctive and remarkable for the predator's fury that it would be a foregone conclusion that Pohlreich's killer hated women, feared women, and flew into rage whenever it appeared that he couldn't readily dominate women. This is a guy we knew would almost certainly strike again. And he did.

FANTASY APPETITES

Like Arthur Shawcross of New York, Randy Kraft of California, Gerald Stano of Florida, and Dean Coryll and Elmer Wayne Henley of Texas, most serial killers have a dynamic aspect to their behavior. Serial killers will constantly experiment with what works and what doesn't, to arouse them sexually and provide them with the greatest thrill and gratification. They will learn from crime to crime what works best for them to achieve the highest level of satisfaction. To achieve gratification, they've pre-scripted their activities from the abduction or break-in right through all the stages of terror and mutilation of their victims. They've rehearsed for this. A prolonged torture or mutilation of any victim energizes the fantasy system of each killer and temporarily satisfies their lust for domination and mastery. Serial killers such as Ted Bundy, John Gacy, and Jeffrey Dahmer have all gone through these stages.

Pumped up into an anticipatory sexual frenzy by a highly specialized fantasy system, probably in much the same way as a heroin or cocaine addict anticipates and even experiences the thrill of a drug even before he takes it, a signature killer such as George Russell first selects each victim with the full arc of his fantasy sexual experience already laid out in his mind. Then, once isolated, he escalates the violence he inflicts upon her to precise circumscribed levels of ritualistic carnage according to the situation and the reactions of the victim. Maybe the victim will strenuously resist; maybe she will be more physical than he anticipated; maybe she will submit or succumb too quickly for him to reach an anticipated sexual thrill level – all of these are part of the situation that may change with each victim. But even as the situation may vary from victim to victim, part of the excitement of the killer's anticipation is the completion of one level and the jump to the next as he gets to know the victim through the course of the crime. The one common strand through all the crimes, however, which serves as the basis for the signature is that the killer approaches each victim, exploiting her naïveté through torture and mutilation, which serve to appease an insatiable fantasy appetite.

In the killer's execution of his crimes, his excitement is at first stimulated and then heightened by his acting out in real time his preplanned, rehearsed, and even researched scenario of his eroticized anger and power. He carries this anger and the erotic fantasies it drives around with him every minute of the day and in the darkness of each arc may be the memory of a victim which stimulates him or, more likely, his discovery of a new potential victim. Maybe as with Pohlreich, Russell picks her up in a bar and she's just responsive enough to his advances to get him going. Maybe, like Georgann Hawkins, she catches Ted Bundy's eye as she walks back to her sorority house or dorm along a dark, quiet street close enough to a parking lot that the killer knows he can lure her, isolate her, spring his trap, and drive away without anyone seeing what he's doing. Or maybe, like Richard Guerrero, who has only a couple of bucks in his pocket and is chatting up guys at the Phonex Bar in Milwaukee, he takes Jeffrey Dahmer up on his offer of going back to his place, watching some videos, and perhaps taking some photos. 'There's some money in it,' Dahmer promised him. By the time Dahmer had handed Guerrero a drink laced with potent sedatives in the basement of his grandmother's West Allis house, Guerrero was as good as dead. Dahmer had done this only two months earlier and would repeat the same scenario again periodically for the next three years until he was caught. For Russell, as for Bundy, Dahmer, and scores of other signature killers, each individual crime is the playing out of a drama in the killer's stage, the three *D*'s of sadism: dependency, degradation, and dread.

Part of the drama the signature killer enacts, once he has his victim, is facilitated by the props the predator brings to the crime scene. The critical prop is a fully equipped murder kit, such as the satchel containing handcuffs, burglary tools, and ski mask that Ted Bundy carried in his Volkswagen Bug, or the duct tape that Nathaniel Code never really left home without. Other killers find it more gratifying to improvise, allowing themselves to be excited by whatever they find at the crime scene, which is what George Russell did at the Mary Ann Pohlreich murder. The implements the killers use themselves have ritualistic significance, because they serve to excite the killer sexually, driving his anticipation of the stalking and the attack about to come or reinvigorating him to a sexual climax in a private orgy after his kill.

SELECTING VICTIMS

Why did George Russell choose Mary Ann Pohlreich to go with him that night at Papagayo's Cantina? What is the spark that turns on the motor of any serial killer as he trolls? Most signature killers are mum about what turns them on, because secretly they are embarrassed about admitting to the sexual fetishes that overtake them.

In most anger cases, we can figure out who in the killer's past pushed his buttons, and therefore, what aspect of the source's personality he goes out to kill when he encounters it. Henry Lee Lucas talked about his Chippewa mother Viola Lucas in Blacksburg, Virginia, who dressed him up as a little girl, and how she beat him and his father Anderson until the two lived in terror of her anger. He once described how she hit him so hard with a two by four that she and her boyfriend had to take him to a hospital, where he remained semiconscious for days. They told the doctor he fell off a ladder. Lucas eventually cut open her throat and she bled to death. Thereafter, women who seemed to him to be on the make or who treated him with disrespect were, in his words, 'as good as dead.'

Arthur Shawcross also talked about his mother and how, shortly after she rejected his Christmas present for her – he had made it in prison shop – as 'tacky,' he killed his first prostitute in Rochester. She made the mistake of laughing at his inability to get an erection. In a similar pattern, Florida killer Bobby Joe Long has talked about his problems with his mother, how she shared the same motel room bed with him when they ran away from his father, how she brought her boyfriends home in the early morning hours for sex, and how she once tried to have a boyfriend beat Bobby up when he wouldn't get up to let them have the bed for themselves. Years later, Long was the subject of an intense manhunt when he was killing women he characterized as acting like prostitutes or described as 'barflies' along the North Tampa strip.

George Russell chose victims who traveled in the same group of young people at the bars and restaurants in Bellevue. He picked up Mary Ann Pohlreich on a night when she had had a lot to drink and was flirting with guys in Papagayo's. There were people all around him, but nobody remembered that he'd taken her out of the restaurant until he was already a suspect. Similarly Ted Bundy isolated Janice Ott and Denise Naslund at Lake Sammamish in a throng of beachgoers, but nobody knew who or what he was. Plenty of people could describe him, but the descriptions didn't help until we already had our 'Ted' case files organized.

The MO of a signature killer changes as he becomes more and more proficient at approaching his prey. The killer will employ tactics that are comfortable for him. When preparing to encounter the victim, the killer can evoke a disarmingly charming manner and dispel most fears of immediate contact with a stranger. Why is it that victims discard their protective armor of resistance when confronted with a charismatic, charming stranger? Probably because the signature killer is a social chameleon who blends so perfectly into the correct surroundings that he actually becomes what the potential victim is looking for.

The main point of the killer's approach, as was George Russell's in his assault on Mary Ann Pohlreich, is to lure the victim in with her guard completely down. In Mary Ann's case, she was in a familiar place doing a familiar dance. This makes the killer's job of trapping her much easier, because she feels secure in her surroundings. Then, the fantasy system is implemented, which the killer has begun by deceiving the victim into letting herself become isolated. Once isolated and trapped, the victim's sudden shift to a state of helplessness and terror heightens the killer's sexual expectations and an extensive bondage and domination scenario is set into motion. Methodically, the love of torture or mutilation is demonstrated through the killer's pre-planned ritualistic acts the likes of which victims will never have imagined in their most gruesome nightmares. This was what Mary Ann experienced after she and Russell set off in his friend's pickup truck. By the time he tried to force her body into the compactor behind the Black Angus, she had become the imprinting murder of a serial spree that would leave the Bellevue Police Department completely stumped until area cops, who had known Russell from his breaking-and-entering days on Mercer Island and other municipalities, pushed his name forward in the investigation. But that was not until at least two other women had been killed.

The Carol Beethe Murder

On August 9, 1990, just forty-seven days after Pohlreich's body was discovered, thirteen-year-old Kelly Beethe found her mother Carol Ann Beethe's battered body in the bedroom of her ranch-style one-story house and immediately called her father, who came over to his ex-wife's house and called the police. Beethe's home was located in a typical middle-class bedroom community and was bordered on each side by neighboring houses. Within the city limits of Bellevue, Washington, Beethe's residence was less than two miles from the Black Angus Restaurant where Mary Ann Pohlreich was found murdered.

Carol Beethe was the single mother of two daughters, ages nine and thirteen, who were asleep in their shared bedroom, only fifteen feet from the entrance of Carol's bedroom, on the night of the murder. Beethe was a white female, five feet two inches tall, 108 pounds, with collar-length light blond hair. She was last seen entering her home alone at 2:30 A.M. on August 9, 1990, by a neighbor who was out walking. Beethe had been visiting a bartender friend of hers at Bellevue's Keg Restaurant, another trendy singles hangout, before going home. Beethe herself was a bartender at Cucina Cucina Restaurant, a frequent nightspot of singles in Bellevue, and was a friend in the group of people who frequented the clubs and restaurants where, it turned out later, George Russell could be found almost every night.

Deliberately arranged by the killer, the crime scene was a ghastly sight. Beethe was carefully positioned in open display on top of her bed. She was lying on her back naked, except for a pair of red high heels on her feet. Her legs were completely splayed and her exposed groin was facing the doorway of her bedroom. Inserted well up into her vagina was the barrel of an over-and-under rifle-shotgun combination, with its stock resting across her shoes. The weapon belonged to the victim. Bellevue Police Department Persons Crime Unit detectives thought for a while that a pillow covering Beethe's face was used to smother her, until they carefully lifted it and found that her head was wrapped in a plastic dry-cleaning bag after she died. Was the intruder readying Beethe's body for removal from her house by placing her battered head in a plastic bag, before he changed his mind and left her in her own bed? Or was he deliberately covering her face so her eyes wouldn't look at him after death? We wondered.

Carol Beethe was savagely beaten – much more than was needed to kill her – with an unidentified blunt object that left forked or Y-shaped impressions all over her head. It was clear from the way Carol Beethe had been beaten, undressed, adorned, and posed that the killer had exercised complete control over the crime scene and had remained in the house for a very long time. He expected no trouble from this victim, and her two defense wounds, one on each hand, showed that he didn't have much trouble. Carol Beethe had been quickly subdued with blows to her abdomen and rib cage, probably knocked unconscious right away, just like Mary Ann Pohlreich, at which point the killer began his overkill and savagery in earnest. Police determined that the gun and shoes were placed in and on the victim after death. The house door to the victim's bedroom was closed; the murderer had come and gone through an open sliding glass door to her bedroom. The murder weapon was not found.

Beethe's murder, like Pohlreich's, was extremely unusual. To the inexperienced observer, they were quite different, although when the ad hoc task force put them together it was clear that they had a common signature. But if one were to rely exclusively on the modus operandi of each murder to determine if they were related, it would be easy to believe that two different killers were at work. Beethe was killed indoors in her own bed with her children sleeping right next door, while Pohlreich, it seemed, had been brought to the alley where her body was dumped outside. The killer's approach to each victim was different. Pohlreich had been picked up on the dance floor of Papagayo's Cantina and induced to leave as if she were going on a date with a guy. In sharp contrast, Beethe was probably attacked while she was asleep in bed. The two women were displayed very differently with different items inserted into their vaginal cavities. To police, who rely on exclusivity of cases, these discrepancies were enough to send them off chasing multiple suspects. In addition, although the cause of death was from blunt impact in each case, the different variety of weapons used influenced the decision of the MO purists that separate killers were in operation. But the signature aspects of both murders should have been more convincing – the extremely rare occurrence of posing, inserting a foreign object into the body, and openly displaying bodies in two murders within fifty days of one another in the same small locality.

Investigators should have concluded that both murders were the work of the same person, the signature of one killer in particular. Unfortunately, Bellevue investigators had drawn different conclusions based on the variance in modus operandi of the two scenes. They looked exclusively for the exact MO from one crime to the next, instead of recognizing that a killer changes his MO as he strives to get more comfortable in successive murders. This inexperience with the signature aspects of murders affected the course of the investigation, since detectives focused their investigation initially on Beethe's boyfriend and refused to back off even when an ad hoc strategy session of local investigators recommended Russell as a suspect. The boyfriend had an alibi for the time of Pohlreich's murder, and at least one police investigator was initially reluctant to accept any theory that Beethe was killed by the same person who killed Pohlreich.

The Andrea Levine Murder

Just when the Bellevue police were coughing up sand in their investigations of the Pohlreich and Beethe murders and taking hits from the Seattle papers, who had been nurtured on Bundy and the Green River killer, another young woman in the area was found murdered. On September 3, 1990, twenty-four days after the murder of Carol Ann Beethe, the body of Andrea Levine was discovered in her ground-level apartment in Kirkland, Washington. Her apartment was within seven miles to the north of the Bellevue Black Angus where Pohlreich's body was found. The municipality might have been different, but the location was essentially the same for the killer.

Andrea Levine, known as Randi, was white, with collar-length dark red hair. She was twenty-four years old, five feet four inches tall, and weighed about 120 pounds. She was last seen alive around midnight at the Maple Gardens Restaurant in Kirkland on August 30, 1990. She arrived with her friends, but according to witnesses, she left alone. Levine had been dead a few days before her landlord discovered her body. When we questioned him, he said it was a few days after he'd chased what he reported as a 'prowler' off his property. Like Pohlreich and Beethe, Levine was known to frequent singles night-spots in Bellevue, but it was also possible that Levine had been stalked and her apartment broken into before her murder.

The display and postmortem mutilation of Levine's body, in ways strikingly similar to Pohlreich and Beethe, confirmed that a sexually deviant serial killer was on the loose in the Bellevue area. Upon the discovery of this third murder, Beethe's boyfriend was dismissed as a suspect in her murder. The real killer would definitely have gone underground after being the central focus of the Beethe investigation, and the boyfriend had been too closely scrutinized to have continued a killing spree with the murder of Levine. At this point, it was obvious whoever murdered Levine had not yet been under police surveillance and was still out there killing. This had to have been a previously unknown suspect.

Levine's body was left supine on top of her bed. A pillow covered her bloody cranium and a top sheet hid her mutilated body. Like Pohlreich and Beethe, the killer had clearly posed his victim. Her legs were spread, an electric vibrator was inserted in her mouth, and the book *More of the Joy of Sex* was cradled in her left arm. She had been bludgeoned about the head violently and repeatedly by a killer who attacked her while she lay asleep. The attack was so swift that Levine probably never even had time to wake up, which was why we believed there were no defense wounds on her body. She had sustained more than 230 small cuts over the entire surface of her body, including the bottoms of her feet. The cuts were all made after Levine was killed, again indicating that the killer had spent a lot of time with the dead victim and was confident about controlling his crime scene. It appeared that a ring Levine was wearing and all the knives in the house had been taken by the killer. The murder weapon was not found. Randi Levine's pickup truck was parked in its normal spot outside and there were no signs of forced entry into the apartment.

THE KILLER'S SIGNATURE

When George Russell, the suspect arrested for the serial murders, was charged, King County Prosecutor Rebecca Roe asked me if I could explain the pattern surrounding his crimes in greater detail. Did the pattern that had confused the police pursuing the investigation make some sense? My answer to her question was a clear-cut yes. There was indeed a very frightening pattern that emerged.

First of all, the Bellevue and Kirkland area of King County had averaged only one murder per year for the preceding ten years. Then, surprisingly, within sixty-seven days, the locale experienced three atypical murders within a five-mile radius of each other. Were these the only crimes in the area? Was there any other activity that should have alerted police to the presence of violence in the community? At the very least, law-enforcement officials should have realized that there was a murder problem beyond normal proportions. Crimes of this magnitude don't take place in a vacuum. The first murder was of such violence and her body left in such an obvious place that it did not fit into a typical homicide. This was no angry boyfriend who'd just committed his first crime. This was something else. Then, when Carol Beethe was found in a posed position, an alarm should have gone off that a series was in progress. Two murders in just a couple of months in locations close together, and where both bodies were obviously posed with their faces covered – the connection should have been clear to homicide cops. Ted Bundy's murders, for example, were part of a pattern of missing women throughout the northwest, all of them Ted's victims. We knew that something was going on because of all the missing persons reports and the similarities among the victims. Again, how many long-haired college coed types have to be missing before one realizes there is a pattern emerging? What we didn't know, of course, was that our suspect in Bellevue would be someone who had read about and admired Ted Bundy. As he began his murder spree, he would tell us, he even compared his crimes and ability to elude police to Ted Bundy.

In the subsequent murder trial of George Russell, my testimony was straightforward: the killer's personal expression was permanently etched on the bodies of Pohlreich, Beethe, and Levine. When I analyzed the murders by type and frequency of injuries and other unique characteristics from the first murder to the third, I drew only one conclusion: they were all committed by the same person. The distinctive aspects of the killer's imprint stood right out at any investigator who had researched or experienced signature murders. Before, I had seen the same type of murders in cases that I studied and at police training seminars. I had discussed extensively with psychologists and psychiatrists these types of crime-scene behaviors. They fall into a pattern.

First, all three victims were intentionally left so someone would find them. They were not concealed or hidden, but were placed in locations where they would be discovered quickly. The killer left them openly displayed, knowing that whoever found them would be shocked, both physically and psychologically.

Second, they were posed in sexually degrading positions: naked, arms spread or folded over as if in deliberate repose, holding or supporting items that revealed the killer's attitude toward them, and legs deliberately spread. The killer obviously received an intense sexual thrill from manipulating their bodies to demonstrate their vulnerability after death. These bodies belonged to him. As part of the pose, only items that the killer found at the crime scene were incorporated into the victim's portraits – the crime shots that he knew would be taken by police photographers. He did this consistently in all three murders. For example, he used a fir cone with Pohlreich so that she was holding it, and a Frito-Lay lid on her head which had been tilted to support it; he placed Beethe's red shoes on her feet with her legs spread apart; and he draped Levine's arm over her book *The Joy of Sex*.

Third, the killer inserted foreign objects into the victims' sexual orifices as part of his protocol. The actual object was absent in the Pohlreich case, but her vagina area showed signs of penetration even though the object was missing. Was this an experiment that didn't work out, or did he run out of time at the crime scene? His intentions would be made clear in the Carol Beethe murder. After the Levine murder, it was obvious that the act of inserting and leaving foreign objects in the victims' mouths and vaginas evolved from the first murder through the third. It became more of a need for the killer to demonstrate his personal expression by leaving a rifle in Beethe and a dildo in Levine's mouth.

Fourth, the collective presence of all three of those relatively rare characteristics in each of the three murders was a very extraordinary occurrence. Notwithstanding the fact that the murders were committed in a small geographic area, the chain of those unusual characteristics was the fundamental aspect of the killer's signature.

Fifth, the strength of the defense each victim was allowed to put up decreased from the first murder through the third. It was as if the killer had gotten his act down more smoothly the more murders he carried out, so that his victims resisted him less with each murder. Pohlreich had multiple defense wounds, Beethe had two small defense wounds, and Levine did not have any defense wounds. The state of the killer's mind was influenced by the struggle put up by the first victim, so subsequent victims were not allowed a chance to fight back. Had he evolved further, Russell would have found ways to move with even more stealth.

Sixth, the killer spent an increasing amount of time with each victim after death, rearranging their bodies in their final death poses. Remaining for any length of time behind the Black Angus Restaurant and at the outdoor scene of Pohlreich's killing was very risky, since someone could come upon the scene and interrupt the killer. He was also in danger of discovery inside Carol Beethe's bedroom; yet he stayed for a considerable length of time. He probably stayed for an even longer period in Randi Levine's bedroom even though he knew that she lived downstairs from her landlord, who had already spotted Russell on the property just days earlier. These increasingly lengthy stays with his victims while he meticulously arranged each crime scene served to heighten his entire sexual experience.

Seventh, the number of injuries sustained by each victim increased from the Pohlreich through the Levine murder. Pohlreich sustained just enough injuries to cause her death, but not much more. The blows to her abdomen lacerated her liver but didn't kill her. The blow to her head knocked her out. She was killed by strangulation, and the time Russell spent with her after death was to pose her, and that just barely, after he found he couldn't get her into the compactor. Beethe was beaten severely, clearly more than was necessary to kill her. Levine was beaten even more excessively than the previous two victims, but the over two hundred cuts Russell inflicted was a clear indication that he was evolving into greater violence. The increasing number of injuries reflected the killer's need to exercise absolute possession by creatively defiling their bodies in a new way each time.

Thus, the gradual increase in the number of injuries in each case, Russell's spending more and more time after her death with each victim, and his reducing the participation on the part of a live victim from the first case to the last were all part of a clear pattern. This pattern, in conjunction with open display, posing, and insertion of foreign objects into the victims' bodies were the specific factors that not only identified the *signature* of the killer in the Pohlreich, Beethe, and Levine murders, but definitely led to the conclusion that all three women were killed by the same person.

THROUGH THE EYES OF GEORGE RUSSELL AT THE CRIME SCENES

George Russell wanted to get back at the Black Angus Restaurant. The place was very important to Russell, because it was one of his hangouts where he held sway and impressed the young waitresses with his phony war stories of working police stings as a deep-undercover narc. But the Black Angus was where cocktail waitress Gretchen Coffin rebuffed him and deflated his ego. When he got angry and threatened her, she got scared and told the manager. He confronted Russell, threw him out, and told him never to come back. Now, with Mary Ann's body alongside him in the truck, he would teach those waitresses a lesson. In his mind, he would show them all. He would dispose of the body right at the Angus, in their very own garbage, and it would be his own private joke. That's what could have been in his mind.

Russell must have been driving around for hours waiting for people to clear out of the alley so he'd have the opportunity to dump Mary Ann there. He must have driven back there more than just once with the body beside him bleeding all over the seat of his friend's pickup. He had to return to make sure the coast was clear for him to dump the body. He probably hoisted it right into the trash compactor – Pohlreich's blood was found on the compactor – where it might have been compressed and carted away with the rest of the anonymous trash, not to be seen again for months or years. Maybe that was his first thought when he contemplated bringing Mary Ann back to the Angus.

But Russell wasn't strong enough to hoist the five-foot-seven, 120-pound body of Mary Ann Pohlreich over the lip, and it was getting quite late. We believe it had to be after 1 A.M. when Russell dumped the body, because the police put her earliest time of death at 2:20 A.M. We think it was after 3 A.M., because the bartender from Black Angus drove into the alley around then and saw nothing unusual, even though when Pohlreich was discovered, she was arranged toward the alley's entrance in plain view. The bartender would have seen her had she been there. We learned that at about 4 A.M., Russell called up his friend Smith McLain on Mercer Island, whose truck he'd taken from Papagayo's after midnight when he picked up Mary Ann, to tell him that he wanted to get his truck back to him. He left the message with McLain's sister. Surely a guy like Russell, who covered his tracks so carefully, wouldn't have called to drop off the truck unless he was ready to drop it off. That is, he had already dumped Mary Ann behind the Black Angus. So, we surmise, very little time was spent arranging her body, probably no more than a half hour, say from 3:20 A.M. Bad planning? No, not if you believe that Russell planned to drop her in the compactor and drive away. But, finding that she was too heavy to lift, and not having any alternate strategies, he decided to leave her where we found her.

Maybe Russell hadn't originally planned to murder Mary Ann when he took her out to his friend's pickup in the parking lot for a quick drink. But because of Mary Ann's behavior on the dance floor at Papagayo's during the night, he felt that he'd been tricked, made a fool of. Mary Ann's roommate told the police stories about how her friend would flirt, physically tease guys, egg them on, then shut them down when it got serious. A lot of guys got pissed off. Other guys just walked away when she got outrageous. But George Russell was a desperate homeless man in his thirties crashing in a condo with four girls who were still teenagers and wanted him back out on the street. He was not going to be turned down by Mary Ann Pohlreich.

He came on to her physically when they were alone in the parking lot, and she strenuously resisted. He punched her so hard in the stomach, he ruptured her liver. She vomited blood as he pushed her into the front seat of the pickup and drove off. At some point he knocked her unconscious. He raped her. He assaulted her anally. He strangled her. His anger then took over, especially after he brought her back to the Black Angus and found that she was still resisting him – after death. After having been beaten, raped, and murdered, she still wouldn't get into the compactor, and Russell wasn't strong enough to get her over the top. He failed again. That was his whole life in a microcosm. But this time it was going to be different. And in his anger he tried to ram something, possibly one of the brooms leaning on the Dumpster, into her vagina. Then his anger abated; he tilted her head away so she wouldn't look at him, put the Frito-Lay dip lid over her right eye, and positioned her arms and legs in mournful, funereal, repose.

Russell had committed his first murder. It didn't take him long at all. Maybe he had been frightened at first when he realized that his anger had taken him over the line into murder; his activities with the corpse in the alley worked through an entire arc of violence in those few hours – an intense sexual frenzy he'd never known before, and complete gratification. That arc imprinted a circuit in his brain. He had learned a new pattern of behavior that brought him pleasure. This first successful murder taught him how to do it. It is known as the imprinting murder.

Possibly as early as ten minutes after he dumped Mary Ann's body, Russell was on the phone to Smith McLain's sister, leaving the message for his friend. He had sewn back together the little rip in his universe during which he murdered Pohlreich. The truck would soon be back in his friend's hands, Mary Ann's blood and vomit would be cleaned off the front seat, and life would pick up exactly where it had left off. Except that he'd gotten away with murder. Just like his idol Ted Bundy, whom he revered and emulated, he would see the Bellevue detectives fumbling around the investigation, looking at wrong suspects, while the newspapers in yuppie Bellevue went into contortions over the unsolved homicide. This was Seattle circa 1974 all over again, only this time the phantom killer was George Russell not Ted Bundy, who'd been electrocuted just a year and a half before. The king was dead. Long live the king. Russell, the sociopath who'd lived most of his teenage and adult life on the con, robbing, breaking and entering, drug dealing, and hustling whomever and wherever he could, would almost certainly kill again.

Russell did kill again, and he spent more time with his dead victim the second time around. He was with Beethe, injuring and arranging her body, for a longer period of time than he was with Pohlreich. This was deliberate. He'd made mistakes with Pohlreich, but he learned a lot in the process. He'd learned never to take the kinds of chances with a dead body out in the open that he did with Mary Ann. He learned that you don't give a victim as much opportunity to resist as he did with Mary Ann.

This is why I tend to think that Russell simply was overtaken by anger when he believed that Mary Ann Pohlreich had tricked him by coming on to him, viciously disabled her with a blow to the stomach as she fought him off, then knocked her out and had sex with her. At that point he was in trouble big-time and had to get rid of her, account for the truck's disappearance during the night, and get rid of the bloodstain. By the time he had gone through the arc of his anger and come out the other side, he had become a signature killer. Then, as he approached the sliding glass door of Beethe's house, it was going to be different. No woman was going to shut him down, tease him and humiliate him, and get away with it. He'd shown them with Mary Ann; as his victim lay sleeping on the bed in front of him, he would show them again with Carol.

George Russell was a breaking-and-entering artist and had been for most of his life. Unless you lived in a vault, there wasn't much you could do to keep him out of your house. He'd learned on Mercer Island as a young teenager that people actually opened doors for you if you knew where to look, and if they didn't, very few houses had alarms. So, when he found that Carol Beethe had left the sliding glass door to her bedroom open for ventilation, he had his way in. But once inside, considering how much time he spent with his victim and what he did to her, you have to ask, what actually motivated him to pick Beethe as his next victim? This is a conjecture of some importance, given the amount of time he spent with her and the attention he lavished at the crime scene.

We know from the police reports that Beethe got home from work at about 7 P.M. and spent time on the phone after making dinner for her daughters and then putting them to bed. At about 12:30 A.M. she left the house. It was sometimes her habit to visit a friend, John Comfort, a bartender in Bellevue at the Keg. She helped him close the bar shortly after two, when they kissed each other and embraced in the parking lot. Kids camping in the neighborhood saw her come home between 2:30 and about a quarter of three. They told police she seemed in a hurry, almost as if she were worried about something.

Friends tell us that like Mary Ann, she was a flirt. Her friends said she liked to have sex, liked to have lovers, but also had a compunction to tell people off, especially men she got angry with. And on the last night of Carol Ann's life, she was out with one of her friends at a bar and came home looking worried. Had she seen something that frightened her? Just about ninety minutes later, after four in the morning, something woke Kelly Beethe from sleep and she saw a man outside her bedroom roaming through the halls of her house carrying a flashlight. She assumed it was her mother's boyfriend, and went back to bed.

We know where Carol Beethe was. Where was George Russell? George and Carol had mutual friends and George frequented both the Cucina Cucina where Carol tended bar and the Keg. We also know that she had at least a tangential connection to George Russell through her friend and Black Angus waitress Gretchen Coffin. Carol Ann had seen Russell at the Black Angus when she was there with Gretchen, the person Russell was hitting on and the very same woman who had gotten him thrown out of the Black Angus for causing trouble. Gretchen testified at Russell's trial that she and murder victim Carol Beethe were sitting at the Angus one night while Russell watched them from across the room, leveling an evil stare in their direction. Quite possibly, he had correctly guessed that Gretchen was telling Carol Ann all about him and fears she had that Russell had been threatening violence.

Had Russell, too, been at the Keg, maybe in the parking lot watching Carol say good-bye that night, and stalked her? We don't know. Did Russell follow her, wait until all the lights were out, prowl around the place looking for an entrée, and then slip through the open glass door over the box fan just inside the bedroom where he found Carol sound asleep in her bed? Was murder already on his mind when he might have tripped over the box fan, awakened the sleeping Carol Beethe ever so slightly, then attacked her immediately, incapacitating her with two blows to her abdomen and rib cage before she had a chance to get up? Between the first and second blows, Carol, suddenly awake, fighting for her life, tried to defend herself by raising her left hand to ward off the next blow. But Russell's punch or kick almost severed the little finger on her left hand. Carol Beethe probably lay unconscious on the bed and all was silent again. We know that robbery was on his mind, because Russell stole Carol's rings as well as her precious bags of silver dollars that she had stashed. But was the robbery the primary cause of Russell's attack, or was it an afterthought to murder?

With her bedroom door closed, the presence of her sleeping children in the house posed no immediate threat of discovery to Russell, who then set about to complete the sexual humiliation of Carol Beethe. He didn't try to rape her or even to ejaculate, which he'd done with Mary Ann. Russell knew about physical evidence at the crime scene, because he later bragged to police that he'd read the standard textbook about it. He also read Larson's and Michaud's books on Bundy and probably thought he knew most of what Bundy did. But he did want to inflict savage humiliation upon her body and pose her in a way that would turn him on at the sight and provide him with some stimulation later when her body was discovered. He liked what he read in the papers about Pohlreich; it gave him something to brag about indirectly, and he didn't take pains to hide it from his friends. So he strangled her until she stopped breathing, then beat her with the Y-shaped object around her head. It was a savage beating that startled police the next morning.

Then, as his rage peaked through its arc, he undressed

his dead victim, spread her across the bed, adorned her feet with the red and white shoes, and then extended her legs to a spread position. He then probably discovered the shotgun under her bed, which he cocked and rammed into her. From the hairs from Russell's head that police discovered in Carol's underpants, we think he even adorned those underpants on his head as he surveyed the scene of his handiwork. Then he wrapped her face in a dry-cleaning bag, probably stepped back again, felt the need to cover her head more, placed a pillow over her as if he were suffocating her, and walked out her bedroom door into the hallway. It was probably just about 4:10, because that was when Carol's daughter had seen him roaming in the hallway outside her mother's bedroom.

George Russell probably didn't even know there were kids living in the house until he read about them in the papers the next day. That's when he realized that he'd been spotted by an eyewitness who could put him right at the murder scene. However, she didn't know who he was and probably wouldn't recognize him again if she saw him. It was a close call and taught him even more about spending time with a victim, and he showed how much he had learned when he attacked his next victim, Andrea Levine.

George Russell knew who Randi Levine was and had even described her sexual proclivities in very disparaging terms to his friends. Why was it important for Russell to disparage Levine to the extent he did before her murder, referring to her as a slut because she was going out with one guy and sleeping with another? Was it because any woman he considered a two-timer was fair game, because she reminded him of the source of his anger? George Russell's own mother had first left him with his biological father while she went off to pursue her career, then moved him to live with her family and left him again, and finally left him with his stepfather on Mercer Island after she moved away with George's half sister. He made excuses about his mother's leaving to his friends, but it must have hurt. When George was in high school, his stepfather married a younger white woman and soon George was thrown out of the house. He told friends he left of his own volition, but he was in fact a homeless person on Mercer Island. George Russell was very angry at women.

Russell's signature and the way his MO evolved through the series suggests that his anger, far from becoming assuaged by his attacks on these women, actually escalated. This is common among killers who retaliate against females. And George Russell did retaliate to a point where the ritualism of the crime intruded into his fantasy and he got off, not just on the overkill of wreaking revenge on these stand-in symbols of his hate, but on the thrill of after-death violence and desecration.

Often, these retaliatory type of killers get so frantically violent they even break the rules they set for themselves. Shawcross crossed racial lines to kill a black prostitute, and Bobby Joe Long picked up a woman who almost overpowered him as he tried to strangle her and had to beat her into submission – not his normal pattern – before strangling her with the belt. Thus, it is consistent with a signature killer pattern that George Russell, living what amounted to a double life, would look for an even greater exposition of his anger and need to transform his fury into the very deviant sexual excitation of ritualistic experimentation with violence. He found it in Randi Levine, whose apartment he might have already robbed. There were persistent reports that Randi had told some friends that someone had been stealing money and other items from her place. She also told her landlord, Bellevue Fire Department Lt. Bob Hays, who lived in the unit upstairs from her, that she was afraid of prowlers and had actually heard a prowler just outside the house around August 25, 1990.

If Russell had been stalking Levine or even robbing her apartment, he probably also knew how conducive

Levine's apartment would be for a killer like him who was looking to spend even more time at the crime scene. She lived alone in a downstairs unit that Russell could get into from the outside. There was a dog that liked to bark, but if he'd already broken in before and no one responded, he could get away clean. Randi seemed to like her independence, and her living situation had already isolated her – an important criterion for a newly emerged serial killer. She was a young woman who had lots of friends and boyfriends and who came and went as she wished and with whom she pleased. That meant lots of false leads for the police to follow.

Randi's aggressive independence with men, her 'cut-'em-off-at-the-knees' attitude toward guys who challenged her, and her willingness to have sexual relationships with different boyfriends at the same time made her an attractive potential victim for Russell, who also probably believed that because he was only on the periphery of her acquaintances he would never be suspected. In retrospect, however, Levine's revealing to friends that things of hers were turning up missing sounds suspiciously like the complaints that followed Russell around most of his life. If he were in your circle of acquaintances and knew where you lived, eventually some of your things would start going missing. Perhaps that's the way it was with Randy Levine who, once she became one of the objects of Russell's anger, might as well have been wearing a bull's-eye, she was that tagged.

Russell thought he'd set up the perfect alibi for the night of the murder, thus giving himself the time he wanted to spend with the victim. He had taken a group of friends over to a room he had rented at a Motel 6 right near Kirkland, where they drank and ate snacks. A little after midnight, Russell announced he'd have to be leaving. He waited, part of the time making out with his friend and former roommate Bobbie DeGroot, until most of the group was asleep. He broke away from Bobbie, telling her he had work to do – office work, surveillance, the stuff he couldn't talk about – and left the motel room after three in the morning. Now the night would be his.

George had the opportunity to spend lots of time with Randi Levine. Her garage was open, he had easy access, and he found Randi fast asleep in her bed after having been out drinking at the Maple Gardens Restaurant until after midnight. Randy drank a lot that night and was so tipsy before she left the restaurant that the person she was with, Cass Hania, expressed concern over her ability to drive home alone. He was concerned enough for her safety on the road that he followed her car home part of the way just to make sure she was okay behind the wheel. She dropped into a deep sleep when she got home. She probably never woke up.

After he broke in, Russell quickly discovered that she would offer him no resistance, and the signature of the attack reveals that's exactly what happened. First there were fifteen separate blows to the head, probably knocking her unconscious even before she woke up from sleep. Prosecutor Jeff Baird pointed out that her torso had been assaulted, the same area that Russell had attacked in the Pohlreich and Beethe murders, but this time he stabbed her with a knife. He stabbed her many times, continuing after she was dead, and then began a cutting process – picquerism – inflicting more than 230 separate wounds. But he didn't stop there. Russell must have turned her over at some point, because he dug deep scratches along the length of her back. Then, while she was still facedown, he jabbed small incisions into her buttocks, anus, and thighs, and all the way down to the soles of her feet.

At some point after she was dead, Russell turned her back over, posed her in a supine position diagonally across the bed with her legs spread apart, draped one arm over a pillow, placed the *More Joy of Sex* book under her left forearm, jammed a plastic vibrating dildo into her mouth, covered her body lightly with a top sheet, and then placed a pillow over her head so that her eyes wouldn't see him. Arranging Randi's body this way, with much more care and attention than he had lavished on victims previously, took a considerable amount of time. Russell's style was continually developing.

We also know that Russell planned for more time with Levine. He left his motel room after three, probably closer to 3:30, hiked the short distance to Kirkland, and didn't arouse the Hays's dog until after five in the morning, when the dog heard him leaving the downstairs apartment. He could easily have spent a good hour with Levine, more than enough time to figure out exactly what he wanted to do as his anger spent itself, and how he was going to experiment sexually by desecrating her body. He also cleaned up after himself at the murder scene, taking care to remove the knives he used, as well as the actual murder weapon.

Just after five in the morning, Randi's landlord and upstairs neighbor Bob Hays heard his dog barking outside. Randi had complained to him before about a prowler, so he ran outside and caught a glimpse of a guy running from the house. He stood there for a bit, quieted his dog, and looked around to see if he could find anything amiss. Nothing seemed to be wrong, so he went back into the house. A few hours later that morning he went outside again and looked through the window where he saw that Randi still seemed to be asleep, undisturbed by the events earlier that day, so he didn't wake her up. That was the morning of August 31. George Russell had once again spent as much time with his victim as he needed, and then escaped the crime scene with only moments to spare. The only person who could have alerted police while George was still in the area wouldn't discover the body in the downstairs apartment until September 3, four days later.

NECROPHILIC FANTASIES OF GEORGE RUSSELL

George Russell was a violent necrophile whose sexual thrills came not only from the anger he vented in destroying his victims but from the postmortem fantasies of posing and humiliating these women. The entire psychodrama was played out in three acts. Russell needed to plan and justify the killing process and takedown of his targeted victim. He initiated this killing process by creating a real or imagined sense of being wronged by his targeted victim. Pohlreich rejected his advances; Carol Beethe and Levine were teasing him sexually; even if they didn't individually target him, Russell believed their sexually teasing behavior was wrong and wanted to punish them for it. Hence, in his own mind, Russell had the justification for hostile aggression against them. For him, the pretense of being wronged hinged on Pohlreich's rejection or Beethe's quick and sarcastic comments. Although the underlying motive for these murders was postmortem secondary sexual actions for Russell, the sequence of hostile aggressions in the act of killing served as a necessary and sufficient precondition for the ritual condemnation of the dead for him. This precedent condition – the justification – along with the stalking and approach comprised act one of Russell's necrophilic psychodrama.

Act 2 was the process of murder: he administered fatal traumas again and again to each victim well beyond the point of death. That the victim suffered torment in the killing process satisfied Russell's immediate angst and hostile aggression. But that same process drove him to a greater frenzy through an arc of violence as he fed on his own anger and the helplessness of the victim. He was humiliating himself by, first, the victim's resistance as she tried to fend off the blows, then by the victim's very lack of resistance after she lost consciousness and lay there at the point of death. In act 2, the anger driving Russell through sexual excitation was coming out of him in waves and bouncing off a surrogate target victim. The woman slumped over Smitty McLain's front seat or lying on the bed in front of him was neither the mother who abandoned him nor the stepmother who moved into his stepfather's house. This was only a symbolic substitute, a placeholder whose promise of sexuality, smirk, or blunt rejection had pulled his trigger. Now Russell, the 'little creep' in their minds, exploded in homicidal rage and was pushing his fury into postmortem sexual experimentation. Once the women were dead, the systematic violation of their bodies allowed him to express hatred and contempt for what each represented. Eventually, he merged each victim into a general group of the hated, his conquests – all of them women who in some way reminded him of the real objects of his rage, the two mothers – his real mother and then his stepmother – who had rejected him on two separate occasions.

In his third act, Russell used posing and paraphernalia such as objects found at the crime scene to degrade his victims and reduce them from human beings to statues or objects. Based upon the evidence of semen in the initial victim, Mary Ann Pohlreich, Russell's first murder was the only one in which he combined primary sexual mechanism – sexual climax – with the secondary mechanism, activities to postpone the sexual climax to a period after the crime had been committed. Through experience, Russell found that secondary mechanisms carried more strength for him in assigning meaning to images, signs, and ritual condemnation. Emotion recollected in tranquillity was more powerful than emotion experienced on the spot and ultimately lost.

Russell selected the phallic-shaped objects (fir cone, rifle, and dildo) placed in or near the body for their implied sexual potency and symbolic meaning. These insertions were used by him to denigrate the victim and present an image of degenerate promiscuity. Likewise, within the behavioral continuum of picquerism, the placement of over two hundred cuts in a polymorphic perverse pattern on Andrea Levine suggested that Russell saw her as sexually contemptible. He displayed her with overtly sexual objects to indicate his belief that she was a discard *because* of her sexuality.

Prior to exiting the crime scene, Russell took great care to pose each victim for maximum effect. In addition to placing them in sexual positions with accentuated arm and leg placements, he added references to, or the use of, garbage and trash to each scene. Russell left each crime scene with the lasting view that the victim, and, by extension, all women, were sexual degenerates who got what they had coming. Because he could not manage the fear and threat of a live potent woman who could, and did in fact, reject him, he hid his fear in hate and visited mayhem on dead bodies which did not resist. In and beyond the necrophilic perversities and potency, Russell's posed message for the police should have been read for its deviancy as a symbol of weakness that reflected upon the messenger.

THE ARREST OF GEORGE RUSSELL

George Russell, the man who was ultimately convicted in the three murders on the basis of evidence and a pattern-murder profile, was a living example of the changing face of serial murder. He was a young black man from an educated middle-class family who grew up in the exclusive upper-class white neighborhood of Mercer Island, Washington, and socialized easily in the Seattle yuppie singles community. Russell could almost be called a *Six Degrees of Separation* killer who recognized no racial distinctions. Just like the Ted Bundys, Jeffrey Dahmers, Arthur Shawcrosses, John Gacys, and other signature killers who live in the communities where they snap up their victims, Russell frequented singles bars and restaurants, dated and lived with young women from different racial backgrounds, and had a practice of turning his friends into robbery victims. It is this background that has me almost convinced that Russell's first murder – the Mary Ann Pohlreich imprinting or pattern murder – was a sexual assault-*cum*-robbery gone wrong when she resisted him after having teased him to a frenzy.

Who was the mysterious George Russell? From police records and interviews given to the press by his mother and natural father, we know he was born in Florida to a woman named Joyce and a father named George Walterfield Russell, who had had an affair and got married shortly before George, Jr. was born. George, Sr. was an employee of a funeral home and was living with his wife and son, who came home one day to find that his wife had left him. He told reporters that when George, Jr. was six months old, his mother left him with her mother when she abandoned the marriage to go back to school. Russell later said he was raised by his grandmother and her sisters in Florida. When Russell was six, he said, his mother, whom he claims had married Wonzel Mobley, but records do not confirm this, had come back for him. She and Wonzel Mobley took him cross-country to live with them in Tacoma and from there, again cross-country to Washington, D.C., then to Maryland, and finally back to Washington State. There they settled on Mercer Island after Mobley completed dental school.

Just after George's junior year in high school, he said, his mother announced that she was leaving Mercer Island for Maryland, giving George, Jr. the choice of staying with Wonzel Mobley or moving back east with her. He says he stayed on Mercer Island by choice. Others have said that Joyce simply moved out and took her daughter fathered by Wonzel with her. George never had a choice. Whatever the case, before long George was roaming the streets at will, getting into trouble, and getting his friends into trouble, and was suspected of stealing from his acquaintances and breaking into houses. George had been raised in the exclusive and affluent community of Mercer Island and blended in perfectly with the other young people in this enclave. He was a member of the club and all doors were open to him.

George never finished high school, although he lived through his teenage years on the island where the beat cops got to know him well. Many times they reported responding to burglary calls in the community and then would see George walking away from the scene. He was never carrying any stolen goods or property, and therefore was not picked up by the police. After a while, though, police suspected that he was ditching the stuff before they could arrive. He always was around when something bad was happening. Soon George's rap sheet was littered with entries for criminal trespass, evading the police, and possession of stolen property. Authorities could not pin a burglary charge on him, so he didn't spend time in prison. All his time consisted of short jail stays, and he was never picked up for a sexual offense.

When he was seventeen and out of high school, George crossed the bridge from Mercer Island to Bellevue, where he lived a transient's lifestyle. He boarded with anyone who would take him in and he could talk himself into almost anywhere. Most of his acquaintances thought that he always had a job – even though we could not find records of long-term employment – because he always seemed to have enough money to get by. Police could locate only two employers, and he was with them for less than two months. Two jobs in fifteen years, yet the man always had money. That's why the police thought he must have been one of the best cat burglars in the area. If he was getting by on burgling and had been for years, why did he start murdering?

Russell became a suspect in the murders after an alert Seattle Police detective, Rick Buckland, discovered that he was investigating Russell for possession of stolen property taken in a burglary of a residence close to the murder scene of Randi Levine. Russell first came to Buckland's attention in May 1990, after police responded to a call of a fight that had broken out between two men in downtown Seattle. As uniformed officers arrived, a black male, who had posed as a police officer to the combatants, was in the process of breaking up the fight. The officers were immediately suspicious of him because he seemed to be hiding something. There was a deviousness about him that set them on alert, so they questioned him further and patted him down. That was when they found the pistol he had concealed. He was arrested for impersonating an officer and taken into custody. The pistol was seized as evidence, traced on the computer by its serial number, and found to be stolen property taken in a burglary in the Totem Lake area north of Bellevue, where Randi Levine lived. They booked him under the name of George Russell.

After Buckland confirmed that the stolen property in Russell's possession came from a Totem Lake burglary near a murder site, he contacted Bellevue detectives Marv Skeen and Dale Foote, investigators in the murders of Mary Ann Pohlreich and Carol Beethe, respectively. Although both detectives had initially looked at other suspects and resisted Russell, they became convinced of Russell's involvement after his name came up repeatedly from other sources, especially Seattle police. They, along with King County Police Detective Larry Peterson, who was investigating the Kirkland murder of Levine, began weaving a tight web of physical evidence around Russell, while hoping they could find another reason to take him into custody and hold him. They were not disappointed, because Russell's murder skein was still under way. The start-stop sequence to the three murders had appeared arbitrary, but it was not. The invisible killer wanted to strike again. His open display of the bodies – a kind of private art form that he was exhibiting – was far from finished. At the same time, Bellevue police were actively searching for some way to catch Russell in the act. They were on the hunt for the man they believed to be their serial killer. Their only question was, would they catch Russell in the act or would they have another murder on their hands first?

Fate intervened on their behalf on September 12, 1990, two weeks after the murder of Andrea Levine. Bellevue police flooded a residential area when a prowler call was sounded. Just as it was years ago on Mercer Island, George Russell was walking slowly away when police spotted him nearby. Russell identified himself, as if he weren't doing anything wrong and had nothing to hide, but the police arrested him on a misdemeanor commitment warrant. Then a startling thing happened. The complaining party was a female who was an acquaintance of George Russell, just as Randi Levine was. The police had no doubt about it – Russell was stopped in the act of stalking his next victim's house. His setup was interrupted by an alert potential victim who called the police and became a living witness. Just as Carol Da Ronch and Nita Neary had identified Ted Bundy, so had this woman identified George Russell and perhaps saved her own life and the lives of many other potential victims.

Now the police pushed their investigation ahead full steam. First, they connected Pohlreich to Russell through a DNA analysis of Russell's semen that was found inside Pohlreich's body. Then, when detectives interviewed Russell's friends, they discovered that Russell had borrowed Smitty McLain's pickup on the night of the Pohlreich murder and returned it with a foul smell inside and a red stain on the seat. Though McLain had the truck detailed twice, the detectives found Pohlreich's blood on the inside of the seat cushions of the truck.

In the Beethe and Levine cases, the physical evidence was not as conclusive as in the Pohlreich case, which made the signature testimony linking all the cases that much more crucial. Detectives found hair in some underwear discovered on Beethe's bedroom floor. That hair was 'microscopically indistinguishable,' the lab report said, from the head hair of George Russell. It remained to be determined, in linking the murders in a series, why Russell had changed his MO, even though his signature had not changed at all.

The Pohlreich murder, we theorized, was more like an experiment at first – a sexual assault or robbery gone wrong because the victim fought him off too hard. Russell might have been surprised by what happened and what he did. Thus, the actual murder itself might have been a mistake, because what he wanted was not what he got. But in the end, the murder gratified him nonetheless. In wanting to control Pohlreich for his own sexual gratification, Russell misjudged her ability to resist his attacks. Then, after he'd killed her and brought her back to the Black Angus, he found he couldn't hoist her body into the compactor and had to throw off police with a different tactic. He hadn't planned on this. After all, he was a quintessential cat burglar, a thief of the night, and confronting someone in an outdoor, nonresidential situation with witnesses who could come around the corner at any moment was way out of his league. But Russell was nothing if not adaptable and quickly learned from his mistake. He also learned that control of the victim was pleasurable. So he changed his method of operation while reserving for himself the pleasure of posing, fondling, having sex with, and controlling the victim after death. He resumed his old method of breaking into homes in darkness to find his victims.

During the course of the murders, Russell stole rings belonging to Beethe and Levine. The theft of the rings was interesting to me, since I felt that most serial killers steal items belonging to victims. Frequently, family members or acquaintances of the killers unknowingly end up with those items as the killer circulates them among his group to get rid of potential evidence while at the same time keeping them in sight. It's a way the killer reinvigorates himself with the thrill without storing potentially critical evidence in his own closet. Detectives Skeen and Foote tracked Beethe's ring to a friend whom Russell had tried to convince to buy it. Larry Peterson recovered Levine's ring, which had passed through several people all the way to Florida.

Russell knew that the police would search his apartment. In a final act of bravado, he called his female roommates and had them present to police upon arrival a 1973 FBI evidence handbook. This was Russell's way of announcing his invincibility by implying, 'You're not going to find anything because I know your business, too.' Russell was still trying to assert control, to maintain his sense of significance even though he knew the police were hot on his trail. But Russell was wrong. This was 1990, not 1973. His edition of the evidence handbook didn't include DNA analysis, nor did he anticipate the thoroughness of the detectives' search for evidence. At Russell's apartment, a gym bag he always carried was recovered, and inside it was human head hair belonging to Randi Levine.

In the subsequent murder trial of George Russell, my testimony was simple: the killer's personal expression was permanently etched on the bodies of Pohlreich, Beethe, and Levine. When I analyzed the murders by type and frequency of injuries and other unique characteristics from the first murder to the third, I drew one conclusion: they were all committed by the same person.

The inception and development of our homicide tracking (HITS) computer program helped catch George Russell even though he was elusive and thought he knew how to camouflage himself in any group. But he played by the rules of the 1970s and didn't understand how his obvious signature made the pattern of his crimes stand out. His hatred of his victims was so evident that police were compelled to act to stop the monstrous killing machine operating in the neighborhoods of Bellevue and Kirkland. He didn't understand this, but he could not have kept hiding from the police once the detectives from the local communities formed an ad hoc task force to share information. That was when his name popped up and he was arrested. At that point, police discovered that Russell had committed the fundamental error of keeping and trafficking in the personal possessions he stole from his victims. These pieces of jewelry connected him directly to the people he killed and became a road map for the police.

Russell didn't simply attack prostitutes on the street like the Green River killer. He broke into people's homes in the night, killed them in their beds, sexually violated their corpses in the most gruesome ways, and then displayed them like trophies for people to find the next day. He degraded his victims by posing them in their full sexual vulnerability. In death, they displayed the helplessness of the final moments of their lives when Russell was beating them until the bones in their skulls shattered. Even the beating was part of his need to control. Serial murderers kill from a need to control, because they can't control anything else in their lives. In those moments just before and after the death of their victim, their need to control reaches its highest point of gratification. And very, very few of these killers know how to cover up their signatures completely once they've expended their lust on a lifeless victim.

The question of why he killed will always remain despite the tantalizing clues in Russell's life that float by. Russell, like almost every anger-driven control-type serial killer I've ever known, experienced abandonment or rejection by his mother at the most critical period of his infancy – within the first nine months. As anyone will remember from Developmental Psych 101, this is not only the period of the first Ericksonian crisis, the crisis of trust, it's also a critical period when the infant's neurological system is developing. Babies during this period are making the important first step of establishing physical boundaries, developing trust and a sense of the outside world. They are making the fundamental distinction between 'me' and 'not me.' Interruptions of this process inevitably lead to trouble down the line that results in problems in socialization, problems in school, problems with the juvenile justice system, and frequent confrontations with the criminal justice system.

In Russell's case, his problems with parent nurturing did not go away; they were actually compounded over and over again. After abandoning him at six months to her mother and family, Joyce left George in his stepfather's care again when he was in high school. Then, after Mobley remarried a young white woman only twelve years older than George, George Russell, Jr. was, according to local police reports, thrown out of the house. He'd been rejected twice, the last time by his stepfather's new wife. If George had had problems with women because of his source, his mother Joyce, he had them again. Women not only abandoned him, they rejected him and threw him out. As George skewed his relationships with women to younger and younger ones, he still found that at a certain point they left or he was shown the door. Was the cause promiscuity? Did he identify that with his mother who left him in Washington State for another man back east? Was there sexual tension in the Mobley household when he remarried? Did George feel two-timed by his new stepmother? Whatever the complex of reasons, it's clear that George was not a guy that could handle being teased by a woman. When he felt that Mary Ann crossed him, he killed her. He knew Carol from Cucina Cucina, knew her reputation, staked out her house, and displayed her in an unbelievably humiliating pose after he killed her. But he saved his most vicious attack for Randi Levine.

In stark contrast to his affluent upbringing on Mercer Island, when George left high school, he became a homeless person who either slept in an outside lair he carved out for himself on Mercer Island or crashed with anyone who would take him in. Sometimes his stepfather would allow him to stay in the house, but he always left the next morning. Every few nights, he had to find a different place to sleep. At the time he was planning the Randi Levine murder, George was bunking with three teenaged women who shared a condo in Bellevue. But he was only bunking, and the girls were fighting among themselves over who would ask George to leave.

George Russell might have emulated Ted Bundy and tried to follow in his footsteps. He might have believed he had the perfect cover – convincing anyone who would talk to him that he was an undercover cop who had to go out at night to work. But he made mistakes that Ted Bundy had always avoided. Ted's life as a stalker and serial killer was completely camouflaged for a very long time. George announced that he knew two of his potential victims and disparaged them to his and their friends. The anticipation of his rage, and the crossing between anger-retaliation and anger-excitation prompted him to telegraph his attacks so that instead of moving off into the darkness, he left a trail that was all too easy to pick up once his name came up as a suspect. Like Code, who made the mistake of killing someone he knew in the house where he grew up, Russell associated himself with his victims in advance so that he was not a stranger killer, but a predator who knew and announced the names of his victims.

Russell was also different from previous prototypical serial killers because in a good-news/bad-news sort of way, he was a product of his times. After the murders of Mary Ann Pohlreich and Carol Beethe, police immediately jumped on two different suspects, both connected to the respective victims, and both white. The official profile that came down from the profile experts told the Bellevue and King County police they were looking for a white killer, because after all, everybody knows that serial killers, except for prostitute killers, rarely cross racial lines. Guess what? They were wrong.

Back in Atlanta in the 1970s, my group of consultants argued strenuously with the officers from public safety that their prevailing theory of a white killer making a politically racist statement by killing black children was just not workable. No white man could simply have walked or driven into black neighborhoods – where the victims came from – and driven out without at least being spotted as an anomaly. We would have had hundreds of witnesses. Also, no white supremacist killer would have made such a statement with a signature murder without revealing some of his racist attitudes. These young boys were the victims of sex crimes, pure and simple. The killer, as we assumed and later found out was indeed the case, blended right into the community because he belonged to the community. He was a young black man named Wayne Williams who was ultimately convicted of murder.

When the police made the same racial assumptions about the George Russell murders, over fifteen years of American social history had washed right by them. George Russell had grown up in a white upper-middle-class community, because George Russell was upper-middle-class. His mother was a well-educated college professor. His stepfather was a well-to-do black dentist in an upscale community where no matter who you were or what you did, your teeth had to be perfect and white, your coffee had to be from Starbuck's, and your suits had to be from Armani. The issue wasn't race, it was the trademark you wore. Seven years after Jerry Rubin claimed to have invented the term, yuppies were alive and well and spending lots of money in places like Mercer Island and Bellevue, and George Russell, Jr., an anger- and impulse-driven, antisocial, violent sexual deviate inhabited the role of yuppie superbly, even though he was a transient who lived wherever he could after his racially mixed stepparents threw him out of the house.

George had cruised successfully with his white friends, both male and female, for years while he was getting into juvenile trouble on Mercer Island. Then he crossed the East Island Bridge and continued the pattern. There's no doubt about it – America had changed, socially at least, if not completely politically, and George Russell was a product of his time. Like the young man in New York who had claimed to be Sidney Poitier's son and preyed on affluent Upper East Side families, George Russell had become the *Six Degrees of Separation* killer, defying the traditional profiles and redefining, at least for law enforcement, how we would have to look at signature crimes in the future.

CHAPTER 9

The Black Hole at the End of the Continuum

Jeffrey Dahmer and Ted Bundy

Sometimes you can't help but be intrigued by a signature crime more bizarre and violent than any you'd seen before. Even though you try to treat it as if it were any other crime you had investigated, the very nature of it grabs you by the collar and drags you along simply because it gives you a glimpse of something on the very fringes of human existence, something you can't believe actually takes place in an American city. You read about modern vampires who drink their victims' blood, and you hear about cases of cannibalism. Then you hear about a case like Jeffrey Dahmer and you have to sit up and take notice because of what it tells you about depraved human behavior. You sympathize with the victims and all their families and wonder just how their paths crossed the killer's. You're forced to research every aspect of the case because somehow, you believe, you just may have to solve something very similar in your own city one day.

Along the continuum of violence, homicide investigators see some of the most incredibly violent acts human beings can perpetrate upon one another, acts that violate not only the law, but some of the most sacred taboos of society. Stories abound in fiction as well as in the history of crime about acts that were so unnatural, investigators had no frame of reference for assessing them. Thomas Harris's Buffalo Bill was one such unnatural killer; Hannibal Lecter was another, who laughed about cooking up one victim's liver with fava beans and a nice Chianti. Remember Lon Chaney, Jr. as Lawrence Talbot, the monster who struck terror into movie audiences back in the 1940s as the wolf man who could see the sign of the pentagram in the palm of his next victim, whose body he savaged during the cycle of the full moon until he was stopped by silver bullet? Remember Count Dracula himself, king of the vampires? We can thrill at the terror of these fictional killers from the safety of a theater seat, or at the other end of a TV remote control, but what happens to our psyches when one of them emerges in real life from the murky depths of the psychopathological ooze where all serial killers lurk to prey upon the living? What happens when he keeps on killing so successfully that nobody can stop him?

Answer: he keeps right on killing; the angry power images feeding his fantasy system cause victims to simply fall his way and play out their roles in his well-rehearsed drama. At his most successful, a killer like this takes his victims and police are unaware of their disappearance. Deep inside him this demented killer wants to cry out, to take credit for the control he's wielding over the entire community, but he can't because it would expose him. He becomes angrier and more contemptuous at the ease with which he succeeds. The sexual thrill he derives from fear may drive him to take even greater chances. What happens to him along the continuum? Where does he go to gratify himself at these heightened levels of violence? What is there for him at the very end of the violent path he's on?

If all of this sounds overly dramatic, think back to the night of July 23, 1991, in the middle of a hot Milwaukee summer. That's when two Squad 31 police officers,

Robert Rauth and Rolf Mueller, were flagged down in the street by a partially clad young black man named Tracy Edwards, who had a set of handcuffs dangling from his wrist, and who told them he'd been threatened with a knife by a crazed white assailant in an apartment, number 213, in a building just around the corner on North Twenty-fifth Street. The real-life drama of a cannibalistic serial killer turned into a grotesque reality that night. The killer's bloody fantasies played across our national consciousness right through the succeeding televised trial, forever changing the landscape of public perceptions of serial signature murders. What we learned about serial killer Jeffrey Dahmer, now dead at the hands of his own murderer inside prison, helped rewrite the book on signature crimes.

With victim Tracy Edwards leaning into their car, Officers Robert Rauth and Rolf Mueller radioed to their District 3 dispatcher that they were investigating a report of a possible assault on North Twenty-fifth Street between State and Kilbourn. The officers let Edwards slide into the backseat, his handcuffs still dangling from his wrist, and followed his directions to the middle of North Twenty-fifth, where they stopped in front of number 924. Then they went to apartment 213 and banged on the door while they visually inspected the numerous locks and the electronic gadgetry that secured the apartment. When a sullen, unkempt young man opened the door and let them inside, they immediately became aware of the foul odor of rotting meat, so overpowering it almost made them retch. Something was very, very out of the ordinary here.

The young man introduced himself as Jeffrey Dahmer, a name that Rauth and Mueller had dispatch run through R&I as a matter of course to see if there were any outstanding warrants on the guy. Bingo! He had priors: sexual assault. And he was still on probation. With the information provided to them by Tracy Edwards,

Dahmer, who'd also told them he'd been drinking alcohol, was violating his probation, at the very least, and would have to be taken into custody. After Dahmer was in custody, hands cuffed behind his back and lying facedown on the floor, the officers were free to look around the apartment and investigate the story Tracy Edwards had told them. No sooner had they begun the search than they found the Polaroids. The photos were scattered about innocently in plain view.

These were horrific pictures of what looked like the living dead: upright corpses in various stages of surgical dissection. Some of the men in the photos were in shackles, possibly still alive or even freshly killed, but not yet dismembered. You want to believe these were faked for shock value, even posed mannequins, but they were all too real. Then, to their ultimate shock, Rauth and Mueller found what people would later refer to as trophy portraits and severed human remains in various states of preservation. These were the human totems, the most prized possessions of a signature killer's war chest, the individual items that proved just how much control he exercised over his victims. Jeffrey Dahmer was so heavily immersed in this control fantasy that it was as if he were living in a crypt with pieces of the dead all around him.

In one particularly grisly photograph, police noticed that a head had been severed from its body, painted gold, and set atop the victim's two hands, cupped with the palms up. It was as if what was living had become a statue in perpetual submission to Jeffrey Dahmer, reducing what was once a vital living person to a piece of sculpture. It was beyond grotesque. In other photographs, police noted evidence of an ongoing mutilation of victims, various stages of bloody dismemberment scattered around like so many postcards. How long had this been taking place? And – they almost didn't want to know – where were the bodies?

'Hey, there's a head in here. This guy's sick.'

One of the police officers tracking the source of the foul, rotting odor, and maybe hoping that it wasn't what he thought it might be, had opened the refrigerator and seen the not yet preserved skull of Oliver Lacy sitting in a box on the bottom shelf. Next to the head, in an all but futile attempt to absorb the odor of rotting flesh, Jeffrey Dahmer had set an open container of Arm & Hammer baking soda. Baking soda is widely advertised to be a powerful absorbent of odors. The box of baking soda attracted particular attention because its presence might mean that Dahmer was aware of the stench of rotting flesh, possibly that it was a giveaway to something wrong in the apartment, and sought to control the odor. Then Rauth and Mueller went into the bedroom where they popped open a fifty-five-gallon drum and found more body parts from the victims Dahmer had lured to his apartment and murdered.

THE MURDERS OF JEFFREY DAHMER

Rauth and Mueller called in their report and the news quickly spread that a major body find had taken place in downtown Milwaukee. Within the next fifteen minutes, as the police sealed off the alley behind the apartments and backed in crime lab vehicles, the whole record book on serial murders was up for a rewrite. As the shining blue and red light bars atop police units threw their patterns across the building's facade and the static of radio transmissions crackled over loudspeakers into the night, residents called newspapers and television stations. Something big was going down on North Twenty-fifth Street, they said; better get your camera crews down here. That's when the mobile units arrived with their satellite dishes, video cams, and production crews. Shortly after midnight, the news that a major serial killer case had been broken in Milwaukee was being flashed to the wire services and to newspapers in major cities.

The mystery of Jeffrey Dahmer that confronted officers Rauth and Mueller began to unravel quickly when detectives Patrick Kennedy and Michael Dubis arrived at the apartment shortly after midnight on Tuesday, July 23, 1991. Rauth and Mueller reported to the detectives about evidence of possible homicides in the apartment, about the human skull they had found in the refrigerator, and about the Polaroids of mutilations of human bodies and human heads. As the detectives took Jeffrey Dahmer into custody and transported him to the Criminal Investigation building, they found a suspect willing to talk to them and reveal the secrets he had been carrying since his first homicide back in Bath Township, Ohio, in 1978, just after he'd graduated from Revere High School. After being read his Miranda rights, Detective Kennedy wrote that Dahmer said that he wished to 'freely make a statement regarding the incident.' He began, according to Detective Kennedy's report, by admitting that he was still on probation for having taken Polaroid pictures of a minor. Then he began talking about his first homicide in Ohio when he was only eighteen, the beginning of his thirteen-year killing spree.

He told the detectives that he was living in Richfield, Ohio, and had just graduated from high school when he picked up a nineteen-year-old hitchhiker named Steven Mark Hicks, whom he took back to his house. They were drinking beer, got drunk, and were having homosexual relations when the hitchhiker got up to leave. Dahmer tried to stop him to prevent him from leaving Dahmer alone. But Hicks was adamant, and when he tried to leave again, they got into a 'physical fight,' during which Dahmer hit Hicks over the head with a barbell, which killed him. Dahmer buried the body outside, let it decompose for a couple of weeks, dug it up, and smashed the bones into small pieces with a sledgehammer. These he scattered in the woods surrounding his father's house. This was the confession to a murder that had gone unsolved for thirteen years, during which time Hicks had been just another missing person. Ohio police didn't even know they had a homicide. Now the case was solved by the only living witness.

Then Dahmer unfolded tales of murder upon murder, killings that took place when he was living in his grandmother's house in West Allis, a murder that took place in a downtown Milwaukee hotel room, and many more murders that took place after he got his own apartment in Milwaukee. He described how he tried to decompose the bodies of his victims by steeping them in acid just like he did with dead animals he found along the road near his house when he was only ten or eleven years old. He told them how he used power tools to dissect bodies and decapitate his victims. Then he explained how he pulled the muscle tissue off the bones of his victims and wore the muscles over his shoulders like a garment while walking around the apartment. He talked about how he painted skulls that he'd preserved after the flesh had decomposed, and how he'd placed them over his bed. He also described how he'd eaten the flesh of his victims and preserved sexual organs he'd cut off some of them in a jar of formaldehyde so he could masturbate in front of them whenever he wanted.

By the time he was finished, Dahmer had revealed one of the most lurid and physically repulsive tales of murder, mutilation, and cannibalism the detectives had ever heard. He had gone so far into the world of fantasy murder, he had gone almost to the end of a continuum of violence and into a black hole which no one had ever explored. He'd gone into the world of the human cannibal and practicing necrophile, a man who trained himself to be a master of guile and camouflage and to live his life inside a tabernacle of the dead.

NECROPHILIA

The first aspect of Dahmer that seemed so abhorrent to detectives was his steady sexual pleasure from the practice of necrophilia, the satisfaction derived from handling and manipulating corpses in various states of decay. Necrophilia is one of the aspects of total control, and it has three major divisions.

First, the corpse's state of decay and odor becomes an acquired fetish for the killer, whose need to consummate an imposed relationship with a fantasized memory of the victim capitalizes upon the signs and symbols of real death. An extreme form is the cannibalistic act of consuming part of the corpse to get into harmony and/or become one with the love object. In another form of cannibalism, the killer, who eviscerates the body, climbs inside and wears the carcass like a buffalo skin. Here, the gruesome scene depicts the killer's attempt to fantasize his unity with his victim in another way. Dahmer engaged in all of these practices inside the tomb that he fashioned out of his apartment.

Second is the 'jackal' who preys upon the dead for forbidden pleasures. Here, while struggling with the morality of adultery, incest, pedophilia, and homosexuality, among other practices, with the living, the death of the victim releases all inhibitions against such acts. The killer can do what he will because the victim will never awaken to see him at his most vulnerable. Now death has transcended the moral plane and allows the killer's unfettered fantasies to become realized with impunity. This process is extremely addictive and seductive to the necrophile, who, because he is in complete control, craves for an increasingly intense gratification from each encounter. Hence, the increasing level of violence that becomes evident in the signature from crime to crime.

For Dahmer, who, according to people who knew him as he cruised the gay bars of downtown Milwaukee, struggled with his homosexuality and had built up a tremendous fury toward other gays, necrophilia provided him the freedom to experiment with his fantasy without the fear of rejection. No one could leave him. No one could make fun of him. A dead victim became the perfect sexual partner.

Finally, the last category is the series of sexual acts with the dead to bolster or feed the killer's need for unconditional and unresponsive acceptance. Here, the killer provides a prepared script of self-validation without the risk of rejection from a live person. In essence, it is the coward's insurance against power emasculation, impotence, and the realization of internal weaknesses. In targeting the corpses of the dead, this type choreographs his ultimate power trip, a drama in five or six acts in which the victims have the script written for them: 'no living humans need apply.'

In this most extreme form of control, the murder itself is an obligatory process to the real satisfaction the signature killer exercises over the completely submissive body of his victim. It is the victim the necrophilic killer fears, or his inferiority to his victim, and therefore he can satisfy his sexual need only with an acquiescent victim who will not reject him or make him feel less than human. The necrophile must own his victim, must never, ever feel as if he can be rejected, and must be able to summon up his victim whenever he wishes.

Dahmer's First Homicide

Jeffrey Dahmer's career was marked by a high degree of organization. Since he'd been experimenting with the disposal of animal remains from the time he was a child, he used the same process to dispose of the body of Steven Hicks, the unfortunate hitchhiker who'd become his first victim. After Dahmer killed Hicks he dragged the body into a crawl space on the side of the house, and using a long kitchen knife, carved the boy's arms and legs off his torso and stuffed everything into plastic bags. These he stuffed into the trunk of his father's Oldsmobile and drove off to the dump. He was still drunk, however, and driving erratically over the center line. On the way to the dump he was spotted by a police car, stopped, and given a drunk-driving test on the spot. He barely passed, and the police told him to be careful. Had he failed the test and been arrested, no doubt the car would have been impounded and its contents searched. The police would have found the body of Steven Hicks, and the serial murder career of Jeffrey Dahmer might well have been stopped after the very first murder. But that's not how it happened.

It wasn't lost on Dahmer that he'd just escaped what could have been a fatal encounter with the law. He turned around and headed straight home, where he took the plastic bags out of the car and lugged them back into the crawl space, sealed them up, and tried to forget about them. But the smell of decomposition wouldn't let him. It was hot that June, and in a few days the whole house was putrid from the stench of rotting flesh. He knew his mother or father could come home at any time and his secret would be discovered. He had to get rid of the body.

First, he tried to stuff the bags into a drainage pipe behind the house, but the bones were too rigid and the bags wouldn't fit. Then he tried to dig a grave right alongside the drainage pipe, but the ground was too tough and rocky. He tried to scoop out enough soil to conceal the body completely, but there were too many rocks and all he could do was scrape a shallow grave out of the soil. He didn't like it, but he was tired, so the shallow grave would have to do for the time being. At least the smell was gone from the house, and with his parents still gone he wasn't in any danger. So Dahmer left the bags under the ground behind his house for the next couple of weeks.

But the panic of discovery began to eat at him again. What if children came to play over in those woods, just as he'd done when he was a child, looking for animal bones or flints? They would find the plastic bags right away and there'd be too many questions to answer. Rather than worry any longer, Dahmer dug up the bags again, and this time, tore into the carcass the same way he'd done when he was younger. First he cut all the body parts into little pieces, then he pared the flesh away from the bone. He used acid to strip away all the flesh and then put the pieces of flesh and organs into jars of acid until they dissolved into a brown murky liquid which he flushed down the drainpipe. Now all he had left were bones: legs, arms, ribs, a spine, and a skull. These he pulverized with a sledgehammer until there was no fragment of bone larger than a small person's hand.

He then took the hundreds of bone fragments, climbed up to a rocky cliff area at the back side of his home, and spread the bones around the area. He stood there on a ledge, he said, and began spinning in a 360-degree circle, throwing the bones out over the ground as he turned. It was almost like a ritual, the spreading of his first victim to the four winds, raining down upon the rocky ground in a grisly shower of human bone pieces. Then Dahmer burned Hicks's wallet and all his identification, took the knife and the necklace that Hicks had been wearing around his neck when Dahmer picked him up, and drove them over to a bridge over the Cuyahoga River. He tossed the knife and necklace into the river, where they were carried far downstream and out of Dahmer's life for the next thirteen years.

In this way, Jeffrey Dahmer's first murder, laid against a background of his childhood experimentation with dissolving animal parts that he'd found along the road, prepared him for becoming one of the most organized and successful long-term signature killers the world has ever known. Over time, that signature evolved into a chilling indicator of the psychopathological inferno burning away at the core of Dahmer's existence. At the same time, it indicated the chilling competence of the man who, after his psychologically gripping trial was televised to the world, would come to his own violent end at the hands of another inmate behind bars in a Wisconsin high-security penitentiary.

THE SIGNATURE ASPECTS OF THE JEFFREY DAHMER CASE

Hatred for His Victims

The types and extent of the mutilation and postmortem manipulation of Dahmer's victims indicated to anyone researching the case that Dahmer clearly displayed an underlying and pervasive deep attraction and hatred for his victims that evolved as his crime spree continued. People who knew him in Milwaukee suggested that Dahmer was hate-driven. In a conversation he had had with John Paul Ranieri, a local Milwaukee counselor known as Brother John who ran a street ministry, Dahmer had talked about his hatred for gays and blacks, the single largest components of his victim profile. That hatred was constantly struggling between the weaknesses and strengths in his personality, or more appropriately, between the reality of his deadly actions and the fantasies that plagued his mind and formed the foundation for his actions. Sitting outside a leather gay bar called the Wreck Room, Dahmer told Ranieri that the gay black men camping it up at the bar didn't know how to behave themselves. Ranieri asked him if he had a problem with blacks, and Dahmer allegedly said, 'According to the biblical stories, they should be all subservient to the whites.'

'Where do you come up with that?' Ranieri asked him.

'It's in the Bible,' Dahmer said, and quoted chapter and verse to the minister about sanctions against sexually deviant behavior. Dahmer continued. 'You know, all of these gays should be dead anyway from AIDS. None of them should live. This is a plague sent by God on the gay community.'

To Ranieri, these were the kinds of comments straight people made about gays, not gays about themselves. And the more Dahmer, by now thoroughly drunk, expounded on the problems of gays and AIDS, the more Ranieri realized that Dahmer was a cauldron of fury bubbling over onto anyone who got close to him. But, at the time, nobody was putting two and two together about the disappearances in the Milwaukee gay community. Ranieri didn't realize until Dahmer confessed to the murders that he was actually talking to an active, stalking serial killer who was at that very moment looking for another victim for himself that same night.

In a bizarre continuation of the conversation, Dahmer lamented that he couldn't get a girl to go out with him. He cruised singles bars, he said, but no girl would give him the time of day. According to the alcoholism counselor, Dahmer's surface problem was drinking. He drank so much he couldn't even stand up straight and acted so much like a geek, girls simply walked away.

But had Ranieri, had anyone known about Dahmer's postmortem activities with his gay victims, he would have realized that Dahmer's protestations about women were simply a part of his conflict. It would have been just as easy for him to pay for female prostitutes had he been heterosexual as it was for him to hustle other gays. His problems with girls were actually not problems at all but easy things for him to complain about. His real problems were with other men and his conflicts about his sexuality.

It was hate that was driving Dahmer, hatred for other men, hatred for his father, and hatred for anyone who was willing to spend time with him. This was a hatred Dahmer exercised through control, mutilation, necrophilia, and cannibalism.

Extreme Control

Among Dahmer's greatest triumphs was his ability to exert control as life fell apart around him. It was paradoxical but typical of a serial killer that the more Dahmer drank and seemed out of control, the more he was actually able to repeat his well-rehearsed pattern of murder. He would find a good-looking stranger near the shopping district downtown, chat him up to see if he was gay and receptive to spending time with him, offer him some money to pose for photographs, take him back to his apartment in a taxi, drug him immediately, kill him, and begin the postmortem activity. Dahmer was still able to function at this game even though people in the gay community had begun to associate him with the disappearances of young men from local bars. John Paul Ranieri himself put the word out on the street, he said, that he believed Dahmer was a menacing and violent individual who was out to hurt people. There were others warning members of the community not to get into taxis with Dahmer because they would be in danger. However, despite the warnings and admonitions, Dahmer was able to function, conceal himself successfully from the police, and satisfy his sexual urges until the very end.

Fetishism

Dahmer engaged in a protracted courtship dance with his prospective victims, picking them out at gay bars, at the shopping mall, and even on the street. He traveled to Chicago to meet companions at the gay pride parade there and brought a victim back with him on the bus to Milwaukee. Dahmer liked to watch his potential victims from afar, follow them with his eyes, and fantasize about which young man would make the easiest victim. This behavior was akin to a type of voyeurism, a signature component he also engaged in after the victim was dead and Dahmer left him propped up on his couch where he photographed him. Dahmer also liked to have extensive physical contact with his victims, such as touching and rubbing after death. He also engaged in oral sex with his victims, fondling them and manipulating their bodies before he cut them up for cannibalism, decomposition, storage, and, in some cases, decoration.

Dominance-Submission

Dahmer took sadistic enjoyment in springing the trap on his victims and in exercising dominance. Early in his spree, he wasted no time in drugging his victims with very strong sedatives, playing with them, then strangling them to death. However, toward the end of his spree, he experimented with handcuffing his victims before he killed them or beginning the process of dominance before the drugs fully took effect. It was as if he wanted to prolong the process of the surrender of the victims, heightening it with the application of bondage devices such as handcuffs. By forcing his later victims to obey him – holding out the promise of letting them go if they did – Dahmer enforced discipline through terror and satisfied his compulsion for sexual sadism.

Cannibalism

Dahmer's indulgence in cannibalism was the umbrella overlaying everything he did. It became part of his maniacal acquisition for power. He always took victims on Friday night so he had the full weekend for the pleasures and cleanup. His cannibalistic tendencies were so pervasive, he experienced two types at the same time: eating for strength from the loved one, his victim; and destroying that same part of himself through devouring it in someone else. For some killers who have all the time they want to spend with the victim or who have secreted the victim's body so successfully that they have no fear of discovery, experimentation with cannibalism is an extension of their compulsion for control. Dahmer carried this much further, however, because he was experimenting at the same time with faster processes he could use to decompose a victim and reduce the bodies to skeletons. Paring muscle tissue and flesh away from bones and handling the flesh provided him with an unlimited opportunity to indulge in his cannibalistic fantasies such as tasting flesh and making living costumes out of the cartilage, skin, and tissue of his victims.

Ritualizations of Victim Body Parts

Dahmer elaborated on his rituals with his victims: he sought multiple victims, tried to get victims to bring him other victims, created living zombies or somnambulistic sex toys by injecting acid into their frontal lobes, decorated skulls of his victims by painting them, posted some of the heads of his victims on his mantel like trophies, and decorated his apartment with an altar to his victims made out of their decorated skulls.

There was overwhelming physical evidence at the crime scenes attesting to Dahmer's interest in the skeleton remains of his victims. He was fascinated with their bones and the varying states of decay of their remains. He singled out for special attention his favorite skull and posed it and others in prominent places. Dahmer's penultimate single signature was the head in the refrigerator. His victims actually became his possessions, but only after they were dead. Thus, in Dahmer's pathological vision of the universe, there was no difference between displaying his hatred toward his living victims and their bodies and his love in preserving them after death and dismemberment. This accounts for the keeping of his loved one and eating his heart. Dahmer did peccadillo types of things, and progressed to cannibalism throughout his killing career.

Tracy Edwards, one of the three living victims of Jeffrey Dahmer, provided insightful details into the hours he spent handcuffed to his captor in the apartment. He described Dahmer's trancelike states as he kept playing the VHS of *Exorist III* on television, and how certain parts of the movie excited Dahmer into holding the knife against Edwards's throat. Edwards told police how Dahmer wanted to listen to his heart beating and then threatened to eat Edwards's heart after he had killed him. This was a kind of foreplay for Dahmer, who would whip himself up into a frenzy and then lapse into dream-like states to subvert the foreplay. It was almost as if Dahmer were looking for specific responses from his victims whenever he adapted something that seemed pre-scripted, such as running his knife over a victim's groin or along his neck. What was Dahmer expecting his victims to say when he told them he wanted to eat their hearts? If he were acting out a fantasy with his later victims, how elaborate did he want it to get, and why did it seem to replace the almost instant kill he was perpetrating on his earlier victims? These are all questions that would provide clues to the evolving signature of Dahmer. He was clearly experimenting with terrorizing his victims as an anticipatory thrill to what he would soon experience through necrophilia, dismemberment, mutilation, cannibalism, and the decoration and adornment of skulls he'd preserved.

The Trial of Jeffrey Dahmer

'Jeffrey Dahmer has a mental disease,' his defense counsel Gerald Boyle told the jury at Dahmer's murder trial, where he pleaded insanity. 'And that mental disease is necrophilia.'

Thus, the stage was set for a classic confrontation between a privileged defendant with all the advantages of one of Milwaukee's best attorneys, and the state. In a trial in which a person with Dahmer's obvious background of affluence sank to such a level of depravity that he not only preyed upon young transient men, he decorated his apartment with their skeletons, Dahmer really had a lot to explain about the 'why' behind his crimes. First, Dahmer came from what might be construed as a typical, all-American, middle-class family. His father Lionel was a chemist, a Ph.D. who had grown up in Milwaukee and had gone to college at Marquette University. Second, Jeffrey was born in Milwaukee; he was a native son of native stock. Third, Jeffrey had family in Milwaukee and had lived with his family while he was committing the first murders. Fourth, Jeffrey had the benefits of what seemed like an all-American home life and the benefits of good counsel when he was convicted of a sexual offense years earlier, and, it was perceived, he was given special treatment in court because of the pleas entered on his behalf. Yet at the same time he was able to camouflage his career as a serial killer, and he emerged from jail only to kill again.

'Jeffrey Dahmer wants a body. A body,' the lawyer continued in his opening statements. 'That's his fantasy. A body.' And he told the story of what happened when Jeffrey Dahmer was fifteen and became obsessed with killing and having sex with a jogger who would run by the house every day. One day he actually acted on those fantasies and sawed off a baseball bat and rode to find the jogger. But he never saw the man again. Boyle contended that might well have been the beginning of Dahmer's obsession with killing and having sex. It was all part of his mental disease.

Milwaukee County District Attorney E. Michael McCann argued that although the confessions of Jeffrey Dahmer were grotesque and even ghoulish, his murders, dismemberings, and sex with corpses were not evidence of mental disease, because Dahmer knew what he was doing at all times and by his own admission understood right from wrong. McCann pointed to Dahmer's own confessions that were read into the record by Milwaukee Police Detective Dennis Murphy. He said that Dahmer not only understood right from wrong, he went to great expense and took pains to conceal what he was doing because he knew he was in the wrong. 'Dahmer stated that he was fully aware that the acts he was committing were wrong and that he feels horrified that he was able to carry out such an offense,' Detective Murphy testified. 'He stated it was obvious he realized they were wrong because he went to great time and expense to try and cover up his crimes. He stated that he used quite a bit of fortune setting up alarm systems in his apartment.'

Boyle sharply contrasted his view of the evidence with the prosecution's, arguing that everything Dahmer did was an indication of his sickness. Unlike McCann, who said that Dahmer liked having live sex partners instead of dead ones, 'preferred the person to be alive,' and 'liked to hear the heart,' Boyle said that Dahmer derived erotic pleasure from dead bodies. 'He did not want to stop what now had become his fantasy, his obsession, his compulsion.' He wanted to create 'zombies,' Boyle said, 'people who would be there for him.'

The ensuing trial was not so much a battle over evidence or fact, but over the meaning of evidence and the interpretations of fact, which is basically how the insanity defense is supposed to work. The entire case is subordinated to the precise legal definitions of insanity which sometimes don't make sense in the real world. Insanity within the legal framework means that the person pleading insane must show that he or she was incapable of understanding right from wrong. The person must demonstrate that some medical condition absolutely removed from him or her the choice of conforming his or her behavior to the law. These are specifics. No one debated whether it was a healthy act on Dahmer's part to cut off a person's skin. No one disagreed that it was evidence of psychological disturbance. However, the prosecution argued throughout the trial that Dahmer not only knew it was wrong to peel a victim's skin from his skull, but that he could have prevented himself from committing that act if he had wanted to. That he was in control all the time, the prosecution experts argued, and that he understood what he was doing meant that he was not suffering from a mental disease that prevented him from conforming his actions to the law.

The defense took the same evidence to show that one might be aware that what one is doing is wrong – indeed, that's what Dahmer himself said to Detective Murphy – but that Dahmer, because he was suffering from a sexual disease, was unable to conform his actions to what he knew was right. He had been traumatized as a child by his fears and was suffering from a mental disease known as necrophilia so that he was incapable of making any decisions regarding his behavior. Therefore, because he was controlled by a disease that prevented him from conforming his actions to the law, he should be found insane and sent to a mental hospital until he was cured.

The two sides fought over the issue of necrophilia and whether that qualified Dahmer as a person with a mental disease. However, some medical experts believed that the definition of necrophilia – a sexual disorder in which the person is sexually stimulated only by corpses – was far too narrow an issue to be debated, because Dahmer had forms of sexual relations with living people and performed oral sex on some of his victims before he killed them. Therefore, the debate over whether Dahmer was a necrophile virtually guaranteed a verdict of sanity, because Dahmer was clearly stimulated by people who were alive.

Where the defense and prosecution differed was on the issue of control. Gerald Boyle argued that control wasn't the critical issue in Dahmer's case; rather, it was Dahmer's substantial inability to conform his conduct to the requirements of the law. When left to his own devices – which I would add includes having a private lair to which to bring back his victims – Dahmer reverts to a creature who may know what he's doing, may be able to control it within a very limited capacity, but ultimately will not be able to conform his behavior to the requirements of the law.

It also all came down to the issue of control. If a person can control his actions, even though they seem bizarre, deviant, and beyond the scope of normal behavior, then the person is considered willful, deliberate, and ultimately sane. Just because Jeffrey Dahmer was a necrophile didn't mean that if a policeman were standing next to him, he couldn't control his impulses so as to prevent himself from getting caught. Thus, the prosecution argument was as simple as it was hard to defeat: if you can control your actions so as to make a behavior choice, then you are in control and not out of control. If you are in control, then you do not have a mental illness and are sane.

The defense's star witness, Dr. Judith Becker, sought to show that Dahmer's pathology was such that although he understood what he was doing was wrong, he was so 'obsessed' with the kind of sex he was compelled to perform, he lacked the capacity to conform to the requirements of the law. For example, he admitted to Becker that he had tried to perform crude lobotomies on his victims because in so doing, he said, he hoped to make them into zombies who would simply stay with him in his apartment and not leave. He became so obsessed with this idea that he had actually drilled holes into the heads of his living victims while they were unconscious. Two of his victims came to after the holes had been drilled, but they had severe headaches. One person actually lived for a whole day but was dead when Dahmer came back the following morning from working the night shift at the Ambrosia Chocolate Factory.

In particular, Dahmer described two homicides that were particularly gruesome, but which helped to explain why Konerak Sinthasomphone – the boy who ran out in the street months before Dahmer was finally arrested, attracted the attention of neighbors who flagged down police, but was released into Dahmer's custody – was unable to communicate with the police. First, Dahmer told Dr. Becker, he was indeed eating portions of victim Errol Lindsey by taking sections of his flesh out of the freezer and cooking them. While he ate, Dahmer said, he would become sexually excited. He also said that he used a handheld drill and bored a hole into Lindsey's skull straight through to the brain. He then injected a large syringe full of acid into the frontal lobe so that the victim, Dahmer believed, would be able to follow simple commands and not resist. Dahmer said that Lindsey awoke after the first injection and had a headache, so Dahmer gave him more sleeping pills.

In describing Sinthasomphone's particularly sorrowful death, Dahmer said that he drilled holes in the boy's skull and filled them with acid. Then the child got up and wandered through the streets. He was completely 'lobotomized' when the police arrived and sat there on the couch in pain and so brain damaged he was incoherent. After the police left, Dahmer gave Sinthasomphone another injection through his lobe, which was fatal. In describing these deaths, Dr. Becker tried to show that the defendant was well beyond the range of any measure of sanity.

District Attorney McCann's main prosecution witness was Dr. Park Dietz, who argued very forcefully for Dahmer's ability to control himself. Dietz, who is probably one of the most experienced experts in interviewing and testifying about the criminally insane, argued that although Dahmer exhibited some profound symptoms of mental disorders, his ability to control and premeditate, camouflage himself, and conceal what he did were all examples of sane, cunning behavior. The evidence provided by Dahmer himself revealed that he disposed of his bodies efficiently, planned different methods of disposal, was able to control his murderous urges for years between crimes – especially when he was in the army – and was able to fool his probation officer and policemen on different occasions; these proved that the man knew exactly what he was doing. Dietz's testimony conforms to the well-established theory that no matter how bizarre, the signature left by the killer at the crime shows that he was not simply a mindless automaton carrying out meaningless commands from a voice echoing in his brain, but an organized predator who might be sick or dysfunctional but is capable of making choices about his criminal behavior and how to conceal it; therefore, he is legally responsible for his actions.

ORGANIZED AND DISORGANIZED SIGNATURE KILLERS

Organization is one of the keys to evaluating signature and legal culpability at a criminal trial. The more methodical organization is, the more it can allow the long-term control-type signature killer to remain on the loose for years, experimenting further and further with his anger-driven sexual murders and evolving further along a continuum of violence until he falls into his own black hole where he experiments with necrophilia, cannibalism, and the creation of a ritualistic lair full of totems. This is what happened to Jeffrey Dahmer, and it was partly the result of his own organizational skills that he reached one of the most bizarre places in the violence continuum. Dahmer was an example of an organized signature killer whose crime scene reflects a rational and measured decision-making process which is orderly, sequential, and self-protective. This is in sharp contrast to the crime scene of a disorganized killer which reflects conflicted planning, impulsiveness, and general disinterest in cleaning up or removing incriminating evidence.

In contrast to the more organized murderer, the less-organized assailant kills and leaves victims at his crime scenes almost exactly where they fell. He exerts little effort to conceal the body and seems to want to run as soon as whatever emotion that drove him to kill is satisfied. Also, the crime scene is within the killer's living and working proximity, and this is an important clue. When we find the crime scene of a disorganized killer, we usually suspect that the killer lives or works nearby, which helps to focus the investigation along a much finer beam.

The disorganized killer's choice of a weapon can be opportunistic – just like Dahmer's first weapon, a barbell – taken from the victim or crime scene. After the killing, the weapon may be located in close proximity to the murder scene. In the most disorganized fashion, the victim's body may show uncontrolled assault. The frenzied attack may have bite marks, insertions, blood or feces smearing, and postmortem exploration of the body. All of it is readily apparent because the killer has not covered his tracks.

Contrary to the organized murderer, the disorganized killer doesn't place a high value on intellectual domination, cunning, or social skills. Instead, he values isolation, nighttime darkness, and self-directed fantasy relationships. As a consequence, his needs are most likely met by menial employment, poor rooming conditions, public transportation, or an older vehicle kept in a slovenly condition. Personally, he may appear disheveled and strange, and look like an outcast. Often, he is viewed as a shadowy person scuttling into darkness. His personal skills are poor. He may retain newspaper clippings related to his crimes. It is important to realize that any classification of a killer's signature will have its variation along the organized/disorganized continuum.

The organized killer is like Dahmer or Bundy, who rehearsed their crimes more than a few times and stayed with the patterns that best served them. They not only knew their haunts and the patterns of their prospective victims, they knew the area well enough to be able to avoid the police. Jeffrey Dahmer's patterns are almost classic. Although he killed while he lived at his grandmother's house, he knew the chances of discovery were high, so he moved out. Once in his own place, he protected it with police locks and all kinds of security devices. He bought freezers and containers to handle the body parts and a huge vat for decomposing victim remains. Dahmer made it a point to be seen for as short a time with his victim as possible, so that he always had the plausibility of denial were he to be questioned. Although there were people who saw him getting into cabs with victims on the way to his apartment, he was killing in a community of transient young men whose comings and goings were generally not tracked. Without the body of his victim in police evidence, it would be almost impossible to pin any crime on Dahmer. In fact, he was so organized that even after he was picked up for the molestation of a minor, his real crimes were never discovered, he was allowed to keep his apartment while serving time in jail, and when put on work-release probation, he was still soliciting young men for sex and manipulating the body parts he had stored.

Like Dahmer, Bundy had a number of dump sites known only to himself. He was driving hundreds of miles with the bodies of his victims that he'd stashed in places so safe he could return to visit them whenever he wanted. He also considered his stash of women's clothing – souvenirs he took from his victims – completely safe in his room, and he even used his girlfriend's fire-place to burn remains of his victims. Bundy was a member of a class, with John Gacy and Jeffrey Dahmer, to which only the most organized and clever signature killers ever belong – killers whose victims simply disappear. Although our King County Task Force would have eventually caught up with him as a result of our computer tracking, history still records that it wasn't until Bundy's own activities in Utah got him into trouble that he came to the attention of the police. But in the state of Washington, at least, Bundy was at or near the end of the continuum of violence just as Dahmer was in Milwaukee on the night he was caught.

THE BLACK HOLES AT THE END OF THE CONTINUUM

If they are not stopped at any point along the continuum, sadistic killers can cross the threshold into the most deviant and horrible of necrophilic psychosexual stages, that of cannibalism. Cannibalism is the devouring or consuming of human blood and flesh to satisfy fantasies which involve harmonizing with their love object. Up to this point, sexual sadists have been identified in varying degrees in their placement along the arc of psychosexual development. We have seen the signatures of the bondage-level offender with Glatman, Cottingham, Pennell, and Spencer, picquerism with Prince and Heirens, and necrophilia with Russell and Dahmer. They all have exhibited the dominance of the killer and the submission of the victims in their signatures. Out along the violence continuum toward the farthest end of the developmental arc, beyond the posing necrophilias of George Russell, is cannibalism, which manifests the most deviant and horrible of behaviors associated with dealing with aggression and sexual functions. And beyond cannibalism, where Dahmer and Bundy were heading, is the physical establishment of an environment fashioned either with or around totems taken from the victims – usually body parts.

Ted Bundy, for example, revealed to me that he would like to have built a crematorium as a dwelling where he could process his victims and dispose of their remains. Burning their flesh and bones to ashes would have been the final act of control that turned Bundy on. Instead of having to venture far out into the wilderness to be with his victims, he would have the luxury of moving from dump site to dump site and finally to his own oven where they would be sacrificed again to his lust. As sick as this sounds, there is a deviant rationality to it that conforms to the kind of deviance Bundy and others of his type exhibit through their signatures. Because extreme long-term successful signature killers consistently evolve toward those behaviors which provide them greater and greater control while at the same time replacing the reality of their lives with fantasy, they seem to live only to reinforce the fantasy as a part of their sexual gratification. Look at long-term killers and you will probably see varying degrees of evidence of this.

Bundy, as he said, wanted to build a crematorium. Gacy, like Dahmer, lived with his victims. While acting out the reality of being a successful businessman and husband, Gacy kept stashing his victims under the floorboards of his house in suburban Chicago, living with them as they decayed, until both his aberrant behavior patterns, witnesses who had seen him with victims, and the odor of decay all combined to send out the alarm. Philadelphia's Gary Heidnik, another sadistic killer, maintained a chamber of horrors in his own basement in which his victims were chained to the wall while he made them watch torture sessions. California's Leonard Lake built a torture bunker on his ex-wife's property in Calaveras County, where he videotaped the torture and humiliation of his female victims before he killed them. These environments represent the killers' ultimate fantasies at the end of the arc of violence where they live with their victims or victims' remains and totems and impart a ritualistic significance to the body parts, clothing, skeletal remains, jewelry, or videos of the suffering victims.

At Dahmer's murder trial, psychiatrist Dr. Becker described where Dahmer was going at the end of his continuum when she explained Jeffrey Dahmer's fantasies about building a kind of 'temple' or altar in his apartment from the body parts, skeletons, and skulls of his victims. He had even drawn her a crude diagram of this temple from which he hoped to receive special powers that would help him financially and spiritually. The temple clearly showed Dahmer's ritualization of his victim's bones, totems he had taken and to which he had imparted a power to stimulate him sexually. They represented control in the extreme. Because Dahmer had no sense of self, he gradually became a devotee of a kind of magical thinking that would imbue him with special powers. This is a very crude and primitive strategy of people who believe they are absolutely powerless in a world that completely mystifies them.

Dahmer was experiencing a straightforward stimulation/arousal reaction which he had engineered into a structure that he drafted for his psychologist. This structure would imbue him with powers, because Dahmer had already become sexually stimulated from the totems that he had taken from his dead victims. Because he was experiencing a form of sexual pleasure, he believed it would give him the power he didn't ordinarily possess in his own life.

AT THE CONTINUUM'S END

It seems clear, especially from the Dahmer case, that when signature killers are so successful they find themselves at the end of their continuum, they have lapsed almost completely into fantasy. A part of them remains in the real world only to navigate through the necessities of living, but whatever heart and soul a signature killer may have is committed to the enhancement of his fantasy environment. He experiments with different and better ways to entrap victims and gratify himself after the victim's death. He seeks to have more intense sexual thrills, whether anger- or fear-driven, much like an addict who needs a bigger and bigger high as his nervous system develops resistance to whatever substance he uses. Consequently, for the signature killer the more elaborate the fantasy, the better.

Perhaps within the context of this fantasy, the killer feels himself growing in invincibility and invisibility so that he actually becomes more vulnerable to the police. Certainly Bundy felt himself to be invincible when he tried to kidnap Carol Da Ronch in broad daylight from a shopping mall in Salt Lake City. Nathaniel Code probably thought he was close to invisible when he went back to the house he grew up in to commit a multiple homicide. Similarly, Dahmer seemed to have completely lost interest in maintaining control over Tracy Edwards, who had asked him if he could go to the bathroom and suddenly found himself no longer handcuffed to Dahmer. This became Dahmer's undoing in the same way that Da Ronch became a living witness in the trial against Ted Bundy.

What brings these signature killers to these ultimate states of fantasy where their signatures actually become their environments? Where does the road start and is it always an inevitable process? We know a lot about signature killers and the processes that drive them from crime to crime once their sprees have begun. But there's still a lot of mystery about the first stirrings of violence. Are they predestined to kill because of their genetic makeup? Is it the environment that pushes them into lives of violence? Or is there a process of clearly recognizable choices in the lives of signature killers that can be roadmapped out for all to see? What is it, we have to ask ourselves, at the bottom of it all that makes signature killers kill?

CHAPTER 10

Why Signature Killers Kill

Why? Because whatever the basis in early childhood, the lives of signature killers represent a total series of decisions directed exclusively toward self-indulgence. The murders themselves are acts representing the absolute of selfishness in its purest, most refined form.

We know, at last, what makes signature killers tick and how they got that way. Since their careers and life-styles have an overall similarity, no matter what their respective MO's, somewhere in this research must lie the core something that all signature killers share, the answer to why these people made the choice to kill. By piecing together the circumstantial evidence that accumulates around signature killer cases like seaweed on a fishing boat's hull and matching the evidence to the histories of other cases and my own interviews with signature killers, we've come up with some pretty good explanations for how their behavior develops and where it goes when it reaches the end of the continuum of violence.

We know that it all begins with the seed of anger, a kind of basic algorithm that drives them from the first ideations of fantasy-violence to the full-fledged commission of felonies, and ultimately to the complete set of ritualized signature murders. No matter whose career I've researched – Jeffrey Dahmer, George Russell, Nathaniel Code, or Ted Bundy – an ongoing nuclear chain reaction of anger seems to be at the heart of the killer's vision of the world and the prism through which he perceives all reality. Looking into these case histories, you can just about see where the anger begins and how it drives the progression of violence in their lives. Somewhere buried in the past of every signature criminal, whether he is a cat burglar, sexual offender, or killer, is the series of events that ignite a fuse of anger that doesn't stop burning until it's put out.

FUSES OF ANGER: JEFFREY DAHMER

In Jeffrey's Dahmer's life, as we will see, anger defined all the actions he took, and the working through of anger circumscribed all the choices he made in life. Even strangers who spoke to him in gay bars in Milwaukee described him as seething with anger. And some even said that he had an anger that had obviously been present from the time he was very young. I would suggest that Dahmer's anger burned so fiercely from the time he was a child that he became a heavy drinker, if not a full-fledged drunk, by the time he was in high school. He medicated himself with alcohol because it probably dulled the anger that was gradually consuming him like a fire and, he must have believed, helped him navigate through life. Whatever sprung the tripwire of his anger, such as Steven Hicks announcing that he was leaving Dahmer alone after they had had sex, became a target of that anger. With little or no resiliency in his personality, Dahmer's first resort was usually to violence. Where did Dahmer's anger originate?

TED BUNDY

Like Dahmer, Ted Bundy was driven by a deep anger that seemed to have started when he was very young. Festering underneath the personas of the loving fiancé who cared for Liz Kendall's children, the college-boy politician on the University of Washington campus, and the concerned colleague sitting across from Ann Rule at a Seattle rape-crisis center was nothing less than a raging monster. Ted disingenuously called this 'the entity' and objectified his crimes as having been committed by a third person, but that was really self-serving garbage. Ted knew exactly what he was doing when he stalked Lynda Healy around the U District for days before he broke into her basement apartment, and Ted knew just what to do – because he'd rehearsed it – when he spied Georgann Hawkins walking back to her sorority house from the library late at night on the University of Washington campus. And of course, Ted was in full knowledge of what he was doing when he committed the murders of Janice Ott and Denise Naslund after he abducted them from Lake Sammamish State Park.

Ted's anger-driven monster was a desperate creature who informed Ted's every action. Cross him, his own fiancée once wrote, and you would see a cold fury pass across his eyes. When he had you in his gaze, the living witnesses from Lake Sammamish told us, he had the spooky eyes of a predator focused on its prey. Very near the end of his life, when in those very same predator's eyes everyone around him had failed and he was left all alone staring at the prospect of death by electric chair, I myself saw that all his personalities seemed to have melted away, leaving a panicked, angry, empty creature gripped in the reality of its own impending death. Like a monster in a horror movie who transforms back to its real self at the point of destruction, so, too, did Ted Bundy.

When I interviewed Ted in Florida and when we saw him repeatedly show up on television and in news conferences, we could feel the anger inside him seething right below the surface. When Ted seemed most in control, those who knew the real truth behind the legalities understood how angry Ted was and how that anger motivated him. At the times when he was most in control, at Lake Sammamish and on the University of Washington campus, he was able to channel that anger into preplanned assaults in which his victims simply disappeared. He visited them at their final dump sites for sexual thrills, even as the forest animals gnawed away their flesh, and experienced the thrill of his anger expressed as total control. But when he was in jail in Utah and Colorado, when he was on the run across the country, and finally, when he was alone and desperate in Tallahassee, at the very points in a fugitive's life when you'd think he'd lie low and try to set up a new life for himself, that was when his anger completely overtook him.

No, Ted wasn't trying to get caught; they never try to get caught. He was, in these last weeks of his freedom, completely overtaken by his anger to the point where he was throwing victims into its flame, almost as human sacrifices. You could see it in the evolution of his signature. The person who, in a bloody fury, bludgeoned to death the sorority sisters at the Chi Omega house in Tallahassee and then bumped into Nita Neary in a hallway and fled was a far cry from the person who quietly dispatched Georgann Hawkins with a single blow from a tire iron in a nearly desolate parking lot, then came back the next day to gather up any remaining evidence right under the noses of local police. Yet he was the very same person. In Florida he was desperate because, as a fugitive with no money and no plan for satisfying his anger-driven sexual passions, he was almost like a trapped animal and was caught driving in a stolen vehicle, a virtual blinking neon sign of incriminating evidence. In Seattle, secure behind the camouflage of his projected personas, he was so in control he was almost invisible. You can see the difference, but you can also see that it was exactly the same person who was able to inhabit both lives. The difference centers on what Ted was able to do with his anger. But, again like Dahmer, where did Ted's anger come from?

GEORGE RUSSELL

George Russell was clearly as angry as both Dahmer and Bundy. The fury he expended at the crime scenes, the obvious lengths he went to show whomever found his victim's bodies the contempt he felt for those women, and the general manipulative superiority with which he treated all those around him bespeak a kind of deep-residing cauldron of anger that's way beyond normality. All of us get angry from time to time, and many of us, battered by our jobs and other vicissitudes, are sometimes pushed to the point of righteous rage. But if we live within the very wide range of normalcy, we amalgamate that rage into our everyday feelings until, maybe months later, it subsides rather than disappears. Maybe it takes us years to get over it and maybe we never do, but we can manage it because we have a personality system that's able to balance feelings. Not so with George Russell. He managed his rage by objectifying it in terms of his victims – of his cat burglaries, sexual offenses, and homicides – and spelling it out for anyone unlucky enough to discover the bodies.

Typical of many serial killers, Russell chose not to confront his anger head-on. It probably overtook him immediately when Mary Ann Pohlreich refused his advances and may even have physically pushed him away when they were sitting in the front seat of Smitty McLain's pickup. But in his attacks on Carol Beethe and Randi Levine, he waited until they were asleep in their beds before he struck. In fact, again typical of many fully emerged serial killers, he probably never even spoke to them. We know that he spied Carol Beethe from afar when she was at the Black Angus talking with her friend about him, and we know that he had made critical remarks about Randi Levine's lifestyle. Both of these women had, in ways not even they themselves realized, pushed his anger/control button, and set him in motion to stalk them until he killed them.

In this way, the anger motivating him was the trigger that set him tracking a victim, and once he'd killed her, the components of anger were the expressions of his signature that he could not help but leave behind. The mixture of components was bizarre. They revealed a mind in pathological torment. They were the leavings of a monster more frightening than any animal, because he was deliberate rather than random. They were so violent in their expression of anger that King County Prosecutor Jeff Baird was right when he told the jury in his closing arguments at the Russell trial that George Russell's message to his victims, to the police, and to the entire community at every crime scene was 'Fuck you, fuck you, fuck you!'

In the afterwash of the cases, one question still lingered in my mind: where did this anger come from? Why was a man from one of America's most affluent communities on the West Coast so consumed by anger that he rejected every opportunity that came his way? His sister, born into the same family, went off to an Ivy League college and a career. Why not George? Again, as in the cases of Bundy and Dahmer, we ask, where did this anger begin?

THE ANGER-DRIVEN PROTOTYPE

Although no two signature criminals are identical, in reviewing the lives of Bundy, Dahmer, Russell, and other sadistic sexual signature killers, we find that certain prototypical issues and events emerge which help define the nature of the anger that drives signature offenders and help us set up a model explaining how the anger we are asking about arises, where it comes from, and where it goes. These prototypical events are important because they tend to set apart the lives of signature offenders from those of others who, although they may have encountered similar difficulties, made different choices. The prototypical events I will highlight aren't mitigating factors in the lives of signature offenders to the extent that they excuse them from responsibility for wrongdoing. They only help explain how the spectrum of choices may have been narrower for signature criminals, even though they still exercised volition over the directions they wanted their lives to take.

For example, Jeffrey Dahmer didn't *have* to kill the young men who became his victims. He was not under a compulsion to walk through each crime as though he were sleepwalking through life. Had that been the case, he would have attempted to commit abductions whenever the feelings came upon him instead of choosing those opportunities when he could best operate. Dahmer was able to control himself to the extent that he could decide when to strike and when not to. This is volition, not compulsion, and the same can be said for Ted Bundy, who successfully knew when to start and stop so as to elude the police during his career. Much the same can be said about Nathaniel Code, who certainly made choices about when and where to strike. The fact that he could wait a year between murders is enough to indicate that he exercised some volition. The prototypical events I'm talking about are the ones that light a fuse of anger that keeps on burning and reveals itself in the *how* and *why* a homicide is committed, as well as in the signature the offender leaves at the crime scene. These are crimes that derive from a series of volitional acts, not the end results of a rage-driven passion that obliterates choice.

Not remarkably, the lives of Dahmer, Bundy, and Russell have strong general similarities. In each case, the families may have seemed privileged and strong from the outside, but from the inside, from the perception of the child growing up in the family, there was an internal weakness. In each case, the child who ultimately became the killer dropped out of that family's structure at such a critical time in his growing up that for the rest of his life, whatever a family was supposed to have provided, it didn't. The way the child ultimately compensated for that deficiency was to become criminally deviant. What that weakness or critical deficiency in the family was and how it came into the child's perception many times varies with each and every family in which a signature offender or suspected offender grows up, but the general similarities are so striking we can actually build a dynamic model to show how it works.

The keystone for our model of a criminally deviant-*cum*-homicidal personality development is the growth of what we call *clinical* anger. It's an anger that:

1. is totally abnormal
2. is constant rather than transient or situational
3. the child, and ultimately the adult perceives as beyond his control or bigger than him, as in Bundy's 'entity'
4. the child or adult never really understands
5. increases progressively and exponentially as the child matures through adolescence and into adulthood
6. cannot be compensated for except by the performance of defiant or violent acts which provide only a temporary release
7. initially becomes the driver for deviant behavior and ultimately violent sexual behavior
8. keeps getting worse until an equilibrium is reached, one that may include the performance of violent acts, sexual crimes, and murder
9. incites the predator into violent retaliatory behavior on surrogate representatives of the

source of that anger or excites the predator into committing violent and criminal sexual acts and even murder
10. even at a low ebb requires medication by alcohol, drugs, other chemical or physical abuses, or deviant sexual outlets such as pornographic fantasy or violent sex with prostitutes
11. becomes imprinted psychologically in such a way that the child or adult develops a pattern of signature behaviors throughout the rest of his life, right through the performance of his crimes.

In its earliest stages of development, the kind of anger we're talking about is probably the natural result of frustration, an emotion that's present in everybody. For example, all newborn babies who require feeding or some form of basic nurturing will cry. The more they are deprived of food or nurturing, the louder and more frustrated their cries become until they are just about howling with infant fury that, if you could translate it, would convey a serious level of violent intent. When food or nurturing is provided, the baby is satisfied and the anger gradually dissipates. That's the way it's supposed to happen until a point in the child's development when he learns to *trust* that those around him – his family – will ultimately respond to his needs. As he gets older, he should learn how to satisfy his own growing needs so that he gains a self-sufficiency which is dynamic, grows as he grows, and becomes the internal gyroscope for his entire psychological balancing system – the coping mechanism of his personality. This is basic Developmental Psych 101. The only problem is it doesn't always happen the way it's supposed to, and that's where the problems start.

THE ANGER-DRIVEN CHILDHOOD OF JEFFREY DAHMER

In a telling interview with the *Milwaukee Sentinel* just after his son's arrest, Lionel Dahmer said, 'Jeff's never been socially adaptive. He's always been out of the social mainstream.' Lionel called his son 'different,' and continued, 'He was a person who was basically kind, but deeply, deeply troubled by something, and he has been for a long time.' Sue Lehr, the mother of Jeffrey's school friend Ted, once revealed that she knew Jeffrey was 'a frightened child.'

You ask yourself how a person can be described as 'basically kind' and then carry on a thirteen-year killing spree in which he methodically disposes of his victims' bodies by dismembering them, rendering down the flesh in vats of acid, and storing the skeletal remains in his bedroom. This is the fundamental paradox at work in the life of a serial signature killer. Sure, he's kind if you're (a) not his immediate victim, (b) someone predisposed to think of him as kind, and (c) a person to whom he's supposed to show kindness. And Lionel Dahmer was (d) all of the above, even though Jeffrey himself disclosed to Brother John Paul Ranieri in Milwaukee during the final phase of his killing spree his feelings of anger and rage toward his father. If Lionel Dahmer were Jeffrey's 'source victim' in the initial retaliatory murder of Steven Hicks, Jeffrey's professed hatred of his father still wouldn't make any logical sense, because within the family Jeffrey Dahmer played out the sibling script of the obedient victim. In his murders, he turned his rage on a secondary target who became the obedient victim during the psychodrama in which he ultimately 'got ritualized' as a painted skull. But Jeffrey Dahmer grew up in a normal, middle-class household in the 1960s and 1970s on the trailing edge of the baby boom. So what happened?

All things being equal, Jeffrey Dahmer should have

had the coping mechanisms necessary to propel him into a productive and successful career. But things weren't equal. What we know is that by the time Jeffrey Dahmer was six years old and in the first grade of Hazel Harvey Elementary School outside Akron, Ohio, his mother Joyce was in the midst of a difficult pregnancy with her second child, David. According to family friends who spoke to the *Akron Beacon Journal* as anonymous background sources after Dahmer's arrest in Milwaukee, Joyce was having a difficult time with the pregnancy. She was already depressed, sources told the newspapers, and had become worried about the delivery. Jeffrey, according to school sources, was also having his own difficulties with his mother's pregnancy and was showing early signs of feeling abandoned. Sources said that he was harboring feelings of ill-will toward his new brother even before he was born on December 18, 1966.

Abandonment is a key word. Here's another: *neglected.* Jeffrey's first-grade teacher made a cryptic notation on Jeffrey's report card that during his mother's illness, the six-year-old school child seemed to feel 'neglected.' Abandonment of the parents often leads to feelings of neglect in the child. Neglect, even if it's only perceived, can lead to generalized progressive feelings of resentment: a smoldering fuse.

A developmental psychologist will tell you that it's probably normal for a young elementary school-aged child to experience feelings of abandonment and even neglect when his mother has a second baby. Suddenly all the attention that the mother showered on the first child is withdrawn because she's involved with a second baby, who by its very nature is more demanding of attention than the older child. Older siblings between the ages of three and six are particularly vulnerable to these feelings because they haven't developed a solid structure of friendships and relationships outside the home. They're still very dependent on the goings-on in the home even though they might be in first or second grade.

Jeffrey Dahmer fell right into this category. However, his feelings of abandonment and neglect might have been exacerbated because of the length and depth of his mother's problems with the pregnancy and the lack of resiliency he may have had as a result of his condition. Whereas most children who perceive a temporary withdrawal of their mother's affection learn to compensate and accept the new family member because they are taught to feel responsible for the new baby, Jeffrey apparently might have compensated by withdrawing from the family himself.

Before the conclusion of his first year in elementary school, the Dahmer family moved to a bigger house in an exclusive section of Bath Township. The Dahmers' next-door neighbor, Georgia Scharenberg, remembered the eight-year-old Jeffrey, and in interviews to reporters after his arrest in Milwaukee, said, 'He always seemed to be alone.'

Friends have described Dahmer as engaging in solitary pursuits and finding enjoyment from the torture of small animals. This is important because it probably means that he had already begun to compensate for the frustration-driven anger he had been feeling from around the time he was six or before, by inflicting pain on weaker creatures. He became fascinated with the death of creatures, and friends began to take notice. During his elementary school years, Jeffrey Dahmer also began collecting dead animal carcasses. 'He had a massive insect collection. He had all these large insects, butterflies, dragonflies.' Then, according to Eric Tyson, one of Dahmer's older friends who was interviewed for the *Akron Beacon Journal*, 'He graduated from large insects to roadkills.' Tyson said that Jeffrey and his friends would walk the country roads of the township looking for rodents and other small animals that might have been killed by motorists.

'He would collect these animals, dismember them, separate them by body parts, and put them in jars.' Eric Tyson said that Dahmer would store the jars in a wooden toolshed behind the Dahmer house that Jeffrey always called 'the hut.' It was an isolated structure way up on a hill on the back part of the property that offered Jeffrey all the privacy he needed to experiment with pickling his animal parts in formaldehyde solution.

'The hut had tons and tons of jars of animals and pieces of animals. And he seemed to be fascinated by the decomposition,' Tyson told the *Beacon Journal*. He said that Jeffrey once took him and another child into the shed to show them the body parts floating in jars filled with a 'murky liquid.' He said that Dahmer held one jar up and said there was a raccoon inside it. They didn't believe him, his schoolmate said. Then Dahmer 'took the jar and smashed it on a rock and the smell was so bad we all vomited.'

Eric Tyson, who grew up across the street from Dahmer on West Bath Road, also remembered Dahmer's collection of dead animals that he organized into a kind of 'pet cemetery.' He told the *New York Times* that Jeffrey had a burial patch for dead animals alongside his house, with actual graves and crosses. He was quoted as saying that 'A number of neighbors have recalled seeing animals such as frogs and cats impaled or staked to trees.' Dahmer had a particularly gruesome habit, friends recall, of burying the bodies of squirrels but impaling their skulls on the little crosses that rose from their graves.

Children from the neighborhood remember that Dahmer would ask them if they wanted to go out and collect road-kill instead of playing. They said that he would take his bike and ride around the back roads all alone looking for whatever he could scrape up off the macadam and bring back to his shed for storage. He experimented with his chemical set, figuring out which substances would dissolve away the flesh and fur and leave only bleached bones as trophies.

As Jeffrey grew older, his fascination with dead animals became more complex and involved. It also seems as if he switched from being a passive collector of road-kill to an aggressive stalker of animals at some point during his early adolescence. Other people from the neighborhood remember that when Dahmer was about fourteen or fifteen, perhaps during his years at Eastview Junior High, there were reports of missing dogs circulating throughout the area. No one knew whether Dahmer was directly connected to the disappearances, but Jim Klippel, who used to be the Dahmer's next-door neighbor, remembered seeing a dog's skull turned into a kind of totem pole in an area only a few hundred yards behind the Dahmer house. Klippel said that he and his girlfriend were walking in the woods when they discovered a dog's head impaled on a stick. The dog's body had been nailed to a nearby tree.

'Somebody must have had a lot of fun with that dog,' he said to the *Beacon Journal*, 'if that's what you want to call it. It was skinned and gutted. And about a hundred yards away there had been a large fire and thirteen little fires around it. It looked so much like cult worship that it scared us to death.'

Klippel had heard the stories of missing dogs and remembered that Dahmer had been associated with them. 'I had heard stories in the area,' he told the newspaper, 'about him going around and doing things to animals. I don't know if he did it. He seemed like such a nice, quiet kid.'

Other friends remember stories about Dahmer's fishing expeditions at a local pond near Medina Road. There, most of the local kids fished just for fun and threw back most of the small bass they caught. Dahmer didn't. Friends remember that he would fillet his catch with his pocketknife. Then he would cut it up into little pieces and throw it back into the water where other fish, driven into a frenzy by fresh blood floating down from the surface, would rise to feed on the remains. Dahmer seemed fascinated not only by the fishes' behavior when blood hit the water, but by the very act of paring away flesh from the bone and dismembering the remains.

'Why do you like to cut them up that way?' one of the kids once asked Dahmer as he watched him become totally fixated on chopping up his catch.

'I want to see what it looks like inside,' Dahmer reportedly answered. 'I like to see how things work.'

One schoolmate also remembers another eerie aspect to Dahmer's behavior. He said that Jeffrey liked to listen to heartbeats by placing his ear against someone's chest. He also liked to touch his friends' veins to feel the way they pulsated when a surge of blood was pumped through. This was almost a foreshadowing of what Dahmer did to Tracy Edwards on the night he tried to kill him. Edwards remembered that Dahmer put his head on his chest, listened to his heart, and told him that he was going to eat his heart right out of him later that night.

If we look at the childhood of Jeffrey Dahmer as kind of a prototype and apply it to Bundy and Russell, here's what we find:

A DESCRIPTION OF PARENTAL NEGLECT

Whether real or perceived by the subject or by those around him, there is a description of childhood in which the subject felt abandoned or neglected by one or both of his parents. No matter how affluent the household, a neglected child is one who may develop a deviant sense of his place in the outside social structure. Or he may never develop that kind of sense at all. The more severe this problem is, the more likely it is that the subject will tend toward sociopathic behavior.

Simply stated in everyday language, sociopaths are individuals who don't respect other people's boundaries. They may steal, cheat, and lie without remorse or feelings of conscience, and they may even commit acts of violence if they think they can get away with it. Sociopaths appear not to have any sense of right and wrong, but that is probably only an illusion, because sociopaths are well grounded in reality and know exactly the level of pain they inflict. More likely, because sociopaths have no sense of personal boundaries, they feel no remorse for the pain they cause when they hurt others, and regard all possessions as their own. People can develop sociopathic behavior patterns if they never learned personal boundaries as infants or young children. If their parents neglected them or, worse, abandoned or abused them, their sense of personal boundaries may be impaired. As a result, as children they may be extraordinarily violent at worst, or at the least they act as if they're completely insensitive to pain and suffering of others. As they grow older, they seem unable to play by any social rules and ultimately may tend to have no regard for law and may be at high-risk for criminal behavior at all levels.

ELDEST AND A PERCEPTION OF BEING THE LEAST-FAVORED CHILD

Many serial killers such as Leonard Lake in California and Arthur Shawcross in New York were least-favored children who blamed their siblings for part of their problems. Lake even murdered his younger brother Donald Lake. In a reverse reaction, George Russell may well have covered up his feelings toward his younger sister by showering her with public praise and extolling her abilities to his friends. In Dahmer's case, he may have perceived that he was the least-favored child or the 'lost' child, because he may have believed that his mother's affections were given without reservation to his infant brother David. If for whatever reason his father had not become the most-favored parent in Jeffrey's own mind, Jeffrey would have grown up in what he perceived was the absence of affection. He would have developed deviant childhood compensatory behaviors to satisfy his feelings of loss, loneliness, hostility, guilt, and shame for not being the child his mother favored. In any event, if he perceived himself as having been put in the position of being the least-favored child in the family, he would have translated it into a severe sense of inferiority. As an adult, victims of a 'least-favored child' complex sometimes develop hostile attitudes toward authority figures and portray themselves as outsiders.

PERCEPTION OF SUBJECT AS AN OUTSIDER IN THE FAMILY

A consequence of the least-favored-child pattern is the outsider pattern. Here, a child perceives himself to be formally ostracized within his own family. He's technically a family member, but he believes that the real love, attention, and affection are directed away from him. What should be a primal social situation enhancing the development of a healthy adult becomes a blueprint for dysfunctional and inappropriate reactions. To gain attention, the outsider and least-favored member of the family must indulge in negative behavior. He withdraws instead of participates and sometimes acts out his most violent aggressive feelings. If unchecked, it results in an adolescent who is incapable of solving his own problems and may seek to medicate himself with alcohol or drugs. This is exactly what seems to have happened in Dahmer's case by the time he entered Revere High School in 1975. It's no surprise that this is also what happened to Leonard Lake, who was actually sent away from the family to be raised elsewhere because the family did not have money for all the children. Lake was allowed to visit for Sunday dinners, and he himself described feeling like an outsider.

EXTREME CRUELTY TOWARD OTHER CHILDREN OR ANIMALS, OR HATRED FOR INANIMATE OBJECTS

In Jeffrey Dahmer's case, the cruelty he expressed toward animals through torture, dismemberment, and rendering their remains was his early indicator of acting out the hostility he was feeling as a result of his perceptions of neglect and abandonment. The more alone and neglected he felt, the more he sought victims to work out his anger. The ritualistic aspects of the cruelty were especially menacing. First, Dahmer sought to make trophies or totems out of his animal victims, preserving them in chemicals and cataloging them in jars. For the animals he was assumed to have killed and buried, he organized their carcasses in makeshift graveyards, experimenting with death as it were, and displayed their skulls above the mounds where they were buried. As a gravesite manager for his own kills, this was the ultimate control that the violent Dahmer could wield over the world around him. His small campfire sites and ritualistic burial grounds were a primitive but organized way for him to channel the escalating hostility he was feeling against the world. His cruelty to animals was a coping mechanism that prevented him from self-destructing when he was very young, but it was ultimately fatal to Dahmer's personality and, of course, to his victims.

By the time he was set to enter high school, fifteen-year-old Jeffrey Dahmer was on a collision course with violence. His patterns of loneliness and hostility were getting the better of him. His lack of emotional resiliency and the gradual failure of his childhood coping mechanisms held him in a form of stranglehold. It would take only a few more factors to set him on a path of violence. Those factors would overtake him in high school: his addiction to alcohol, his parents' divorce, and his complete and total abandonment. By the time he was eighteen, he would be almost completely alone in the world and would have become a cold-blooded killer.

BACKGROUND SIMILARITIES AMONG DAHMER, BUNDY, AND RUSSELL

The Dahmer story is a good working prototype for comparison purposes because his life, while debunking some of the standard myths about serial killers, embodies some of the most important features about the backgrounds of signature killers. Most significantly, it shows how a child can develop within a relatively financially well-off family and, for a variety of reasons, still never learn to manage anger and frustration, and wind up making the kinds of choices that lead to a life of violent crime.

When you compare Dahmer's background with George Russell's the importance of the similarities becomes even more apparent. By this comparison, the anger-excitation and anger-retaliation models for signature sexual crime and signature murder just about jump out at you and almost answer the question for themselves: where did the anger come from?

I ask myself these questions: Did George Russell perceive parental neglect, did he perceive abandonment, did he believe himself to be the least-favored eldest child, and was he an outsider in his own family? Russell's story speaks for itself. By his own account, his mother left him with his biological father when she left the marriage and returned to place him with relatives. He was abandoned with relatives when he was small and abandoned again with his stepfather when he was an adolescent. He was actually abandoned in favor of his younger sister, who went with his biological mother while he stayed with his stepfather. Then when his stepfather remarried, George, already an outsider in his own family, was an outsider in his stepfamily. He wound up becoming such an outsider that he was literally homeless in Seattle with a family who lived just over the bridge on Mercer Island.

I suspect that George Russell embarked on a life of juvenile crime so early in life that socially deviant criminal behavior became his anger-compensatory mechanism rather than experimentation with violence on small animals. He was able to violate other people's boundaries by breaking and entering and staking out houses so easily that it became a form of retaliation and revenge. No need to run over a dog when you can vent anger on human beings. George actually got away with it and convinced the local Mercer Island police to make him kind of a junior detective, snitching on friends and ingratiating himself with the very authorities he was trying to deceive.

However, the history of Dahmer's cruelty to animals does provide an intriguing similarity to Russell's persistent inclination to play with people – and in turn be cruel to people – much younger than himself. Both Dahmer and Russell needed to exert control to compensate for the lack of control, frustration, and downright anger they experienced in their lives. Dahmer, shunned by his peer group and completely unsocial, chose to exert his control over animals. Russell, very much a part of his peer group at first and needing social interaction, if only as a camouflage, chose to exert his control over people. Rather than render animal flesh in jars of acid, Russell became manipulative and sought to get others into trouble, and in so doing render, as it were, their personalities down in vats of his own acid. The older Russell got, the more the anomaly of his dealing with younger people became apparent. At the time of the Bellevue, Washington, murders, Russell was crashing with girls who were just a little older than teenyboppers. It was simply a basic way for Russell, like Dahmer, to exert control over an entity weaker than himself.

Both Dahmer and Russell were quintessential outsiders no matter how hard they tried to be members of the club. Dahmer became the class clown. Constantly sedated with alcohol from the time he was in junior high school, Dahmer would show off by pounding back six-packs of beer that he sneaked into the building in the lining of his specially modified ski jacket. Dahmer would clown in public, in school, and even in the local shopping malls. His antics became so famous among members of his crowd that making a public display to attract attention just for fun became known as 'doing a Dahmer.'

George Russell, too, became kind of a leader at first. He liked to portray himself as the bravest when it came to showing off, but usually wound up turning in his friends. He was always chatting up people, hanging around their houses, and trying to impose his friendship, but in the end he wound up being very much alone. When friends bounced him away, he found others to latch onto. He was forever looking for relationships in which he could sponge off the person he was calling his friend. While he was living with his stepfather, he got away with it. After he was kicked out of the house, it became much harder to do. However, even on the night of his last murder – partly, I'm sure, to provide himself with an alibi – he hosted a party with his younger friends in the motel room he rented for all of them.

In researching the Russell story I was particularly struck by Russell's idolizing Ted Bundy. How odd. Why would anyone idolize someone as thoroughly miserable as Ted Bundy, who probably never experienced a happy day in his entire life? Makes no sense unless you realize what Russell was truly after and why he identified with Bundy in the first place. If it's possible, George Russell was even more unhappy than Ted. At least Ted had a girlfriend, the outward trappings of a family, and something of a career. He didn't inhabit any of these or invest them with any reality, but at least he went to college, held down jobs, made friends, and went to law school. Russell had none of this: no family, no friends, no job, no anything. Thus, he held Ted Bundy as a kind of hero, someone he could emulate who eluded police and wreaked vengeance upon the types of women who wouldn't even give George a chance, women like his stepmother. In some small way, therefore, George Russell believed that he was following in Bundy's footsteps by sharing the same mission as his dead hero. It was also another reason to stay angry at the world in general and at women in particular.

Maybe George Russell sensed that he and Ted Bundy had more in common than most people realized. In both their lives, they were subordinate to dominant mother figures who relocated them into new families and had the ability to change the environments around them. Ted, for example, was born in Vermont as Theodore Robert Cowell, then had his name changed to Nelson; then, when he was five years old, Ted's mother moved him to Washington, where she got married and changed his name again to Bundy. I suspect that both Bundy and Russell developed a similar kind of anger and frustration directed at a mother figure who could so capriciously – in their eyes – yank the stability of a family away from them and create a new family. Bundy, in particular, even though he was still living in Seattle, seemed almost rootless, according to the FBI timeline, in his traveling back and forth from coast to coast and up and down the West Coast after he graduated from high school in Tacoma in 1962.

Bundy's frustration and anger also translated

themselves into his inability to hold down jobs for long periods of time, his self-stated difficulties with relationships, and his ultimate career as a cat burglar and thief both before and during his long-term career as a serial killer. Like George Russell and almost all other serial killers, Bundy seemed to have no respect for other people's property and stole from others to satisfy his own needs. He stole from lockers at the Olympic Hotel in Seattle and was fired because of it, stole during the period he was living with fiancée Liz Kendall, and lived on stolen credit cards and vehicles during his final murder spree in Florida. Bundy was a thief who, despite all the effort he put into looking and acting normal, was thinking about murder and sexual behavior with the bodies of his dead victims just about every minute of the day.

The more I got to know Bundy during my years tracking him and then talking with him about serial murder, the more I realized that Bundy had a hole right through the center of his life that no amount of murder, necrophilia, burglary, and violent behavior would ever fill. Bundy wasn't stupid, even though he was never as smart as he tried to convince people he was; but he still couldn't figure out until close to the end that there was no release from the roiling anger that kept erupting inside him. He could throw anything into the burning pit – relationships, career, any chance he might have had for a normal life – but it didn't work. In the end he was consumed by the very anger that killed over thirty young women during the course of his career as a serial killer. Even in the final minutes of his life, confessions of murder were spilling out of him as if he couldn't stop thinking about the one thing that had turned him on for most of his forty-three years.

Bundy and Russell, it seemed, were frustrated and angry as a result of a dominant woman figure in their lives, probably their mothers, who was the controlling element. Dahmer, on the other hand, seemed to be reacting to a dominant male figure. The reverse imprint of that anger was the infliction of pain and suffering upon victims who embodied the relationship between the killer and the dominant figure he was reacting against. The signature reflects the working out of that anger, whether as sexual excitation or as direct retaliation upon the victim. The more experimentation over the long term, the more the dynamic signature evolves and leaves traces of where the killer began and the directions he is taking.

Bundy, Dahmer, and Russell were all sexual killers whose crimes reflected the translation of anger into explicitly sexual offenses. Their backgrounds were all generally similar, and we can account for the anger that motivated them. We can relate their lives and crimes very easily to the life and crimes of Nathaniel Code, who was also separated from his family and who, upon returning to his grandfather's house and seeing that his place as a child had been taken by the visiting children, forced his grandfather to witness the torture and murder of those children before Nathaniel murdered him. His life fits into the same prototype derived from the story of Jeffrey Dahmer, in which anger drives the subject's actions.

Jeffrey Dahmer and his brother David lived in the same house with the same parents, but turned out very differently. The night that Jeffrey Dahmer was left alone in his home when his parents separated and David was taken away by his mother was the night Jeffrey Dahmer killed for the first time. California serial killer Leonard Lake was sent away from the family while his brother Donald, who also grew up in a difficult environment, was allowed to stay. Both had severe sexual dysfunction, but Donald never became a killer. In fact, Leonard murdered him after he suspected the younger man of making sexual advances toward their sister. Leonard Lake eventually committed suicide while in police custody. But the question remains, why one brother and not the other?

This is one of the key issues for determining why signature killers kill.

THE PSYCHOLOGICAL DEVELOPMENT OF A SIGNATURE KILLER

In the strictest of legal terms, there is a fundamental difference between signature killers and those people further back along the spectrum who may display dysfunctional behavior, even dysfunctionally sexually deviant behavior, but who don't kill. That's pretty basic. For me, I carry a badge. I get there only when there's a dead body. I don't get called when somebody *may* someday become a serial killer or when a supervisor at a local post office or a bicycle messenger service humiliates, tortures, or obsessively controls his subordinates. Maybe I should, but that's not my job. Because of the legal distinction between those who kill and those who don't, the fact that very similar behavior may include signature killers and a group of people who exhibit sexually deviant behavior in a signature pattern is too often unnoticed. Accordingly, we criminologists tend to exclude from a research group the very behavior we need to study if we're to figure out why signature killers kill. Theoretically, if we look at the types of signature behavior of people who don't kill or who may be on the road to killing but who haven't killed yet, we might get some insights.

What I believe from all the behaviors and cases that I've researched is that it's not just a matter of chemistry or parental abuse or head injuries. It's not whether someone's an alcoholic or a drug abuser or whether he's been beaten up on the job. Every one of these is a challenge, an issue that shapes behavior, but what it really comes down to is choices. Jeffrey Dahmer made conscious decisions to kill or not to kill, how to dispose of bodies, and how to escape detection. Ted Bundy knew that no matter how much his 'entity' demanded satisfaction, the choice to break into Lynda Healy's apartment or to stalk Kimberly Leach as she walked along the street was his and his alone. Leonard Lake made a virtue out of rape, robbery, and murder and consciously recognized the steps he had to take to make it seem as though the missing persons – his abductees – were still alive and communicating with their families. George Russell chose to leave his parents' house and sponge off friends, chose to strike Mary Ann Pohlreich out of anger and strangle and beat her until she was dead, and chose to stalk his victims Carol Beethe and Andrea Levine. Whatever happened in his life, Russell made choices at every juncture that took him along the road that ultimately led to a life sentence in prison.

Maybe the choices signature offenders make are across a very narrow spectrum of possibilities, or maybe in other cases, they're very broad. In life some choices are easier than others and some are close to impossible to make. But in every case, there's a choice 'to be or not to be,' to kill or not to kill. And it's that choice and the factors leading up to it which require investigation and understanding.

When you examine the lives of signature killers, you find that there are certain basic similarities in their histories and behaviors. Although their specific signatures may differ, it seems as if many start from the same premises concerning self-worth, relationships with their parents, relationships with childhood or school-age peers, expectations regarding the outside world, attitudes toward authority, and, obviously, attitudes regarding sex and sexual partners. In fact, I believe the general similarities are so strong, we can even construct a working model of how these premises get into place and what constellation of factors results in an individual's going over the line to become a sex offender, and from there a signature killer.

It's a very faddish thing in typical true-crime stories to go back to a killer's childhood and from there to catalog all the incidents that seem inevitably to lead to the tragedy of a murderer's career, which is exactly what we've done with Russell, Dahmer, and Bundy. The problem with taking an inevitability theory at face value, however, is that it presupposes that it was external or environmental forces that pushed the subject into committing murders, rather than the killer's own choices. But we can show that a workbench model for signature/deviant behavior is far more prevalent than most people think, and that much of the same events that shape the life of a signature killer potentially shape the lives of the majority of people who don't become criminals. In so doing, we can look at the types of specific choices signature killers made, and in some cases we can begin to explain why they killed in the first place.

THE SIGNATURE BEHAVIOR MODEL

Our model begins in early childhood, when a number of preconditions are established that initially set forth a spectrum of choices that each of us has to make, the normal as well as the deviant. And as you will see, there are probably far more people either at the extreme ranges of normalcy or even out of the range of normalcy than anyone might expect. That number is growing.

Early Childhood

The first nine to twelve months of an infant's life are absolutely critical in helping to develop an individual's preliminary life script. What we now know about how newborns develop, their resiliency, their need for sensory feedback from parents and others around them, and the kind of imprinting that takes place during this period provide us with a kind of roadmap for possibilities in a child's life. We know, for example, that there are two essential processes that take place within the first nine or so months after birth.

The first is a neurological and physiological process. The infant's nervous system continues to develop, the brain is growing, and the child's still-developing sensory system is responding to all kinds of external stimuli. This process has already begun before birth – we know that newborns respond to the human heartbeat, to vocalizations from their mothers, to loud noises, and to a wide range of neurochemical reactions that course through the mother. After birth, the same process is even accelerated as infants experience more sounds and a whole range of tactile stimulation, proportionately the same kind of stimulation that all mammals from cats to dolphins to apes provide to their young. In human beings, this kind of stimulation is more than important; it's life sustaining. Children who are kept from reacting with their environment as newborns, either because they're institutionalized or because their parents simply neglect them, have to enter their childhood years with an enormous handicap that impedes their ability to become socialized members of a community.

Simultaneous with a newborn's neurological development, a psychological component of development kicks in through which babies actually learn whether to trust their external environments. *Trust* is a powerful word, but that's exactly what happens. By learning how adults around them respond to their vocalizations, babies test the reliability of their external environment. An outside world that's reliable is one that can be trusted. An outside world that's nonresponsive or is simply not there because the parents are not there – neglect, abandonment, or the simple, selfish unwillingness to interact with a child – cannot be trusted, and babies eventually adjust to that as well, but with potentially negative consequences.

In the normal course of things, newborns require lots of handling. They have to be carried, fed, changed, picked up, soothed, and nurtured. The mere act of picking up and holding a child physiologically and emotionally stimulates both the child and whomever is doing the picking up, usually the parent. In families where babies are held and touched a lot, physical development is stimulated and the children seem happier. In families where babies are not handled as much, babies are usually crankier and sound frustrated, and development is slower. All of this is within the range of normalcy, however, and depending upon the family and the child's preschool years, a lot of readjustment can take place because children have a natural resilience.

Infants also establish their boundaries through organized vocal feedback. Unless there's some physical impairment, newborns naturally vocalize. They've been hearing – and learning – sounds through the walls of the mother's womb for months and vocalize meaningfully – fright, pain, and discomfort – within the first moments of birth. Just as immediately, the environment around a newborn is supposed to form itself to respond to those vocalizations. Frightened babies get soothed, uncomfortable babies get changed, hungry babies get fed. All of this stimulates both parent and child and teaches infants within the first six months of life that there is a dependable quality to their environment. They can make expectations about what their actions will initiate. This doesn't mean that parents have to jump up from their chairs as if they've been ejected from a navy jet every time their newborn makes a peep. Different families have different responses and babies adapt to their environments. Ultimately, the way the family responds to a baby's vocalizations will train the baby in forming expectations, and gradually a pattern of behavior will develop. This is also how they learn what to expect based on what they do.

This type of physical and vocal feedback is a fundamental factor in helping to establish a child's sense of reality, its estimation of self-worth, and, accordingly, its self-esteem, the core premises from which most choices are made. Self-esteem, a belief in the validity of oneself, is vital and is directly related to the physical and vocal feedback that should typically take place during the first six months of an infant's life. Without this feedback, a pattern of deviancy begins, which if not reversed or balanced through later intervention narrows the choices older children make and can lead to conflicts with authorities and ultimately the juvenile justice system.

If you look at the prison population in the United States as a control group, you will see that the overwhelming majority of felons not only have little or no self-esteem, they usually have no basis from which to judge themselves. They're sociopaths with no sense of boundaries. They know right from wrong, but having no boundaries leaves them with no compelling reason to share or to respect what is not their own. They are selfish in the extreme and respect only the immediate gratification of their needs.

In very severe cases where children are separated from parents during the birth to nine-months period or where parents leave children almost completely alone, there can be a deprivation of sensory input in the form of touching and vocalization. This type of impairment can be critical and can create severe psychological damage. The child's growth and maturation can be retarded, and its participation in a social order, which most of us take completely for granted, can be an arduous chore for this type of person. Children this deprived usually require special education, if not outright institutionalization, and have severe problems with authority figures. More often than not, it is harder for them to make the necessary choices to obey the law, but they can be trained to do so.

Individuals who develop sociopathic behavior as children or as adolescents and who run afoul of authority figures usually have had some significant problems during early infancy relating directly to some deprivation of important sensory input. This may have happened as a result of forced hospitalization in which they've been taken away from their parents; parents may have abandoned the child; or parents, because of their own difficulties may have neglected the child so that there was no interaction. Children who are moved a lot, shifted from parent to parent on an inconsistent basis, who are left with relatives, or who are just left alone with a babysitter all can develop this kind of deviant behavior early on. What happens during early childhood can help reset the balance or exacerbate the problem.

As the child gets older, the behavior that's been shaped during his first year forms a basis for behavior once the child is ready to encounter other authority figures such as leaders in his peer group, older children, teachers, and other adults. This early childhood socialization is also important because it presents the child with real choices about how he will interact with others. Children who are products of a home life in which they benefited from interaction with their parents surely have an easier time than children from families where they were deprived. There's a wide range of normalcy and deviance at either end. Overindulged children are just as likely to have problems as children who experienced a deprivation of interaction. Gradually, as the child reaches five and six, he faces choices about how he will react in groups with his peers. Children with little or no self-esteem will be less likely to venture out to socialize than children with a strong sense of themselves, because the more deprived the child's background is, the more fearful he is of being vulnerable to new social situations. Interacting with others, initiating relationships, stepping into new territory outside the family all involve psychological risk. Children who are prepared because their parents have given them the attention they need to develop a sense of themselves are able to step over the fear to make new relationships and possibly put themselves at risk of rejection. They are confident. Children who are not prepared shun relationships because they're afraid of the risk. They are afraid of encountering new people and choose to retreat into a different world.

This does not mean that children so challenged as newborns automatically become signature killers or even sex offenders. In fact, given a variety of environments, children who don't learn to trust or who have a low self-esteem can actually surmount their challenge and grow up to achieve great success. By overcoming it, they turn their weakness into a strength. They have hard times experiencing or even recognizing happiness, and for the rest of their lives they may exhibit a telltale predatory behavior, but it need not destroy them. They may become successful executives inside an already predatory corporate world or emerge as financial sharks who stay just inside the law. It's a large playing field and environment, and learning how to make choices can make the difference in one's life.

The Diphasic Personality Formation

A diphasic personality is one in which there is a split development into two phases. One phase consists of a construction and retreat into a fantasy world where it's safe and the child is in complete control. He can crawl into that world in his mind whenever he wants and never have to confront the trials that are out there in the real world. The other phase of the child's personality development takes place in the real world. He may not commit very much of himself to this personality, because it's only out there as a placeholder. Because there's little or no commitment, it's as if the child's not really there at all. Here is how the formation of a diphasic personality takes place.

Fear of social interaction, whether you see it in a child among a play group of two-year-olds or much later in an adult who's so withdrawn he lives within his own fantasy world, is one of the potential results of an early childhood in which the infant receives less than minimal attention and nurturing from his parent. Children who aren't inbued with the core confidence that parents can give them, or who, because they've been sequestered from a parent for one reason or another, feel abandoned enter their preschool years with a kind of psychological hesitation that can impair their chances to reach to members of their peer group. Humans are social animals who perform in groups; that's how we survived as a species, and an unsocialized person does not have the same tools for survival as a socialized one. Thus, we adapt as best we can by making choices throughout our lives within the spectrum of what we have to work with. However, among the more severe forms of adaptation is a retreat from reality into fantasy and the formation of cover or placeholder personality to protect the fantasy world we've created. Sound sophisticated? It is, but that's exactly what some children can do as early as five years old to protect themselves from the vulnerability of entering into new relationships.

As a child who has developed a diphasic, or two-pronged personality, progresses through elementary school where he keeps one foot in reality and the rest in a fantasy world, how much mental energy the child imparts to that fantasy helps determine how much he will ever grow out of it, if ever. Again, it's a matter of choices and opportunities. If a child is lucky enough to encounter someone during elementary school – a peer or adult – who can coax him out of fantasy into accepting the vulnerability of dealing in the real world, that's positive. If, however, the child's frustration and anger at himself for not participating in the real world grows to a point where he retreats even further into fantasy, it's negative. The deeper into fantasy he goes, leaving a cover personality which he may barely inhabit for real-world business, the greater the effort it will usually take for him to pull out, and the more alone he may feel during the process. This certainly describes the young life of Jeffrey Dahmer, who, by the time he reached the early elementary grades, was going out on his bike to examine roadkill on the rural roads in his neighborhood. Soon he graduated to bringing them home, mounting them, and experimenting with how they decomposed. This became the fantasy existence into which he would eventually retreat as he grew older, and where he actually lived when police arrested him in Milwaukee.

The progressive development of a diphasic personality requires a great deal of energy, builds up tremendous stress, and, accordingly, generates anger as energy. I've found that much the same engineering principles that have to do with the dynamic structure of a human personality encountering the vicissitudes of life apply to most engines or anything with moving parts. You have to have something that will bear the stress or dissipate the buildup of friction and stress, or else the engine will simply seize up and stop working. When you look at the lives of signature killers, you can see that that's exactly what's happened in many instances. The formation and development of a diphasic personality structure – retreating into fantasy while throwing a phantom personality projection into the real world where it cannot compete – drives anger and frustration to the point where the personality cannot shed load any longer. Ultimately, the selfish decisions made to protect the self that is as deeply imbedded as a black hole push the individual into a complete fantasy existence where the resulting anger outcrops as confrontations with authority. This can happen as early as six or seven years of age and usually requires professional medical intervention before the child reaches adolescence, when another engine starts up – one with more serious consequences for the individual, because a series of chemical reactions takes place that alter the behavior of the child before he even realizes what's happening.

Adolescent Development

As the diphasic child gets older, his retreat into fantasy retards his normal maturation process. Children mature socially as they grow physically, learning how to work and play in groups and fit into the normal pecking order. Diphasic personality types tend not to fit in because they don't commit socially. Fear keeps them out of situations, and rather than compete in the pecking order, they withdraw into a world of their own creation. But they're still growing in anger and usually display an ill-concealed surface hostility, a short temper, an overly violent reaction when challenged, and a fear of new situations and new people. If the anger reaction in a diphasic personality type is like a spinning gear in a child's early years, then by the time he reaches adolescence it reaches a new level. Suddenly sexual urges seem to arise out of nowhere in an adolescent, physical passions triggered by other people that the adolescent can't control at first. For children who have been socialized and who don't fear vulnerability, the sexual passions of adolescence are gradually internalized as the child learns to cope.

For the diphasic, however, it's a completely different reaction. Suddenly it's as if the ever-present but free-floating anger now has a focus. The adolescent wants something, wants to gratify these physical urges, but doesn't have the social skills to manipulate the situation. For the heterosexual diphasic male, girls seem to float by him, but because he is nonsocial, they're a threat. He can't figure out how to talk to them, how to get them to help him satisfy his desires, and so he's afraid of them. He retreats further into fantasy, where he may indulge ideations of either revenge or inappropriate forms of violent gratification. He's afraid of no control, so his ideations focus on control. Anger and revenge are one form of control, especially if he already has a target victim like his mother or father. But control takes many forms, and in his fantasy world the diphasic may see violence as a kind of indulgence. It's safe, he doesn't have to venture out into the real world, and the girls who cross his path easily float into his dream world where they belong to him. He retreats even further, but can't escape the anger that identifies objects that hold out the promise of gratifying the feelings that overwhelm him.

The translation of anger into sexual reactions begins in preadolescence, because that's when the chemical reactions first begin that will bring about the resulting physiological and emotional changes. However, psychological roots of anger reach back into very early childhood when the individual's basic concepts of self, esteem, and confidence were ill-developed and he held himself back from the normal socialization process. As the child reaches later elementary and intermediate grades, it becomes increasingly his responsibility to recognize that something's wrong and to make the choices, however painful, that will integrate him into a social structure. In other words, either the adolescent, the teenager, or the young adult is still making choices and is still capable of deciding whether to risk the social interaction, or fearing that, to retreat into a fantasy world where he believes he can exercise complete control.

Some adolescents may become violent; others seek control in different ways. Dahmer was a prankster even though he was fascinated by death. What if he were fascinated by controlling people through his pranks and through laughter directed at himself? Couldn't his life have gone another way if he had just had a receptive audience? Many an entertainer has described a difficult childhood and adolescence in which his or her only means of control was to always keep 'em laughing. They may survive quite nicely in the paranoid world of show business by the very skills that helped them cope when they were children. The closest they may ever come to breaking the law is to cut into the carpool lane on the San Diego Freeway.

Nevertheless, you can see from the lives of Jeffrey Dahmer and George Russell and from the numerous interviews given by Ted Bundy that there is a carryover effect from childhood through adolescence and beyond, where adolescent urges, frightening and compelling because they threaten to overwhelm the individual, translate quickly into adult problems where they're exacerbated because they haven't been dealt with in adolescence. It's as if the adult has grown up physically but not psychologically, because the individual is still reacting as if he is dealing with raw sexual energy and unmitigated anger and frustration. What happened to the normal maturation process? It never took place because the diphasic personality type never really committed to the real world, but stayed within the safety of his fantasy existence. He didn't mature because choosing to live in his fantasy world allowed him to stay a child with no respect for the consequences of his actions. It's when he reaches young adulthood that the problems begin in earnest.

CHAPTER 11

The Beginning of the Continuum

Crossing the Line: The Adult Diphasic Personality at the Beginning of the Continuum

Society imposes upon adults the burden of having matured through the behavioral extremes of early teen years to the point where one's primal sexual energy has been managed. That's the ideal. But for it to work the individual must have some method of admitting to himself that he is capable of trust and vulnerable to intimacy, and his boundaries are porous enough to allow him the interchange of feelings which may put him at risk. The further away one is from that ideal, the more resistant one is to social interchange and the more one confines himself to psychological isolation. Because the diphasic personality type has a fundamental inability to admit vulnerability and allow trust, he in fact remains in a form of psychological isolation where the only feedback he receives is the energy from a fantasy system that from adolescence has an anger-driven sexual component that permeates his consciousness.

How much does this affect his behavior or, more important, tilt him toward deviant behavior? In the direct proportion that his fantasy replaces reality and creates false reality, does his behavior become increasingly deviant – which is not to say it's necessarily criminal, only deviant? There's no law against indulging in a fantasy world until the borders of that fantasy intrude upon the rights of others or violate the law in another way. By extension, using the argument of 'what if a tree falls in the forest and no one is there,' if an anger/fantasy-driven recluse, otherwise minimally functional in the real world, takes pleasure from the security of a rear window or a balcony in simply watching the comings and goings of his female neighbors, he's probably broken no law. Hey, a cat can look at a king, right? But when he takes aggressive actions to peep into their lives, the problems begin.

THE ARC OF FANTASY ANGER-DRIVEN FEELINGS FROM SIMPLE INTRUSIONS TO VIOLENCE

Where did Jeffrey Dahmer cross the line? Where did Russell and Bundy? We know about Jeffrey Dahmer, at least from his own confessions to police about his first murder. From a child who had conflicts with school authorities again and again and medicated himself with alcohol, itself a misdemeanor, to a high-school graduate whose parents fled from the family in separate directions after what must have been an awful fight, Dahmer was left absolutely alone. In their haste to escape the house, his parents simply abandoned their eighteen-year-old. Maybe it was like waking up one morning, finding out you're all grown-up, but also finding out you're all, all alone on a vast ocean. So you go out looking for a friend, find one, and become intimate with him; then he, too, decides to leave. What did Dahmer choose to do? Rather than simply go out and find someone else – face the fear of intimacy and rejection – he killed his new hitchhiker friend, disposed of his body in the ways he had practiced in his fantasy world, and kept the murder to himself for the next thirteen years. It took Dahmer only one day to evolve from an abandoned child in the mist of his fantasy of playing with the dead to a full blown bludgeon-murderer who then defiled and chopped up the body of his dead victim.

From what the official case records tell us about Ted Bundy, the first murder ascribed to him was the death of Lynda Healy in her basement apartment in Seattle's U District. What preceded that murder that made it so easy for Ted to kill and establish a pattern that allowed him to kill in five states over the ensuing couple of years? We learned about Ted that his cousin had been a roommate of Lynda Healy's current housemate and that Ted and Lynda had been registered in the same classes at the University of Washington. We also learned that Ted and Lynda had cashed checks at the same Safeway supermarket within four hours of each other on the day Lynda disappeared. In other words, Ted probably knew Lynda because they were in the same classes and had probably been at some of the same parties through the roommate connection. Had Ted asked her out and been rebuffed? We have no way of knowing, but we surmise that Ted could very well have been stalking Lynda Healy before he broke into her apartment and killed her. He lived close enough to her apartment to have been familiar with the area and probably even knew the layout of the house itself. We also learned about Bundy that he had been a cat burglar during his murder spree and probably before, and had no difficulties with breaking and entering into houses.

'The killer knows the victim, but the victim doesn't know the killer.' That's what Ted told me when he evaluated our HITS form, and I never forgot it. Did he mean that he knew he would be Lynda Healy's killer before he killed her? How long did the stalking go on? Had Ted's fantasy ideations of Lynda Healy grown so intense that he stepped over the line from following her to keep her in view to actively stalking her, and thence to breaking and entering and murder?

We know from the way Ted liked to bludgeon his

victims that breaking into a domicile at night when the victim was asleep and bludgeoning her into unconsciousness or death was his method of attack in the Chi Omega murders in Florida. But we know from the Lynda Healy murder that the killer spent quite a bit of time with her at the actual murder scene. He undressed her, hung her bloody nightgown in her closet, and made her bed in his own unique style. There were signs of a struggle in Lynda's bed, but it was probably over very quickly, because no one heard Lynda scream. Ted's intention was to spend his time with dead victims, not put himself in jeopardy by dealing with live ones. That's why he knocked his victims out almost immediately, transported them to a dump site, and murdered them so that he could experience sexual gratification through necrophilia. Therefore, murder was a threshold that Ted crossed in his fantasy about controlling his dead victims to actually exercising that control. All he needed was a safe place to leave the bodies, preselected or opportunistically delivered victims, a pre-scripted and well-rehearsed approach to his victims, and escape routes to and from his dump sites which would provide him some security from detection. Maybe the availability of Lynda Healy and the fact that he seemed to have spent more time chasing her than the others makes her case a likely candidate for the first Bundy murder in Seattle. I still have my doubts and believe there were previous murders, but the pattern of how Ted crossed the threshold seems clear.

What also seems clear is the pattern of violence and criminal behavior leading up to George Russell's first murder. Here's a guy who studied Ted Bundy's methods from various books about him. Here's a guy with resentment building up in him for over twenty years and who's been in conflict with all sorts of authorities from the time he was a preadolescent. He was a cat burglar, a kid who ratted on his friends after he probably led them into committing crimes, and a kid who desperately tried to belong to any group that would have him even if it meant lying his way in. Because so many people knew him and crossed his path as he continued to fail socially among the different herds migrating from singles bar to singles bar in Bellevue, he got angrier and increasingly aggressive. As women his age or just a tad younger kept rejecting him, he began sending out danger signals of impending violence, but everyone thought it was just talk until the horrible truth sank in.

I'd hypothesize that as frustrated and fantasy-driven as Russell got, he was probably still at the edge of his comfort zone until he encountered Mary Ann Pohlreich one night at Papagayo's, got teased into a frenzy by the victim, then got humiliatingly rejected when they were alone, and broke through the wall of fantasy. We know from how Pohlreich was murdered that after Russell hit her, he still had choices to make. She was probably still alive as she lay across the front seat of the truck Russell had borrowed, and maybe even barely conscious. She certainly was bleeding and probably throwing up after Russell beat her. Maybe he panicked and thought he had to kill her to keep her quiet, and having made the decision, indulged in his fantasy of destroying a woman. Or maybe in that very moment when Pohlreich pushed him off her, satisfying the anger that had been a part of him since he was a child was more important to him than anything else.

In an act of utter selfishness, the killer withdrew to a universe of one, and his impulse took precedence over another's life. Russell had been satisfying his impulses to the exclusion of everything else throughout his whole life: taking what he wanted whenever he wanted, observing no boundary between other's property and his own wants, going wherever he pleased even when he was not welcomed. The threshold of violence and then murder, although bright red boundaries to us, might have been only a small step to Russell who, in that moment with Pohlreich, had already made a decision to punish this woman for humiliating him. Once dead, the victim became a tableau for the killer to express visually the message he had for the world in general, and women in particular. He savaged her, leaving a distinctive signature of transgression and defilement, as an expression of the fantasy world in which he lived. It may have been the first time that the 'real' George Russell ever expressed himself, but it was also the basis for a signature analysis which ultimately led the police to identify the killer.

THE ARC OF VIOLENCE FROM SEX CRIMES TO MURDER

It's misleading to imagine that the developmental process of the signature killer is like a well-marked road which begins with a dysfunctional or wildly deviant childhood and leads inevitably to the kinds of graphic murders we see in George Russell or Jeffrey Dahmer. The important thing to remember is that because these diphasic types have committed to a world of fantasy rather than reality and develop a cover or camouflage personality as a real-world placeholder, they can move back and forth with greater facility the more practiced they become in bringing back trophies from the real world to their fantasy world.

Jeffrey Dahmer, for example, actually managed to stand up in court, plead for mercy in front of a judge, get sentenced to a modified form of supervised probation/incarceration, and still go right on killing and bringing the bodies back to his apartment. For his part, Ted Bundy never stopped thinking about death and killing even while he was so much involved in the world of politics and work that he was able to ride his bike through a police crime-scene security detail on the University of Washington campus the day after he'd abducted Georgann

Hawkins from the exact same spot. He lifted evidence of the crime right off the ground while the police were milling around, and fit right in. The same is true for Nathaniel Code, who watched the police at the crime scenes of his murders from the safety of a crowd while they searched the area for clues. And George Russell openly bragged about the success of Ted Bundy to friends while all of Bellevue was shocked at the discoveries of Pohlreich, Beethe, and Levine. Even people who knew Russell, and that includes some of the police, believed that he was only a petty thief incapable of the kind of violence at the crime scene. Russell's camouflage personality as a deviant burglar actually covered his fantasy of self-importance and control over women.

Most signature killers indulge in behaviors along the continuum of violence even while they're in the midst of their killing sprees. Russell, Code, and Bundy all stole and broke into houses throughout much of their adult lives, especially while they were killing. Signature killers don't just stop at one crime and begin another. As they evolve along the arc of violence, they experiment with new ways of satisfying themselves to achieve sexual gratification. Some rapists who display signatures of bondage, torture, or humiliation, but don't kill, reveal by their signatures their evolution toward homicide. Even after they commit their first homicides, they may continue to rape without murdering the victim even if it's sometimes only a matter of opportunity. The general tendency among signature criminals is to evolve, because it's through the evolution of sexual experimentation that signature criminals believe they will find their gratification.

THE COMFORT ZONE

Moving out along the continuum of potential violence, not all diphasic personality types cross over the threshold into criminal behavior. In fact, the overwhelming majority of potentially violent people find their needs satisfied at a point somewhere between the edge of normalcy and the borderline of criminality. Even though many of these types have fully developed fantasies to which they're committed more than to the risk of interacting socially, they've developed a host of compensatory behaviors that allow them an exit before criminal behavior. This is why even though children may come from very similar types of families in which they've experienced neglect, abandonment, and sometimes outright child abuse, most people come to rest at a level where they balance fantasy and reality, and may have difficulty in the real world but develop behaviors which allow them to compromise.

It is the types who don't kill in whom we see the psychological elements underpinning the signature of a control-type serial killer turning up in many personalities in a variety of situations, albeit without the overt violence. We may see all the potential for violence there and probably lots of elements of the behavior as we brush against watered-down versions of the three *D*'s in many otherwise normal encounters with people. We may even have a vague feeling that something about this person is wrong, but we don't see their problems for what they are: the telltale signs of a disturbed personality. It's no crime to be disturbed or unhappy, nor is it a crime to take it out on others.

How many stories have we heard about supervisors at work who routinely terrorize their subordinates with demands that cannot be met and arbitrary behavior? Nonresilient people locked into the security of a bureaucracy can respond to perceived threats to their job safety or encroachments into their bailiwick with abnormal levels of hostility and promises of retribution that can make the lives of people around them miserable. Stories abound of postal workers or other civil servants who are harassed at work by supervisors who seem intent on inflicting psychological pain and physical violence.

Many of these stories are actually descriptions of people who use control as a weapon over others because they are afraid they really have no control in their own lives. And this extreme, control behavior can often manifest itself into a psychologically abusive form of the three *D*'s in which the abuser becomes a cruel, petty tyrant inflicting a sense of dread, forcing a dependency, and routinely degrading anyone unfortunate enough to fall within his or her sphere of influence. Ironically, it's not uncommon for these abusers to be rewarded by their supervisors for knowing how to crack the whip over their underlings, thus escalating the level of abuse in direct proportion to the reward until something gives under the strain. Or they may be terrorized in turn, racketing up the tension on everybody until something snaps. Abusive spouses and sometimes even abusive parents can also fall into this category and keep on inflicting terror until someone stops them.

There is an entire spectrum of three-*D* behavior that ranges from hostile to clearly pathological. People may suffer just below the surface for all their adult lives, never committing crimes, but abusing all those around them. Maybe these desperately unhappy people have a kind of support system within the workplace or within the family that keeps their real deviant tendencies in check. However, if that support system fails, if a loved one or family member dies, or if the person gets fired, it can be the triggering mechanism which lets the fantasies loose and the ideations of violence begin. And even then, if the person has lived within society's conventions for most of his life, his fantasies don't get much beyond violent thoughts. He may seethe with hatred and fear, but he only consumes himself. It is only the tiny percentage in which the fantasies turn to reality and the beast within is unleashed that terrorize communities by preying on the most vulnerable victim pool that fits the profile of a signature.

The key for people researching in this field as well as for investigators seeking a broader perspective on signature murder is to recognize that serial signature behavior, especially the anger-excitation or anger-retaliation reaction, is not restricted to killers, rapists, or other violent offenders. Most sexually abusive behavior has its roots in an anger-excitation reaction. For example, a college professor who continually makes sexual advances toward his female students, debasing them while at the same time looking for sexual favors; a manager in an office setting who routinely abuses his female colleagues; or anyone, for that matter, who uses a position of power to exploit others sexually while humiliating or degrading them is displaying an aspect of an anger-excitation reaction. The important elements are that the person is using his power as a means to exploit someone else, exert control, instill a sense of dread, force a dependency, and degrade the person under his control, and out of which he will experience some degree of sexual gratification. I believe this behavior is far more prevalent than any of us realize and is probably the underpinning for a large measure of abusive and tyrannical behavior in the workplace and in domestic situations.

I'll go out on a limb even further. I believe that it's a mistake to believe that there is a fundamental gap between signature killers and a group of people who display what I call signature-pattern abusive behavior. Legally, of course, killers commit murder and have to be prosecuted. But I believe that there are many individuals far closer to the act of murder than most of us are willing to admit. And I'm not including the population of serial rapists, arsonists, or even cat burglars. I'm talking about people in the general population who exhibit a consistent pattern of signature abusive behavior which tends to get worse when the person is under stress but never really disappears even in the least stressful situation. I'm talking about people who have abnormally short tempers, who snap at those around them when under stress, who are prone to violence as a very first resort, who vent their rage on inanimate objects, who become physical under stress, and who are almost pathological about exerting control over others and over events around them. On a sliding scale, the less resilience these people show under stress, the more likely it is they retreat to ideations of violent sexual fantasies, especially fantasies about exerting sexual control and humiliation. Whether they actually cross over the great divide between fantasy and reality to commit criminal offenses depends on many, many factors such as how close they are to the line. Do they act out fantasies with people in their daily lives without actually committing a crime? Do they commit a variety of borderline unlawful acts that function as a stress-relieving safety valve? Have they found a safe enough niche to enable them to act out fantasies without consequences, i.e., abuse of female employees during the day and violent sex with prostitutes after hours? Do they actively troll for potential victims, but pull back because the trolling is excitation enough? Do they medicate themselves with drugs or alcohol to the point where they diminish the inhibitors that keep them from causing violence?

I think I've described a basic personality type in our population, a personality type that's been around for a long, long time. This is a good-news and bad-news situation. The good news is that although these types populate all workplaces and neighborhoods, they don't commit crimes and certainly don't become signature killers. They abuse their employees or subordinates, may become difficult people to deal with in the workplace, may even enter the professions where they use their professional position to try to humiliate their clients, but that may be as far as they go. We hear the story of the therapist or counselor who may go very far out, gaining sexual control over his patients, placing them into an emotional bondage, gratifying himself through exploiting them, and even acting out a necrophilic scenario with a drugged patient, but we hear it only when he's confronted and it makes the news. There are probably all varieties of this type of person all around us, eking sexual gratification out of whatever situations they can exploit, but we don't really know what we're looking at.

They may stay safe at their compensatory levels until the stress becomes too great and they need to move further along the continuum, or the anger stirs up to the surface like an eruption. Incidents in which these people become victims, either of unfortunate situations, crimes against them or family members, or other kinds of tragedies, also present them with a revised set of choices. Do they remain in the comfort zone? Can they still find the gratification they're looking for in the equilibrium they've established? If their answer is no, they move out along the violence continuum where they may establish a new level of equilibrium – probably short of homicide – where they believe they're safe.

THE VIOLENCE CONTINUUM

Signature sex offenders, including murderers, behave across a clearly identifiable continuum of criminal violence which begins with the most deceptively innocuous acts, such as voyeurism, but extends through all types of physical assault to homicide. A signature criminal such as Ted Bundy, for example, will say that he is psychologically compelled to act out his episodic crimes which are just like dramatic scenarios in which the killer performs specific behaviors in specific patterns that constitute the signature. Bundy's signature was apparent to us only in what we were able to glean from witnesses who saw and heard him and from the crime scenes when we finally found them. George Russell left a more visible signature at his very public crime scenes, as did Nathaniel Code. Dahmer, on the other hand, was almost completely invisible until investigators searched his apartment. But these are the killers. Voyeurs may say they feel compelled to stalk subjects passively in their neighborhoods or local schools, where they revisit specific spots on a regular basis according to the schedules of their unknowing victims. Peeping Toms may simply look and do nothing else, but their presence is unsettling. Voyeurs may go out of their way to cross the paths of the people they're watching, never interfering directly in their lives, but only becoming a nuisance once they're spotted.

Peeping Tomism and voyeurism are usually against the law in most jurisdictions, and depending on their repetitive nature or frequency, may be classified as a sexual offense. The lengths to which a voyeur may go to observe a victim may also involve trespass, breaking and entering, invasion of privacy, or a host of other violations that may make for a long arrest or offense record, but rarely trigger a red flag for most authorities. In reality, however, these are the very signs that an offender is on a continuum of violence which usually escalates until the offender is stopped or killed. Many early offenders do wind up becoming victims of violence themselves because they're placing themselves at risk. Others simply bounce in and out of the criminal justice system, picking up whatever skills they need to navigate in society, but because they are usually sociopaths, the skills are aimed at helping them commit crimes more successfully.

Peeping Toms and voyeurs may become passive stalkers, watching, trailing, but never physically confronting their victims, content to look and to fantasize as they learn more about their victims' behaviors. Sexual offenders on the continuum of violence like to experiment with their fantasies, seeing what brings them more gratification and how they can tweak the most out of a potential encounter. It is in these experiments that sexual offenders evolve, some to burglary or breaking and entering; others to luring their victims into meetings where they might steal a small possession as a memento imbued with some aspect of the victim that now drives the offender's fantasy.

Those who move out along the violence continuum are essentially cowards with absolutely no sense of self or, accordingly, self-worth. They are hollow, and in the resonating emptiness of their beings they express a deep anger at everything and everyone who is not them. They fluctuate between true submissiveness in relationships and a false sense of power and domination. They are rarely on an equal footing with those around them and retreat into fantasy for solace or gratification. Those who successfully experiment with sexual encounters may gradually escalate their levels of violence again, becoming more confrontational with objects of their fantasies until they graduate, always by choice, to full-scale sexual assaults.

The more they lapse into sexual crime and the more the sense of gratification, fleeting though it may be, increases, the more the offender will experiment: restraint, bondage, torture, infliction of pain, and finally, actual homicide. But they don't stop there. Like drug users after a bigger and bigger thrill, signature killers can seek to experiment with activities which allow them to vent their rage on dead victims or subsume victims' flesh into their own bodies. The violence continuum incorporates all types of postmortem deviances including necrophilia and, ultimately, cannibalism, the outpost of human deviance where some of the most notorious killers in history, including Jeffrey Dahmer, reside in our memories. These are the types of killers who lurk out there in the darkness of an urban tenement, trolling in their cars along a desolate street following a hooker around the next corner, or, twisting in the darkness of their own mind, boiling with an all-consuming sexual fury until they can find their next victim.

SIGNATURE CRIMINALS IN PRISON

Lying beneath the bravado and cruelty of a signature sexual offender is a monumental terror of making decisions in the real world. That's why from a very early age, that individual created and retreated into a fantasy world where he was in complete control. Because he probably was ill-parented or unparented when he was a child, signature offenders tend to gravitate toward parental or authority figures as adults, even though they severely challenge and test both so as to destroy any meaningful relationships they develop. Prison is another matter. In prison, signature offenders incorporate their minimal needs very quickly into a rigid, authoritarian, rule-driven, but capricious system so as to become model inmates. Prison provides for all their wants and needs such as shelter, food, activities, and a basic shape to their lives. They exist in fantasy worlds anyway, which they're free to do in prison, because docile inmates make the corrections officials happy. As inmates, signature offenders can indulge themselves in books and magazines, feed their fantasy from violence-related events in their memory, learn sexual gratification techniques from other inmates and people just like themselves, and devote time to playing mind games with the prison psychologists. Even their anger is under control because, since how they express that anger is a matter of choice, a draconian prison system forces them to keep it largely under control.

Signature offenders adapt so well to a prison regimen that even though there is little hope of ever rehabilitating them, sentencing guidelines, overcrowding, and the need to make room for additional prisoners under 'three strikes and you're out' or other laws mean that lots of these sex offenders will be given time off or receive other forms of reduced sentences. Also, to the inexperienced eye, they sometimes look like excellent rehabilitation possibilities. When you know what to look for and what to ask, however, you realize that there is no cure, certainly not chemical castration or physical castration, and they will ultimately graduate to more violent crimes. Once they're released, since nothing has ever addressed the underlying cause of anger, the same forces that shaped their decision to move along the continuum in the first place are still at work. After a prison experience, however, younger signature offenders have learned a lot more; they've been mentored in many cases by the lifers and understand how to commit their crimes better. They have more material to experiment with and the experience of more successful inmates. The result is that these guys get out, better criminals than before, and are looking for action. Unfortunately, we don't realize it until years later, when they're brought back and we review their criminal records from different jurisdictions, so the problem just keeps getting worse.

Once you see the magnitude of this problem you wonder why the legislators who enact the laws regarding sentencing of prisoners and the administration of correctional systems don't spend as much time worrying about the prisoners getting out as they do about the prisoners going in. If they did, they'd be horrified to find out that a majority of released inmates are worse off than when they got in five or so years earlier. A minority of prisoners are rehabilitated, to be sure, but these aren't the signature sex offenders who look at prison as a vacation from the street or, in the case of someone like Bundy, a sabbatical from murder.

Ted knew he could never be rehabilitated, and he certainly didn't want to die, but he was able to make a life for himself on death row. He analyzed other serial killers, was infamous enough to garner their respect, and fed his own fantasies on their stories as well as his memories of where his secret stashes of bones and bodies lay. What I found out was that for a signature killer who's led a successful career, the mere fact that he knows things you don't about whom he killed and where they are is a level of control he exercises over you. Prison doesn't shut off the signature killer's control mechanism, because it's all within his fantasy world and he never gives it up. That's why when a signature sexual offender is released, what he has learned makes him more dangerous.

THE GROWING MENACE

There are at least two issues when we look at the apparent problem of the increase in signature crime, especially murder. The first issue is whether signature crime is really on the increase at all, or whether we are merely more aware of it, know what to look for in a crime report, and therefore categorize it as a signature crime when just fifteen years ago we might have called it something else. We know that traditional homicides seem as though they're on the decrease if you look at the trends in the national crime statistics over the past few years. So why does everyone assume that signature crimes, particularly murder, are bucking the trend? Can we attribute it all to a recategorization of crimes so that there is a statistical bump while the larger picture shows a decrease?

From my experience, I don't think that's the case. I think there truly has been an increase in signature crimes, maybe not as dramatic as some would say, but an increase nevertheless. Over the longer term, however, say thirty years, you can see a dramatic increase in signature crimes – control-driven cat burglaries, control- and anger-driven sexual assaults and homicides. This broad-term increase seems to indicate that unlike more traditional felony murders (a clerk is killed at a twenty-four-hour convenience store during a holdup), bank robberies, drug murders, gang-related assaults and murders, stranger murders such as freeway shootings after a traffic confrontation, or deaths resulting from bar fights or street brawls, signature crimes are not environmentally sensitive to such relatively short-term things as shifts in the economy, availability of drugs, police presence in a gang-infested community, deterioration or gentrification of urban neighborhoods, and personnel level of social workers to monitor and intervene in parental child abuse cases. Any increase in signature crimes over a thirty- to forty-year period reveals a much more significant problem in society itself, that it could cultivate, just like a bacteria, the forces that allow signature criminals to flourish. What are these trends and what can we do about them?

Some people take the 1950s as a benchmark, probably because it's my generation doing the benchmarking, and ask why the incidence of signature murder has increased since the 1950s. First of all, I believe that signature murder was on the increase by the 1950s, certainly by the 1960s, and that for our purposes the 1950s are not as meaningful as some point before World War II. For a better perspective on what I think is a clearer explanation of the increase of signature murder in terms of a generational shift, a better starting point is probably at a time before the great depression but after the beginning of the century, say 1925 for argument's sake, when the forces were already under way that would cause a fundamental shift in the values of what we most hold dear.

In the twenties, right up through the stock market crash in October 1929, while America's major cities were adjusting to the impact of successive waves of immigration during the early part of the century – families who brought with them traditional Old World family values – the rest of America was still largely rural, the farm was an important family business, and the agrarian lifestyle could allow extended families going back three or four generations to live in the same household. Children were raised not just by their parents – today over fifty percent of American children are raised by one parent and a growing number are raised by no parents – but by their grandparents, great-grandparents, or aunts and uncles. And although families were larger seventy-five years ago, children weren't neglected because there were so many family members to care for them. Instead of being relegated to nurseries, nannies, foster parents, and day care, children were integrated into the family structure and raised by the family, and they grew up in the family because they had chores and jobs to do. If a parent had a problem such as alcohol abuse or something that got between the parent and child, an aunt or a grandparent, sometimes an older sibling, took over the child-raising chores. Families stayed together no matter what, so children learned commitment.

This is like a simple engineering case study. It's a hard job growing up and integrating oneself into a tricky social world. Human beings were never meant to be loners; they originally survived by the social order of extended families or clans and by related or affiliated clans that formed tribes in which there was something of a political and generational hierarchy. When tribes settled down to occupy a territory, there were land management issues, the requirements of a common defense, and protection against environmental disasters and the vagaries of climate. Related tribes became confederated tribes, and thus began the issue of primitive government. At the bottom of it all, giving it meaning and shape, was the family structure, the means through which new generations were integrated into the social pecking order. In other words, it did take a village to raise a child, because it was the only way the community could sustain itself and provide for continuity.

The result of this was that child care was not random. If a parent couldn't do it, then someone else in the family did. Even through the 1930s, and especially in families that emigrated from Eastern Europe at the turn of the century, where you see eight to fifteen children in a family, the chances are that the youngest kids were raised mostly by the other siblings under the mother's eye because of the sheer size of the family. Children were raised and the socialization of the child was a family function not relegated to a television or to whomever happened to show up in school. Children were fed, talked to, nurtured, held, carried about, integrated into family activities, and given – at the very earliest ages – a sense of family responsibility and importance to the family. That instilled an important sense of confidence and self-esteem, and kids grew up knowing who they were and where they belonged. Religion, expressed as the inculcation of moral responsibility for one's actions, was as much a part of education as learning to read. In other words, during the early part of this century in America, at least, the family structure raised the child who was so locked in that he couldn't veer very far off course. In the majority of cases, problems were nipped in the bud, and it was usually where you could point to the collapse of an individual family structure that you could predict difficulties for a growing child if someone didn't intervene on his behalf. That was then.

So what happened? Between the years 1930 and 1950 and the interventions of a great financial depression that changed the nature of American society, and World War II, which removed an entire generation from society and brought it back fundamentally changed, a paradigm shift took place in American culture that altered our social family structure and set into motion trends that are still playing themselves out. These trends so undermined the structure of the American family that defining what a family is and what it does have become issues of academic debate. To put this into clearer baby boomer perspective, take a quick snapshot of dinner at the Waltons and dinner with the Bradys. Get the idea? Three generations live on Walton's Mountain and John-Boy gets to watch the respect his father pays to his father. The elder siblings help raise the younger kids and the socialization of all the children is the family's responsibility. In the Brady household, Alice, who's a worker for hire, mostly raises the kids, mediates among her employers instead of parenting the children, watches Mike and Carol lead their separate lives, and worries about Sam the butcher. In the Partridge family there is no father; the mother serves the narcissistic values of the children. The group is almost completely rootless and travels mostly by bus from one single-night stand to another. The Simpsons, admittedly a cartoon, are intergenerational predators who battle one another for food scraps, perpetrate violence upon each other, and revel in the cartoon-within-cartoon torture, humiliation, gore, and dismemberment of Itchy and Scratchy. Have I made up this degeneration played out on our TV screens? I don't think so.

The point here is not a quick walk-through of family television as life over the past thirty years, but a snapshot of how our interpretations of family and its inherent values are projected through the lens of our popular culture. Leslie Fiedler says we can do this. Our values have changed, and with them the values we place on the structure of the family and the way children are raised within the family. The shift from three-generation households to two and now to one is alarming, because it means that children are probably getting less care. As a consequence, I believe, the incidence of violence perpetrated upon children is appalling as is the incidence of violence perpetrated by children upon one another. Homicide rates may be dropping all over the country, but they're rising in lower and lower age groups. That means that unless children at ages ten and eleven are put away for life, they're going to be coming out of prison probably dangerous and very easily armed. Whereas these children, already terminally angry, have women as their source victims, other women will almost surely become their secondary victims. Whereas these children band together, not as families but as hordes of individual criminals and gangs, their propensity for violence increases exponentially and we'll see a higher incidence of gang rapes, violent assaults on women, or the kinds of 'wildings' like the brutal beating of New York's Central Park jogger.

I'm also suggesting that parents themselves, especially the parents in my generation, have abdicated too much responsibility in child raising. If the overriding image of the Dahmer household on the night of his first kill – both parents fled the house, leaving the teenage son alone to do whatever he wanted – is a defining metaphor for our generation, our selfishness in pursuing our own aims to the detriment of our children is an indicator of what our children are learning. In Los Angeles, for example, local news broadcasts delight in playing tapes that parents make, through a hidden teddy-bear camera, showing how a nanny they've hired abuses their child. The black-and-white grainy image of an employee, usually an undocumented alien with no formal training in child care, slapping around a crying one- or two-year-old while the parents cluck to themselves on the other end of the camera and then file charges against the nanny – while an all-too-sympathetic news anchor comments in a mincing voiceover – is so common that it's more than disturbing. Has anyone thought to ask where the parent is? Have we actually stopped raising our kids and relegated the task to hired workers, teachers, and the state, and then send the tapes to *Hard Copy* when something goes wrong? Whatever happened to staying home and raising the child?

Similarly, on *Politically Incorrect* recently, the normally sanguine Bill Maher was uncharacteristically incensed over an article in *Harper's* magazine about a student who had killed his music teacher because the teacher had not allowed him to play in a band or something. It seems that in a yearbook entry about the accused, his fellow students had written jokingly about his habits of killing small animals and starting fires. 'It's okay,' so the paraphrase goes. 'Even though you murder and torture small animals and start fires, we still like you.' Endearing enough. But isn't that what they said about Jeffrey Dahmer when they wrote about him? At what point do we publicly recognize that cruelty to animals – in any form – starting fires, cruelty toward other children, and abnormal levels of violence are all precursors of core signature behavior? These kids grow up to the point where they make the choice to commit sex crimes. That's what's just over the generational horizon. There's an epidemic of violence sweeping across the generations of high school through elementary-grade children and nobody, not teachers, not parents, not the political candidates preaching family values, is doing anything about it. It's all dumped in the lap of law enforcement and the justice systems, which are completely overloaded and can't stop the tide because it's already too late. Our society has both abdicated and abrogated its responsibility to raise its own children, and this shift in family values from the 1930s to the present is so apparent that it almost begs the question to ask why signature crimes are on the rise.

Concurrently, the whole concept of marriage and relationships has undergone a fundamental shift since before World War II. Part of the problem is that of course, there's no one willing to take the ultimate responsibility for raising a child within a family, because family members themselves are retreating from the responsibility of maintaining the family. Look at some of the statistics: one-third of all children born in America in 1994 were born out of wedlock and into single-parent families. Compare that with five percent in 1960. One of every two children born in the United States in 1994 will live through his parents' divorce, and today six of ten children will spend time living with a single parent. The childhood of George Russell is more than instructive in this regard.

It seems that serial murder is on the increase, in part because serial marriages and relationships are on the increase. We can't complain too much about children not taking responsibility for making choices in their lives if no-fault divorce laws remove the responsibility of choice from their parents. We are in the midst of an age of administrative blamelessness where no one is picking up the slack, but successive generations of children are left at risk. I actually think that during this century we have witnessed such a fundamental resocialization and restructuring of the family that it has truly outpaced our species' ability to adapt physiologically and psychologically to the change. We've become so trapped in our social hyper-evolution that our children have lost the concept of self, and violence is the only way they have of establishing boundaries. When people ask about the reason for the growing number of signature crimes, people have to look at the collapse of the traditional family in America and judge for themselves the very far-reaching consequences it's having on all of us.

THE IMPACT OF PORNOGRAPHY

As if to exacerbate this generational shift in family values, we are living at a time when pornography and violence on television are available to children of all ages. Despite the minimal safeguards against exposing children to violence or explicit sex, the stuff is not only blatant and rampant, it plays directly to school-aged audiences for whom, coming off television, it has an hypnotic effect, depressing psychological and social inhibitions to violence and making it palatable for everyone, including potential predators. Ted Bundy once told an interviewer that he indulged in pornography and that it incited him to commit violence. What he said was taken at face value and then largely discounted, because pornography itself couldn't be responsible for the creation of a serial killer. But I think Ted was actually saying something else, and it made sense.

I don't believe for an instant that there's a direct one-to-one correlation between seeing a violent act on television and committing one in the real world. It implies that there is no responsibility on the predator's part; he only saw it in the movies. However, I do believe that repetitive violence, especially violence perpetrated on women, has a cumulative effect that desensitizes a viewer over time to what should be an abhorrence of violence. If it's now formulaic to terrorize women, because we see it in just about every movie of the week, in grade-B and low-budget movies, and off and on in various series, the pattern of perpetrating that terror goes into a common culture. Sure, elementary school kids know how to commit violence. They see it every night on TV as well as in the theaters. Set fire to a New York City subway token booth? No problem! Just watch how they do it in the movies. Like Bart Simpson's Itchy and Scratchy, we are desensitized to the impact of the violence on human beings because on television human victims are reduced to cartoons.

Most children growing up watching this stuff don't know what it's like to hurt another human being. Surely most don't know the size of hole a 9mm round makes when it goes through a chest and takes out most of someone's lung, or what an M16 or AK47 round does to someone's leg right above the kneecap – just about blows it off. The amount of blood that human beings shed when they're hurt or wounded is also astounding if you've never seen it before. Blood gets slippery and you can't stand up in it. It gets sticky when it dries, adheres to your flesh, and doesn't come off easily. It also smells. But watching Chuck Norris on television take a blow to the head, shake it off, and keep right on kick boxing is to believe that in a world of nonimpact, it's all a video game.

In Joseph Pearce's *Evolution's End*, he talks about the repetitive effect of television as the passive programming of neural fields that are created by the watching of television itself. There are visceral responses to product advertisements, reactions to scenes of sex and violence, and a host of subliminal messages translated through imagery. Like the reinforcement of suggestions to a subject whose logical skepticism has been neutralized by the seizing of his attention, television creates a neural network in which the subject believes whatever it's shown. Ad agencies know this. Programmers know this. I would suggest that if there's any doubt about this, you spend some Saturday morning from eight until noon watching children's cartoons, where you'll find a four-hour info-mercial for product interspersed with scenes of violence and destruction that play directly into the fantasies of children who are not grounded in reality. Even normal children are programmed to want, frustrated at what they cannot get, and consistently desensitized to the effects of violence upon others. Imagine the effect this has on children who have impaired real-world skills because they've been hiding behind their own fantasies. These kids are constantly frustrated, and beyond a certain point, choose to take from others what they cannot get for themselves. Their wants have been so programmed by what they see on television, and they are so ill-equipped to mediate their emotions, they simply suffer. It's as if we're programming future generations of sociopaths who know only how to want and not how to work for what they want.

By the time children reach adolescence, the amount of suggestive sexual and violent material they've been watching on television starts up a whole new level of programming. It's one thing to be stimulated by beautiful women and romance, but it's quite another to be handed a video manual for how to kidnap, beat up, rape, assault, murder, and humiliate a woman. In addition, much television and movie programming contains what amounts to little more than a stereotyping guide for how to handle women who are too aggressive, promiscuous, pushy, contrary, and however else women can be categorized. We know that programs that sexually stimulate fare better than shows that don't, but given a growing population of adolescents who don't know what to do with the feelings they're experiencing, programmers don't understand that they're playing with fire. There's an almost direct correlation between what judgmentally incompetent viewers see and what they think they can do. Much of the sexual programming on television, especially that which has to do with perpetrating violence on women, instructs as much as it stimulates. The limits that industry standards and practices exercised in the past over violent and sexually stimulating material have been so eroded that certain television programs are nothing more than accelerated particle-beam weapons aimed right at the most receptive areas of viewers' brains. Short of arguing for a kind of censorship, which, by the way, was exercised without apologies during the 1950s, we should be looking at programmers for a minimal understanding of the kind of sexual violence television is actively promoting and an expression of some kind of responsibility for addressing the problem.

If television and motion pictures as art forms lay out a format for committing sexual crime and actually provide it as a no-consequence option for viewers already living in fantasy worlds where they hide away from real-world vulnerability, then the current movement toward transgressive art exacerbates an already exacerbated problem. Literature about the so-called moral validity of serial murder, as in *American Psycho*, and art that glorifies self-mutilation and the inflicting of pain as worth elevating serves as a tableau for future generations of individuals in whose fantasy worlds art and reality merge. Signature killers already believe that some murders are okay. They don't need a Bret Easton Ellis to give them permission. In fact, they may even see their own murders as art, especially the killers who gratify themselves by posing their dead victims.

Was Stephen Pennell, at least in his own mind, creating an art form by posing a victim whom he'd defiled and mutilated? Did George Russell see himself as a kind of sculptor fashioning a message out of the corpses of Pohlreich, Beethe, and Levine? What did it mean to drape a victim's hand over a copy of *More Joy of Sex* as if the whole scene were a living snapshot of murder? Similarly, Jeffrey Dahmer's photographs of victims propped up as if they were still alive, yet horribly mutilated, was one stage of ritualistic expression. His proposed tabernacle of skulls was another. This is the real transgressive art, a killer who designs a scene with his victim's corpse, not in the stillness of repose, but as *stasis*, an action arrested in time, frozen in an instant by the exercise of the killer-as-artist's control. These mimetic dioramas are the real thing, truthfully capturing at once the forces at work in the killer's fantasy and his idealization of sexual gratification, death, and pleasure into a monument of putrifying flesh. It's sick, but it's on the increase because we don't have the means to do anything about it except clean it up and put the perpetrator in jail.

If the structures that trained our children to succeed in the real world are failing, if the psychological chain between generations is eroding to the point where it's no longer functional, who will take up the burden? Freedom of expression works in the context of society primarily because generations of adults coming of age have learned the social restraints necessary to exercise it. Perhaps that's what Judge Robert Bork is describing when he says that society has gone so far to remove restrictions, especially in the 1960s, that it's brought us close enough to a state of moral anarchy to worry about what to do about it. On the Internet, for example, there are newsgroups with instructions telling you how to kidnap young girls, how to kill people silently, how to abuse young girls and frighten them into silence, how to conceal weapons, how to fabricate homemade bombs and use them in terrorist attacks, and where to swap photos of young boys and girls in sexually degrading positions. There's always been pornography and sexual deviance. The problem is that it's so accessible and potentially so responsible for an increase in transgressive violent behavior that it's as if the center does not hold.

THROUGH THE LOOKING GLASS INTO THE FUTURE

We live in an age of dramatic potential. Our understanding of science and medicine allows us to look seriously at different types of cures and even vaccines for cancer and types of heart disease. Our life spans are increasing. Our awareness of the dangers to the environment have resulted in air and water cleaner than they were a hundred years ago. Education is accessible to greater numbers of people than it has ever been. As optimistic as we should be about the future, we are nevertheless more fearful than ever. We're afraid we'll get shot on the freeways, afraid that the child sitting next to ours in the school cafeteria is carrying a gun, and afraid to drive down to the ATM because we don't know who's lurking in the shadow just beyond the circle of the halogen lamp. We live in fear; yet it's a fear that is partly of our own making.

Even as the numbers of reported crimes go down and

cities seem safer, we're getting worried because somehow in the increasingly violent signature crimes we read about, we wonder whether a generation of criminals has broken out. What's clear is that some component of society has to take responsibility for the growth in sexual signature crimes, especially homicides, because frankly, there's no excuse not to. We know how signature crimes are committed, we understand how signature killers evolve and what makes them kill, we understand the origin of clinical anger, and we should know what the indicators are for potentially violent people.

Because we know that signature crimes are essentially anger-driven and that anger, a kind of friction between the offender's real world and a fantasy existence, starts very early in childhood, we should be able to address it. Granted that most signature types, even people who later in life may employ dread, dependency, and degradation to humiliate those around them, never become criminals; many of them will. Many people exist on the very borderline of criminal behavior, slipping one way and then another unless they're stopped. What separates the signature killer from the dysfunctional person who doesn't kill? Nothing more than a choice; nothing more than a decision about how selfish to be at any given moment. The threshold is so frighteningly narrow and the numbers of people right on the edge so great, our understanding of what makes signature crime may be our only weapon of defense. But if we continue to be afraid to address the central issues about ourselves and our society that speak directly to the underpinnings of signature crime, we'll soon become like Pogo, who said, 'We have met the enemy and it is us.'